The Phonology of Classical Latin

T0385859

Publications of the Philological Society, 52

The Phonology of Classical Latin

András Cser
Pázmány Péter Catholic University

Publications of the Philological Society, 52

WILEY
Blackwell

This edition first published 2020
© 2020 The Philological Society

John Wiley & Sons

Registered Office
John Wiley & Sons Ltd, The Atrium, Southern Gate, Chichester, West Sussex, PO19
8SQ, United Kingdom

Editorial Offices
101 Station Landing, Medford, MA 02155, USA
9600 Garsington Road, Oxford, OX4 2DQ, UK
The Atrium, Southern Gate, Chichester, West Sussex, PO19 8SQ, UK

For details of our global editorial offices, for customer services, and for information about how
to apply for permission to reuse the copyright material in this book please see our website at
www.wiley.com/wiley-blackwell.

ISBN 978-1-1197-0060-9
A catalogue record for this book is available from the British Library.

Set in Times by SPS (P) Ltd., Chennai, India
Printed in Singapore by COS Printers Pte Ltd

1 2020

The Phonology of Classical Latin

András Cser

Pázmány Péter Catholic University

Andreae Mohay, magistro optimo

THE PHONOLOGY OF CLASSICAL LATIN

András Cser

Pázmány Péter Catholic University

CONTENTS

List of figures
List of tables
Abbreviations and symbols
Acknowledgements
1. Introduction
1.1. Aims and scope | 1
1.2. Previous research | 1
1.3. The language, the data and the form of writing | 2
1.4. The framework | 7
1.5. The structure of the book | 11
2. The segmental inventory | 13
2.1. Introduction | 13
2.2. Consonants | 13
2.2.1. General distributional regularities in simplex forms | 16
2.2.2. The question of the labiovelar(s) | 20
2.2.2.1. The issue of frequency | 22
2.2.2.2. Phonetic issues | 22
2.2.2.3. Geminates | 23
2.2.2.4. Positional restrictions and stop + glide sequences | 24
2.2.2.5. The question of [sw] | 25
2.2.2.6. Verb root structure | 26
2.2.2.7. Voicing contrast in clusters | 26
2.2.2.8. Alternations | 27
2.2.2.9. *Ad*-assimilation | 30
2.2.2.10. Diachronic considerations | 30
2.2.2.11. Poetic licence | 30
2.2.2.12. Further remarks on the voiced labiovelar | 31
2.2.2.13. Summary of the labiovelar question | 32
2.2.3. The placeless nasal | 32
2.3. Vowels | 34
2.3.1. The nasal vowels | 35
2.3.2. The question of diphthongs | 37
2.3.3. Hiatus | 43
2.4. The phonological representations | 44
2.5. Conclusion | 46
3. The phonotactics of simplex forms and resyllabification | 48
3.1. Introduction | 48
3.1.1. Excursus on metrical evidence | 50
3.2. The presentation of the consonant clusters | 51
3.3. The analysis of the consonant clusters | 51

3.4. Syllable contact and the interaction between place of articulation and sonority	67
3.5. Resyllabification and extrasyllabic [s]	70
3.6. A note on words written with initial ⟨gn⟩	74
3.7. Conclusion	81
4. Processes affecting consonants	82
4.1. Introduction	82
4.2. Contact voice assimilation	82
4.2.1. Excursus: loss of [s] before voiced consonants	84
4.3. Total assimilation of [t] to [s]	85
4.4. Rhotacism	86
4.5. Degemination	89
4.5.1. General degemination	89
4.5.2. Degemination of [s]	91
4.6. Nasal place loss before fricatives	92
4.7. Epenthesis after [m]	92
4.8. Place assimilation	94
4.9. Dark and clear [l]	96
4.10. Final stop deletion	99
4.11. Liquid dissimilation	100
4.12. Conclusion	103
5. Processes affecting vowels	104
5.1. Introduction	104
5.2. Alternations in vowel quality	104
5.2.1. The Old Latin weakening	104
5.2.2. Synchronic alternations between the short vowels	106
5.2.2.1. Alternation in closed vs. open syllables	106
5.2.2.2. Lowering before [r]	108
5.2.2.3. Word-final lowering	110
5.3. Vowel–zero alternations	111
5.3.1. Before stem-final [r]	111
5.3.2. Prevocalic deletion of back vowels	112
5.3.3. Vowel–zero alternation in suffixes	114
5.4. Length alternations	114
5.4.1. Shortenings	115
5.4.2. Lengthening before voiced stops	115
5.4.3. Coalescence with empty vowel	118
5.4.4. Coalescence with placeless nasal	119
5.4.5. The *abiēs*-pattern	121
5.5. Conclusion	123
6. The inflectional morphology of Classical Latin	124
6.1. Introduction	124
6.2. Allomorphy in the verbal inflection	126

6.2.1. The general structure of verbal inflection   126
6.2.2. Affixes immediately following the infectum stem   127
6.2.3. Affixes immediately following the perfectum stem   131
    6.2.3.1. Classification of affixes   131
    6.2.3.2. The general pattern of affix alternations   132
    6.2.3.3. Vowel deletion after [s]   135
    6.2.3.4. Hiatus and *i*-final perfectum stems   135
    6.2.3.5. The non-alternating suffixes   137
6.2.4. Affixes following the extended stems   139
6.3. Allomorphy in the nominal inflection   141
6.3.1. Introductory remarks   141
6.3.2. Case endings and allomorphy: nominative and
accusative singular   143
    6.3.2.1. Phonological alternations in the nominative singular 144
    6.3.2.2. Gender marking   145
6.3.3. Case endings and allomorphy: the remaining cases   146
6.4. Morphophonological analysis: inflectional allomorphy
and the vocalic scale   149
6.5. The vocalic scale and sonority   150
6.6. Conclusion   152
7. The phonology of prefixed forms   153
7.1. Introduction   153
7.2. The prefixes of Latin   155
7.2.1. Vowel-final prefixes + *prae*   156
    7.2.1.1. *dē-*   156
    7.2.1.2. *prō-*   156
    7.2.1.3. *sē-*   157
    7.2.1.4. *ne-*   157
    7.2.1.5. *re-*   157
    7.2.1.6. *ambi-*   158
    7.2.1.7. *ante-*   159
    7.2.1.8. *vē-*   160
    7.2.1.9. *prae-*   160
7.2.2. Prefixes ending in [r]   160
    7.2.2.1. *per-*   160
    7.2.2.2. *super-*   161
    7.2.2.3. *subter-*   161
    7.2.2.4. *inter-*   161
    7.2.2.5. *por-*   161
7.2.3. Nasal-final prefixes   161
    7.2.3.1. *in-*   161
    7.2.3.2. *con-*   162
    7.2.3.3. *an-*   165

7.2.3.4. *circum-*   165
7.2.4. Coronal obstruent-final prefixes   166
   7.2.4.1. *post-*   166
   7.2.4.2. *ex-*   166
   7.2.4.3. *dis-*   168
   7.2.4.4. *trans-*   169
   7.2.4.5. *ad-*   170
7.2.5. Prefixes ending in [b]   172
   7.2.5.1. *ob-*   172
   7.2.5.2. *ab-*   173
   7.2.5.3. *sub-*   175
7.3. Generalisations   176
  7.3.1. Assimilations   176
   7.3.1.1. Voice assimilation   176
   7.3.1.2. Place assimilation   176
   7.3.1.3. Total assimilation   177
  7.3.2. Non-assimilatory allomorphy   179
   7.3.2.1. [s]-allomorphy   179
   7.3.2.2. Vowel-triggered allomorphy   179
   7.3.2.3. [b]-allomorphy   180
  7.3.3. On the nature of prefix-variation   180
7.4. Conclusion   183
8. Conclusion and conspectus of the phonological rules   184

Appendix 1: The textual frequency of consonants in Classical Latin
Appendix 2: Authors and works mentioned in the text
References
Index of Latin words
Subject index

LIST OF FIGURES

1 The Classical Latin consonants and their spellings   14
2 The Classical Latin vowels and their spellings   32
3 The structure of vowels and glides   46
4 The structure of consonantal segments   46
5 The structure of a consonant with secondary articulation (velarised [l]) 47
6 The structure of the placeless nasal   47
7 First classification of clusters   58
8 Final classification of clusters   63
9 Distribution of single consonants   64
10 The general syllable template   65
11 The structure of the cluster [ŋks]   67
12 Heterosyllabic cluster types in simplex forms   69
13 Resyllabification   71
14 Assimilation in *in*+⟨gn⟩   80
15 Assimilation in *con*+⟨gn⟩   80
16 No assimilation in *re*+⟨gn⟩   80
17 Contact devoicing of obstruents   83
18 Total assimilation of [t] to [s]   87
19 Rhotacism   89
20 [p]-epenthesis in the environment [m]_[t] and [m]_[s]   94
21 Place assimilation 1   95
22 Place assimilation 2   95
23 Full structure of plain [l]   98
24 Full structure of velarised [l] (=Figure 5)   98
25 [el] → [ol]   99
26 [el] → [ul]   99
27 Lengthening concomitant on devoicing   117
28 ABLSING affixation of a-stem   118
29 ACCPLUR affixation of a-stem   118
30 Coalescence with placeless nasal and the representation of a nasal   120
   vowel
31 Derivation of nasals before stops: underlyingly placeless vs. full   121
   segment
32 The general structure of Latin verb forms based on the infectum and   127
   the perfectum stems
33 The environments of Type 1 vs. Type 2 allomorphy   130
34 Formal types of affixes immediately following the perfectum stem   132
35 The environments of -*is*-class vs. -*er*-class allomorphy   135
36 The vocalic scale   149
37 Total assimilations at prefix–stem boundary   177

38 Systematically attested place assimilations between stops and between 178
   fricatives at prefix–stem boundary
39 Ratio of *con-l*-assimilation   181
40 Ratio of *ad-t*-assimilation   182
41 The frequency of consonants, in order of decreasing overall frequency 187
42 Initial, final and medial frequency separately   188

LIST OF TABLES

1	Summary of the labiovelar question	32
2	Distinctive features for Classical Latin consonantal segments	44
3	Distinctive features for Classical Latin vowels and glides	45
4	Initial clusters	52
5	Final clusters	53
6	Medial clusters	54
7	Extrasyllabic [s] in non-neutral position in poetry	72
8	Extrasyllabic [s] resyllabified	75
9	Extrasyllabic [s] not resyllabified	76
10	Type 1 affix variants immediately following the infectum stem	128
11	Type 2 and other affix variants immediately following the infectum stem	129
12	Affix variants immediately following the perfectum stem (preliminary)	134
13	Affix variants immediately following the perfectum stem (revised and extended)	139
14	Affix variants following extended stems	140
15	Nominative and accusative singular endings	144
16	Genitive, dative and ablative singular endings	146
17	Nominative and accusative plural endings	147
18	Genitive, dative and ablative plural endings	148
19	Summary of inflectional allomorphy	150
20	A conspectus of the phonological rules	184
21	Alphabetical list of authors	203
22	Chronological list of authors	205

ABBREVIATIONS AND SYMBOLS

1	1st person	Neut	neuter
2	2nd person	Nom	nominative
3	3rd person	Nu	nucleus of syllable
Abl	ablative	obs	obstruent
Acc	accusative	Ons	onset of syllable
Act	active	p. e.	personal ending
Adj	adjective	Part	participle
C	consonant	Pass	passive
CL	Classical Latin	Perf	perfect
Co	coda of syllable	PIE	Proto-Indo-European
Dat	dative	Plur	plural
Fem	feminine	Ppf	pluperfect
Fr	French	Pres	present
Fut	future	Rh	syllable rhyme
Gen	genitive	Sing	singular
Imp	imperative	son	sonorant
Impf	imperfect	Subj	subjunctive
Inf	infinitive	Sup	supine
Interj	interjection	V	vowel
Masc	masculine	X	skeletal slot
N	nasal consonant		

[...]	phonological representation
⟨...⟩	orthographic form
>	developed into
<	developed from
>>	is higher (on some scale) than
~	alternates with
*	reconstructed form
**	ill-formed or non-existent form
+	morpheme boundary (in polymorphemic forms)
#	word boundary
→	is the morphological basis of; in phonological rules: is replaced by
←	is morphologically based on
x.x	syllable boundary
{s}	extrasyllabic [s]
σ	syllable

Names of ancient authors and titles of their works, occasionally abbreviated in the main text, are listed in Appendix 2.

ACKNOWLEDGEMENTS

I extend my gratitude to those colleagues with whom I discussed various parts of this work while it was in progress over many years, and whose remarks and suggestions were helpful at earlier stages: Péter Siptár, Péter Szigetvári, László Hunyadi, Krisztina Polgárdi, Donca Steriade, Ádám Nádasdy, Béla Adamik, Tamás Adamik, Péter Rebrus, László Kálmán, Miklós Törkenczy, Giampaolo Salvi, Zsuzsanna Bárkányi and Zsolt Simon. I am also grateful for the invaluable comments and suggestions of two anonymous reviewers of the manuscript. Part of the work was written while I was on the Hajdú Péter Research Grant at the Research Institute for Linguistics (Hungarian Academy of Sciences), and thus relieved of my teaching and administrative duties at Pázmány Péter Catholic University between February and June 2014. I thank István Kenesei, then director of RIL, and Marianne Bakró-Nagy, then head of the Department of Historical and Finno-Ugric Linguistics at the same institute for this opportunity and for providing a friendly atmosphere of scholarly collaboration not only during this period but for many years before it. I have, on several occasions, received financial support from Pázmány Péter Catholic University that made my participation at international conferences possible. My thanks must also go to Péter Balogh, who first introduced me to the Latin language more than thirty years ago; and to András Mohay, an outstanding teacher, whose absence from academia is a huge loss to classical studies. And, of course, I am very grateful to my parents, who decided that all of their children must learn Latin, no matter what.

But most of all I thank Emese, my *uxor carissima*, who has borne most of the burden of my general distraction and occasional absence from family life. I hope she will not feel that it has been in vain.

Akadémiai Kiadó has kindly permitted me to reuse substantial parts of two of my previously published articles.

1

INTRODUCTION

1.1. AIMS AND SCOPE

This work is a comprehensive corpus-based description of the synchronic segmental phonology of Classical Latin, and of those aspects of its morphology that interact with its phonological structure in important ways. The goal is not only to give a description; the goal is to highlight how the patterns and processes described and the new research results that they lead to contribute to phonological theory. This contribution is meant to work in two ways. The analyses presented here are informed by specific hypotheses about how phonological representations are structured and about how phonological rules work; and in that way my findings corroborate these hypotheses. But the description to be presented also provides raw material for researchers of phonology and morphology, regardless of what framework they work in at present or will work in in the future.

The scope of the work encompasses the complete segmental phonology, including patterns and processes, syllable structure and alternations; it does not cover strictly speaking prosodic issues, i.e. word stress and intonation. As regards word stress, what is commonly known will be taken for granted and mentioned where appropriate without argumentation; it was not among my goals to produce new research in that area. The treatment of morphology is confined to two major areas. I give a full description and analysis of the morphophonology of regular inflection, and I discuss prefixation, which also provides important insight into phonological patterns.

The discussion is primarily not diachronic; this is not a historical phonology of Latin. Mention will be made of several phonologically interesting preclassical and postclassical developments at certain points, but as a matter of principle, the focus is on Classical Latin, and my analyses are not informed by etymological considerations.

1.2. PREVIOUS RESEARCH

Research on Latin phonology was purely diachronic for many decades since the nineteenth century. The presentation of sound changes leading from Proto-Indo-European to Latin, and then from Latin to the Romance languages, encapsulated most of what there was to say about the phonological structure of the language.

The great historical grammars of Latin (Sommer 1902; Meillet 1928; Leumann 1977; Sihler 1995; Meiser 1998; Baldi 2002; Weiss 2009) include an immense wealth of information about how sounds and sound patterns developed, but they usually discuss synchronic regularities as remnants or consequences of diachronic changes. *A fortiori* the same is true of works dedicated solely to historical phonology (Niedermann 1953[1906]; Juret 1921; Kent 1932; Maniet 1955). The latter group partly overlaps in its content with works whose focus is on the reconstruction of the pronunciation of Latin (and, by implication, its sound system; Sturtevant 1920; Allen 1978). Other works focus on prosodic issues but discuss much of the segmental phonology of the language, especially those aspects that are connected to syllable structure, vowel length and phonotactics, largely in structuralist-type frameworks (Zirin 1970; Pulgram 1970, 1975; Allen 1973; Devine & Stephens 1977; Lehmann 2005). Two works have attempted to take broader scope over the phonology of the language (Ballester 1996; Touratier 2005; Oniga 2014 is a generativist introduction to the Latin language with chapters on phonology and morphology on pp. 9–171). In recent years two works stand out as treatments of aspects of the historical phonology of Latin informed by the most current work on phonetics as well as phonology (Stuart-Smith 2004 and Sen 2015). Works whose topic is of a narrower scope are not listed here but are referenced at the appropriate points in the discussion.

My own research has focused on Latin phonology for many years now. Much of what I have published over the past decade and a half can be seen as preliminary studies to what I am presenting here. I revisit several questions, and often find new answers to them; and even when the answer has not changed, the discussion is significantly updated and augmented with new data, new ways of description and modelling. I do not list specific bibliographic items here; they will be referenced at the appropriate points.

1.3. THE LANGUAGE, THE DATA AND THE FORM OF WRITING

The subject of this work is the language referred to as Classical Latin. It is therefore appropriate to begin by delineating this object and defining to the necessary extent what is meant by it. Classical Latin is, of course, not a language in itself but a variety of a language: it is the (spoken as well as written) Latin of the Roman élite of the late Republic and the early Empire, the variety of Latin that emerged and crystallised by the first century BC, became, in a standardised form, the vehicle of a vast amount of literature as well as non-belletristic writing and was then transmitted in established forms of schooling for centuries. It can be delimited temporally as well as sociolinguistically, and this is most pertinent to the present discussion because it involves the delimitation of the data I use.

The beginning of Classical Latin in the strict sense of the word is traditionally placed in the first half of the first century BC. The grounds for this are provided symbolically by the public appearance of Cicero (dated 81 BC), a figure of paramount importance in the crystallisation of the linguistic norm. The Latin of the third and second century BC authors shows phonological, grammatical and lexical peculiarities that are absent from the middle of the first century on, either because the spontaneous course of language change replaced them, or because they fell victim to the conscious efforts of selection and elaboration on the part of Cicero and his influential contemporaries. Since, however, the language of official documents begins to show marked consistency already before the first century BC, it is 'categorically not the case that the process of standardisation belongs exclusively to the final years of the Republic and the early Empire, even if this was a particularly important, even climactic, phase in the development of the language in its higher written forms' (Clackson & Horrocks 2007: 90).[1]

In the other direction the cut-off-point is even more difficult to determine. Traditional histories of Latin, which refer to the first two centuries AD as the 'silver age' or the 'postclassical period' establish these stages on literary rather than linguistic criteria (e.g. Palmer 1954: 140 sqq.). The form of the language standardised by the first century BC was perpetuated in the written medium for centuries, and it is clear that it gradually drifted away from the realities of the spoken language. It is also clear that expectations and tastes changed in literary forms too, but that will not be my concern here. Highly schooled native speakers of Latin were able to write in Classical Latin well into the sixth century AD (such as Boethius). At the same time, we know for certain that important and far-reaching sound changes had been completed or progressed considerably by this time, e.g. the neutralisation of vowel length or the palatalisation of coronals and velars. Also, there are signs that some inflectional patterns and categories began to break down in later imperial times, and noticeable shifts were underway in derivational morphology too. These changes were, by and large, kept out of the more elevated styles of writing, which contributed to the widening gap between the standardised (by this time chiefly written) form of the language and its spoken varieties.

The collapse of the institutional background that had made the preservation of the linguistic norm possible was complete by the end of the sixth century AD all over the territory of the (Western) Roman Empire, including its last stronghold, Italy. Familiarity with Classical Latin vanished quickly, to be more or less restored by artificial measures in a process that began in Charlemagne's Frankish Empire in the late eighth century, by which time, it is argued by authorities, the Latin language of Antiquity, as preserved by the Church, had ceased to be understood in Gaul. It appears that comprehensibility broke down in Spain and Italy later, maybe only in the tenth century.[2]

---

[1] For the unfolding of this process and the emergence of the classical norm see Clackson & Horrocks (2007: 77–228) and Rosén (1999), two comprehensive works. On the issue of dialectal divisions and regional diversity within Latin the authoritative work now is Adams (2007), on social variation Adams (2013).

[2] For treatments of the question of the 'end of Latin' see Herman (1996; 2000), Wright (2002), Clackson & Horrocks (2007: 265–72).

In terms of data, the present work is based on volume 1 of the Brepols Corpus (CLCLT-5 – Library of Latin Texts by Brepols Publishers, Release 2002).[3] In selecting the data I have by and large confined myself to the period between 100 BC and 400 AD. I do note data that are phonologically interesting and relevant from earlier, and occasionally from later times, but when making generalisations, I disregard these. This means not only individual words but also patterns such as the metrical structures of pre-classical (scenic) poetry. I further disregard loanwords that were, in all likelihood, not yet 'naturalised' in the period under discussion, such as the *pn*-initial technical terms borrowed from Greek, which are found in e.g. Vitruvius's *De architectura* or Pliny's *Naturalis historia*. It goes without saying that it is impossible to be certain in all cases when a loanword has been fully incorporated into the vocabulary of the receiving language (and, by consequence, perhaps changed its phonological patterns). But there is a clear difference between loans like *bracchium* 'arm' or *poena* 'punishment' on the one hand and *aer* 'air' or *pneumaticus* 'concerned with air pressure' on the other in that the latter two are not only more recent but also much more restricted in terms of register, and therefore they will not be cited as evidence that e.g. [pn] is a licit cluster in Latin or that it is usual for a long vowel (least of all [aː]) to be found before another vowel.

There are two partial corpora that I also made use of. In order to calculate the textual frequency of consonants (reported in Appendix 1) I created a selective corpus of 191,025 words (1,101,173 characters) representative of a variety of authors and genres. All the texts in this corpus date from the first century BC and the first century AD.[4] Finally, the term 'poetic corpus' in this work refers to the entire corpus of the poets Lucretius, Catullus, Vergil, Horace, Propertius, Tibullus, Ovid, Silius Italicus, Persius, Lucanus, Martialis, Statius, Valerius Flaccus, and Juvenal.[5] I used this corpus whenever I needed data for specifically poetic use.

Naturally these aspects of the delimitation of the data can be criticised and, as I said above, in the absence of clear and well-defined boundaries I could not argue with equal force in each and every case for the – tacit or explicit – dismissal of certain forms. It is also well known to everyone who works with extinct literary

---

[3] The database includes over 47 million words altogether, and covers all works from the classical period (more than 5 million words) based on highly regarded textual editions, supplemented with extensive bibliographic infomation.

[4] This corpus includes the full text of the following works: *Res gestae divi Augusti* (also known as the *Monumentum Ancyranum*), Julius Caesar's *Commentarii de bello civili*, Cicero's *Brutus*, *De legibus*, *Pro Archia poeta* and *Pro Quinctio*, Ovid's *Amores*, Persius's *Saturae*, Sallust's *Bellum Catilinae*, Statius's *Silvae* and Vergil's *Georgica*. Since calculating frequencies could not be fully automated, using the entire Brepols Corpus was impracticable.

[5] The poets are listed in chronological order of birth to the extent that it is known. Lucretius was born in the first years of the first century BC, Juvenal died some time in the first half of the second century AD. Together they practically cover the entire surviving poetry of these two centuries. In culling the data I consistently excluded works by these poets denoted as *dubium* or *pseudo-* in the Brepols Corpus.

languages that isolated and odd pieces of data can always turn up, whether in minor texts that one has accidentally overlooked or has not had access to, or in variants of better-known texts. I nevertheless hope that the overall picture that emerges does justice to the language and does not give a skewed presentation of its phonological and morphological patterns.

The next point to consider concerns the availability and the reliability of the data. It is only one part of the problem that data for Latin exist only in writing. The other part is that even the documents in which the language has been preserved come overwhelmingly from periods later than that in which Latin was actually spoken and in which the originals of these documents were composed.

The written sources of Latin thus fall into two major groups. A smaller part has remained from Antiquity without any mediation, since these texts were written on durable materials such as stone or metal, or were preserved due to extraordinary circumstances on some less durable material, such as papyrus, wax or wooden tablets. Texts of this kind, except papyri, are referred to as inscriptions. The larger part, by contrast, i.e. manuscripts in the narrower sense, do not physically date from Antiquity (with a handful of exceptions) but have been transmitted via copying by hand, the only method of transmission until the appearance of the printing press. The vast majority of extant Latin texts fall into the latter category and, by consequence, they do not always reflect faithfully the form of texts as originally produced by their authors. The changes introduced in the course of copying are studied and, if all goes well, detected and reversed by practitioners of textual criticism, who produce editions of texts from extant manuscripts (which editions, in turn, are incorporated into electronic databases). What follows from this is that the linguist who studies Latin (or the literary critic, or the historian) has to rely on a large corpus of texts that are burdened with varying degrees of uncertainty of an elementary kind. Of course most texts, especially from the classical era, have been restored with high fidelity and very good editions have been around for some time. But one always has to bear in mind that some of the data are conjectural, and some of the conjectures are not necessarily right, though most linguists (or literary critics, or historians) are not in a position to judge these for themselves, especially on a larger scale.

A case in point is here taken from Plautus (cca. 254–184 BC; see Reynolds & Wilson 1991: 23). In his famous play *Miles gloriosus*, l. 1180, a person is described with the phrase *exfafillato bracchio* in some manuscripts, in some *expapillato bracchio*, in some *expalliolato bracchio*. All three readings can possibly go back to Antiquity (the earliest extant manuscript dates from the fourth century AD, that is, about six hundred years after Plautus's death), and the latter two can be easily interpreted as 'bared to the breast' and 'not covered by cloak' (scil. *bracchium* 'arm'), respectively. Textual critics, however, have settled for the first as the authentic reading. The word *exfafillato* presents interesting linguistic and philological problems: (i) this is its only occurrence in the extant corpus; (ii) consequently its meaning is unclear, but it is generally interpreted as 'uncovered' or 'stretched out from under the cloak' by modern authorities; (iii) it involves a phonological curiosity, namely a word-internal [f], which is very unusual in Latin; and (iv) the reading is unassimilated ⟨exf-⟩ instead of the more usual ⟨eff-⟩ or ⟨ecf-⟩. The latter two are phonological issues I will discuss in some detail later (see Chapters 2 and 7), and specific textual problems I encountered are mentioned at various places. The point I want to make here is simply that the set of data on which conclusions are based in any discussion of Latin is inevitably incomplete, partly conjectural and somewhat contingent.

The form of writing I use throughout this monograph is what can be regarded as the standardised writing of Latin as generally used in textual editions, textbooks and dictionaries. It is interesting to note that this writing does not originate from the high classical era (that is, the middle decades of the first century BC) but is somewhat later. It is based on the official practice of the late and post-Augustan era,[6] roughly the first century AD, also referred to in literary terms as the 'silver age'. Its distinguishing features include, among others, the consistent use of ⟨u⟩ for short [u] (as opposed to earlier ⟨o⟩ after ⟨u⟩ as in ⟨seruus⟩ vs. ⟨seruos⟩ 'slave', ⟨uultus⟩ vs. ⟨uoltus⟩ 'face'), the consistent use of ⟨qu⟩ for original [kʷ] instead of ⟨c⟩ before rounded as well as unrounded vowels (as in ⟨equus⟩ vs. ⟨ecus⟩ 'horse'), and the consistent use of ⟨i⟩ for [iː] instead of ⟨ei⟩ (as in ⟨pueri⟩ vs. ⟨puerei⟩ 'boys'). At the same time it must be borne in mind that there being no standardised spelling in the modern sense of the word, archaic spellings are attested in inscriptions and papyri well into the imperial period. Furthermore, modern editorial practice departs even from this silver-age standard in at least two ways. One concerns the marking of length, which is systematically omitted from edited texts (except dictionaries and some elementary textbooks), though it was present in many inscriptions, albeit not very consistently. The other concerns the writing of the two glides [j w], which were not distinguished from the corresponding vowels [i u] until the sixteenth century.

The exclusively written sources, of course, lead to another question: how does one interpret the data phonetically? How does one know how the words actually sounded? With Latin we are in a relatively fortunate position, since the wealth of data of various sorts does not leave much unresolved.[7] First of all, given that spelling was not standardised, and even in official use it only achieved comparative stability by the early first century AD, it can be safely assumed that writing was not so far removed from pronunciation as the ossified traditional spelling of many European languages, and the relation between the two was

---

[6] Perhaps the most emblematic representative of this style of writing is the text called *Res gestae divi Augusti*, composed in several stages probably during the last fifteen years or so of Augustus's reign (d. 14 AD), and then augmented with additions commissioned by his successor, Tiberius. This text was carved into the walls of several temples and public buildings all over the empire and, most notably, into bronze pillars (now lost) in front of Augustus's mausoleum. The best exemplar of the text is found in Ankara, Turkey, hence the alternative name *Monumentum Ancyranum*.

[7] The items in the list that follows will be exemplified at various points in the following chapters.

much more consistent and closer to an ideal of biuniqueness. The lack of a standardised spelling is a blessing in this case, because the vast amount of variation found in contemporary writing (inscriptions, papyri) is indicative of interesting details. Second, direct references in ancient grammarians' works are numerous, though not always easy to interpret (see Vainio 1999: 97–107; Adams 2003: 433–5). Third, versification is indicative of vowel length and the syllabic affiliation of consonants (including their absence, such as that of word-final [s] in preclassical poetry). Fourth, puns and other kinds of poetic invention that crucially depend on sound shapes may also be of use. Fifth, transcriptions to and from Greek also provide invaluable information about the pronunciation of both languages (see Adams 2003: 40–67). Latin loanwords in other languages dating from ancient times give further insight into original sound shapes. Finally, the evidence of related languages as well as of the Romance languages also contributes to our understanding of the sound system of Latin.

1.4. THE FRAMEWORK

The framework I chose for the description and the analysis may be called fairly conservative. The presentation of phonology is rule-based; not primarily because I believe that rule-based frameworks are more suitable for the description of natural languages than others, but because the results thus presented are interpretable for adherents of the most varied theories and can easily be reformulated in different frameworks if necessary. The few specific assumptions I make about how phonological rules work are those of 'classical' Lexical Phonology (Kiparsky 1982a; 1982b; Mohanan 1986; Goldsmith 1990: 217–73), all very basic: (1) phonological rules are arranged sequentially and may operate on each other's output; (2) there is a distinction between phonological rules that interact with morphological structure and those that do not, i.e. (2a) different morphological domains may define different sets of phonological rules that operate in them and (2b) a subset of them are subject to the Derived Environment Condition, i.e. they are not triggered by environments that emerged earlier in the derivation, including lexically given environments.[8]

The representations I assume are geometrically characterised, that is, segments have a hierarchical internal structure in which the terminal nodes are (binary) features. Root nodes attach to skeletal nodes (timing slots) and it is through these that segments are organised into syllabic constituents. Details of the specific feature geometry that I use are explained in section 2.4, including the fundamental assumption that the place nodes and features of vowels vs.

---

[8] On the Derived Environment Condition see Cole (1995), more recently as Non-Derived Environment Blocking in Baković (2011: 15) and Inkelas (2011: 80–2); originally called Strict Cycle Condition, as in Mascaró (1976) and Kiparsky (1982a; 1982b).

consonants are organised differently; my analyses depend on this assumption crucially, and also corroborate it.

As regards morphological structure, my approach is, in a way, minimalist. The structures I discuss are all concatenative (including reduplication), with morphemes being realised in each case by phonologically specific, concrete entities (admitting the possibility of zero variants). My focus is on the phonological conditions that obtain in various morphological constructions, meaning both the phonological conditioning of allomorph choice and the phonological conse-quences of morphological operations. Various instances of lexically or grammat-ically conditioned morphological variation will also be presented, but these will not be in the focus in the same way as phonologically relevant variation. A fundamental dichotomy that is observed in the organisation of the material is that between simplex vs. non-simplex (or complex) forms. Simplex forms are not necessarily monomorphemic; indeed monomorphemic forms are relatively rare in Latin. They may have suffixes of any kind, may show fusional exponence within the stem, or may be reduplicated. Complex forms include prefixed words, cliticised words and compounds (the latter two discussed only tangentially).

It is important to realise that much of what is traditionally discussed under the rubric of Latin (inflectional or derivational) morphology is etymological informa-tion whose relevance to synchronic morphology is questionable.[9] Take the following example. In the verbal sub-paradigm *amamus, amatis, amant* 'love' 1PLUR, 2PLUR, 3PLUR, respectively, and corresponding sub-paradigms of any other verb, it is very easy to identify *-mus, -tis* and *-nt* as cumulative exponents of person and number. But how about the vowel [a] before them? Does it have morphological function, is it a separable morphological constituent? Since it appears in all forms of this particular verb,[10] but does not appear in the related words *amor* 'love' and *amicus* 'friend(ly)', one could feel justified in calling it a verb-forming suffix. In the formally similar verb *secare* 'cut' → *secamus, secatis, secant* the same vowel is found only in the forms based on the infectum stem, not in those based on the perfectum stem (PERF1SING *secui* as opposed to *amavi*) or those based on what is called the third stem (e.g. *sectus* PASSPART), or in derivationally related words (e.g. *segmentum* 'segment, slice'). Thus the *a* in *secare* could be seen as an infectum suffix. In a third verb, *fugare* 'put to flight' → *fugamus, fugatis, fugant* the [a] appears in all verb forms as well as the noun *fuga* 'flight', but it is not found in the related verb *fugere* 'flee'. So, it may seem reasonable to say that the [a] in *fugare* is a noun-forming suffix and the verb is derived from a noun. Finally, in a verb like *nare* 'swim' → *namus, natis, nant* the same [a] is found in all forms of the verb and there is absolutely no derivationally

---

[9] The descriptive tradition of Latin inflectional morphology as it is today is basically a distilled version of the vast amount of diachronic work going back to the nineteenth century. For excellent recent histories of Latin see Sihler (1995), Meiser (1998), Baldi (2002), Clackson & Horrocks (2007), Weiss (2009).

[10] For 1SING *amo* see 5.3.2.

related word that does not include it. Therefore the only viable option is to say that it is not a suffix — indeed, if it was a suffix it would leave us with an absolute stem consisting of a single consonant, definitely not a desirable option. Now this [a], which is shown to represent four different types of morphological entites, if one insists on an exhaustive morphological analysis of that kind, behaves in exactly the same way phonologically: it shortens before 3Sɪɴɢ -*t*, 3Pʟᴜʀ -*nt* and drops before the 1Sɪɴɢ suffixes -*o*, -*or* as well as before the -*e*- of the subjunctive, thus *amemus*, *secemus*, *fugemus*, *nemus*, etc., and it triggers the same kinds of allomorphy in each verb. How then does one analyse these forms? How many morphemes do they consist of and what exactly are those morphemes? In my view, these are largely lexical matters from a synchronic perspective and do not form part of productive morphology (certainly not inflectional morphology). As a consequence, many time-honoured terms of morphological analysis will not be found in this work (e.g. thematic vowel), simply because I have found them useless for my purposes.

But it is necessary at this point to briefly explain and illustrate how I conceive of the relation between morphology, phonology and the lexicon. As will be clear from the preceding paragraphs, morphology as the term is applied here is primarily concerned with structures and allomorphy. Structures may be concatenative or fusional (with the latter type not discussed in the present work in detail). Morphological regularities, whether of structure or allomorphy, are typically morpheme-specific, or take scope over small, grammatically defined sets of specific morphemes. Such regularities are not phonological even in those rare cases when it is possible to make phonological generalisations about them.[11]

Rules of allomorphy may involve three kinds of conditioning. They may be phonologically conditioned, such as the choice of the future marker -*b*- vs. -*ē*- after nonhigh vowels vs. after high vowels and consonants, respectively.[12] They may be grammatically conditioned, such as the choice of the 1Sɪɴɢ marker -*ō* vs. -*m*, of which the latter is never found immediately attached to infectum stems, only to extended stems.[13] They may also be lexically conditioned, which means neither grammatical nor phonological factors can be identified as corresponding to the choice of allomorphs.[14] In the third case then it is a feature somehow represented in the lexical makeup of a word which particular morphological variant it will exhibit.

---

[11] For instance, if there is a difference in vowel length in the infectum vs. the perfectum stem of the verb, it is nearly always the former that has a short vowel and the latter that has a long vowel, e.g. *agere* ~ *ēgi* 'do', *emere* ~ *ēmi* 'buy', *fodere* ~ *fōdi* 'dig'.

[12] *Ama-b-is* 'you will love', *vide-b-is* 'you will see' vs. *capi-e-s* 'you will catch', *ag-e-s* 'you will do'. All types of allomorphy will be amply illustrated in the following chapters.

[13] *Vide-o* 'I see' vs. *vide-re-m* 'I would see'; in fact, the choice between the two allomorphs after extended stems is already phonologically conditioned, but pure (i.e. unextended) stems categorically exclude the choice of -*m* (more on this in Chapter 6).

[14] See the difference between the two stems in the case of *fodere* ~ *fōdi* 'dig' vs. *amare* ~ *amavi* 'love'.

Phonological rules, by contrast, are generalisations that ideally only make reference to phonological units. They make reference neither to grammatical structures, nor to particular morphemes. Under the assumptions adopted here, they may make reference at most to a distinction between derived and non-derived environments (see above), and to word boundaries. That said, it is possible for a phonological rule to have exceptions, it is possible for it to be restricted to a certain morphological domain, and it is possible for it to have apparently narrow scope resulting from lexical contingencies (small number of lexemes including a particular phonological configuration that triggers the rule).

These distinctions are here illustrated with a small set of verb forms, five lexemes represented by the present infinitive, the perfect 1Sing form and the passive participle.

(1) INF   PERF   PASSPART   gloss
     vomere   *vomui*   *vomitus*   'throw up'
     emere   *ēmi*   *emptus*   'buy'
     sumere   *sumpsi*   *sumptus*   'take'
     premere   *pressi*   *pressus*   'press'
     mittere   *mīsi*   *missus*   'send'

For simplicity, let us assume that the infectum stems (i.e. what is found before the -*ere* ending) do not contain further morphological elements. (This is neither obvious, nor is it in fact true for many other Latin verbs.) If we now compare the perfect to the infectum-based forms, we see at least three different ways they are distinguished. *Vomui* has an -*u*- suffix; *ēmi* has vowel length (i.e. fusion); the other three seem to have added an -*s*- suffix, but *mīsi* also has a long vowel just like *ēmi*. Whether a verb has the -*u*- suffix, the -*s*- suffix, fusion or some other way of differentiating the two stems is synchronically a lexical matter; it is simply part of the lexical makeup of the verb.

Passive participles are all affixed with -*tus* or -*sus*; the choice between the two is again lexically given (though -*sus* is very often found with verbs whose infectum stem ends in a coronal stop). But note that *vomitus* has an intervening [i], whereas *emptus* and *sumptus* have an intervening [p].

The precise relation between the forms is determined by an intricate interplay of lexical, morphological and phonological factors. *Sumpsi* follows strictly from the concatention of *sum*- and -*s*-, because a phonological rule (see 4.7) inserts a [p] in this environment; the same is true of *sumptus* and *emptus*. In *vomitus*, the choice of -*itus* rather than -*tus* is lexically conditioned allomorphy. Unlike *sumpsi*, the form *pressi* does not follow from *prem-s*-, and neither does *pressus* from anything like putative *prem-sus*. In their particular form, they are arbitrary and unparallelled, which means it is not only the choice of -*s*- over -*u*- or anything else for the perfectum stem and the choice of -*sus* over -*tus* for the passive participle that is lexically given, but the entire form of the perfectum stem and the passive participle. *Missus* follows from *mitt*+*sus* by the application of two phonological rules, degemination (4.5.1) and assimilation of [ts] to [ss] (4.3); *mīsi* shows the application of the same rules plus the degemination of [ss] after long vowels, also a phonological rule (4.5.2), but the latter crucially depends on the presence of a long vowel in addition to the -*s*- suffix in the perfectum stem, which are both purely morphological markers (whose choice is lexically conditioned, as seen above).

The reader will see that there are significant differences in the generality of the proposed phonological regularities, and also in how intimate their relation to morphology is. In some cases it may be in doubt whether a pattern is part of phonology or is a case of allomorphy. I think in the case of a work like this it is better to err on the side of generosity and include the phenomena in question if they conform at least to a certain extent to more general phonological regularities of the language, or if they appear to cross the boundaries of well-defined morphological categories. But inevitably opinions may differ as regards some of what is presented in the pages that follow.

At certain points I will argue that particular phenomena belong to the lexicon rather than the phonology, in other words that particular patterns or forms have been lexicalised rather than produced by active phonological rules. The arguments, which are generally based in these cases on productivity in the broad sense, may be found to be more persuasive in some cases than in others. But no principled attempt will be made in the pages that follow to strictly separate what is lexicalised and what is not. Under current views it is entirely possible that the output even of productive rules could be lexically listed (see e.g. Bermúdez-Otero 2012), just as it is possible to conceive of phonological regularities as patterns obtaining over sets of lexical forms rather than as input–output processes or as constraints (see e.g. Rebrus & Törkenczy 2015a; 2015b). These (meta-)theoretical issues will not be settled here.

1.5. THE STRUCTURE OF THE BOOK

Chapter 2 describes the segmental inventory of Classical Latin, with a detailed account of basic distributional regularities and an analysis of controversial points (nasal vowels, diphthongs, labiovelars). The same chapter presents in detail the phonological representations used throughout this book. Chapter 3 is a phonotactic analysis, based mainly on the distribution of consonants in clusters, with a focus on non-nuclear syllabic constituents. The interaction between sonority, place of articulation and syllable contact is also explored here, as is resyllabification and – as a short diachronic detour – the history of the phonotactically odd cluster written ⟨gn⟩. Chapters 4 and 5 analyse consonantal and vocalic processes, respectively. Chapter 6 elaborates the structure of regular inflectional morphology (both nominal and verbal) in terms of morpheme variants and the phonological conditioning factors that define their distribution. Chapter 7 leaves the domain of morphologically simplex forms entirely, to discuss the phonological behaviour of prefixes and prefixed forms. Chapter 8 concludes the book and provides a conspectus of the rules. An Appendix provides data on the frequency of consonants in a corpus of Latin texts (described above in 1.3), another Appendix lists the ancient authors and their works that are referred to in the book.

2

THE SEGMENTAL INVENTORY

2.1. Introduction

In this chapter the segmental inventory of Classical Latin will be established on the basis of surface contrastivity and phonological behaviour.[15] Thus the discussion here and its results serve as a preliminary to everything else that follows. At the same time, several problems of analysis arise in their own right already at this stage. These concern contour segments on the one hand: how does one decide if the entities traditionally called diphthongs and labiovelars are segments or sequences? On the other hand, one needs to argue for segments that are not represented in an obvious fashion either in the spelling system — which is fairly phonological in Latin — or in the philological tradition. In my analysis the latter case involves the placeless nasal and the nasal vowels.

Besides problematic points of segmental analysis, basic distributional regularities (word-level phonotactics) are also presented. A detailed explanation of the phonological features as well as of the representations to be used concludes the chapter.

2.2. Consonants

The surface-contrastive inventory of Classical Latin consonants and their usual spellings are shown in Figure 1. The Classical Latin consonant system is typologically very simple and parsimonious. Voicing is contrastive only for stops; fricatives are redundant in their voicing, sonorants are redundantly voiced. Three places of articulation cover all consonants but one; [h] is the only glottal segment in the system, while there is no velar fricative in the language at all.[16] Whether the coronals [t d s n l r] were dental or alveolar is difficult to establish with certainty, and nothing hinges on it in this work. The glide [j] was phonetically palatal, and [w] was labiovelar.

---

[15] Portions of this chapter first appeared, in somewhat different form, in Cser (2012a).

[16] Since, however, the only reconstructible historical source of Classical Latin [h] is Proto-Indo-European *[gʱ], it is probable that there was, at some point between the two stages, a velar fricative in the system which then developed into [h] (see e.g. Sihler 1995: 158 sqq. for a classic handbook-type summary; Stuart-Smith 2004 is a work devoted in its entirety to the development of Proto-Indo-European aspirates in Italic, with the problems surrounding Latin [h] discussed on pp. 43, 47 and passim).

Segment	Spelling	Example
[p]	⟨p⟩	*pars* 'part', *quippe* 'naturally'
[t]	⟨t⟩	*tegere* 'cover', *caput* 'head'
[k]	⟨c⟩ mostly ⟨q⟩ _[w], i.e. ⟨qu⟩ = [kw] ⟨k⟩ in some words ⟨x⟩ = [ks]	*cicer* [kiker] 'pea', *hinc* 'from here' *aqua* [akwa] 'water', *quippe* 'naturally' *Kalendae* [kalendaj] '1st day of month' *dux* [duks] 'leader, guide', *rexi* 'I ruled'
[b]	⟨b⟩	*bibere* 'drink', *imber* 'rain'
[d]	⟨d⟩	*dare* 'give', *quod* 'which, that'
[g]	⟨g⟩	*gravis* 'heavy', *agger* 'heap'
[f]	⟨f⟩	*frangere* 'break', *fuit* 'was'
[s]	⟨s⟩ ⟨x⟩ = [ks]	*spissus* 'dense' *dux* [duks] 'leader, guide'
[h]	⟨h⟩	*homo* 'man', *vehere* 'carry'
[m]	⟨m⟩	*mensis* 'month', *summus* 'topmost'
[n]	⟨n⟩	*nomen* 'name', *annus* 'year'
[l]	⟨l⟩	*linquere* 'leave', *puellula* 'little girl'
[r]	⟨r⟩	*rarus* 'rare', *cruor* 'blood'
[j]	⟨i⟩ or ⟨j⟩ _V (depending on editorial tradition) ⟨e⟩ V_C and V_#	*iungere* or *jungere* [juŋgere] 'join', *ieiunus* or *jejunus* [jejju:nus] 'hungry, fasting' *aes* [ajs] 'bronze', *stellae* [stellaj] 'stars'
[w]	⟨u⟩ or ⟨v⟩ _V (depending on editorial tradition) ⟨u⟩ V_C and V_#; #[s]_ and [k]_ (=⟨qu⟩)	*uelle* or *velle* [welle] 'want' *haud* [hawd] 'not', *suavis* [swa:wis] 'sweet'; *aqua* 'water', *quippe* 'naturally'

Figure 1. The Classical Latin consonants and their spellings

			labial	coronal	dorsal	glottal
obstruents	**stops**	**voiceless**	p	t	k	
		voiced	b	d	g	
	fricatives		f	s		h
sonorants	**nasals**		m	n		
	liquids			l r		
	glides				j w	

There is a tradition of analysing glides as positional variants of the respective high vowels (see e.g. Hoenigswald 1949a; or more recently Ballester 1996; Marotta 1999; Lehmann 2005; Touratier 2005). While their environments are partly predictable, cases of contrast are far too numerous to be dismissed. Some of these cases can be explained away with reference to morphological structure (*vol*[w]*it* 'he rolls' vs. *vol*[u]*it* 'he wanted' where the [u] is a perfectum marker, or *s*[w]*avis* 'sweet' vs. *s*[u]*a* 'his/her', where the [a] of *sua* is a feminine marker), some cases clearly cannot: *bel*[u]*a* 'beast' vs. *sil*[w]*a* 'forest', *q*[w]*i* 'who/which' vs. *c*[u]*i* 'to whom/which', *ling*[w]*a* 'tongue' vs. *exig*[u]*a* 'small', *co*[i]*t* '(s)he meets' vs. *co*[j]*tus* 'meeting', or *aq*[w]*a* 'water' vs. *ac*[u]*at* '(s)he should sharpen'; or consider the possibilities of representing the difference between *inicere* [injikere] 'throw in' vs. *iniquus* [iniːkwus] 'inimical'.

The consonant [h] does not condition or undergo any phonological rule in Latin and this has led some linguists to the conclusion that a complete description would be equally feasible without it (as in Touratier 2005 or Zirin 1970; in the latter work /h/ is appropriated as a phonological symbol for hiatus). The phonological inertness of [h] may well be a sign that by classical times this sound was lost completely. Yet the morphological behaviour of two verbs (*trahere* 'drag' and *vehere* 'carry') militate against this conclusion. These verbs are inflected in the infectum-based paradigms exactly as other consonant-stems (e.g. 3Sɪɴɢ *trahit, vehit;* see Chapter 6). If the putative [h] at the end of the infectum stems (*trah-, veh-*) was completely inert, these verbs would be inflected as *a-* and *e-*stems (3Sɪɴɢ **trat, **vet), respectively.[17] Apart from this, the behaviour of (etymological) (V)[h]V is no different in any respect from that of plain (V)V.

There seems to be good evidence that the orthographic sequence ⟨gn⟩ denoted phonetic [ŋn] rather than [gn], at least word-internally.[18] The evidence is surveyed in Allen (1978: 22–5) and most handbooks, and involves the general phonotactic patterns of Classical Latin (on which more will be said in Chapter 3), diachronic developments, and inscriptional as well as ordinary spellings. The major points are the following.

(i) In the prehistory of Latin, there was a tendency for stops to be nasalised before nasals (e.g. [pn] > [mn], as in *swepnos > *somnus* 'sleep, dream', cf. Old English *swefn* or Greek *hupnos* 'dream', or [tn] > [nn], as in *atnos > *annus* 'year', cf. Gothic *aþn*).

(ii) Inscriptional evidence includes several forms like ⟨INGNES⟩ for *ignes* 'fire(s)', attesting to the outcome of the nasalisation of [g] before nasals.

(iii) The sound change [e] > [i], which was conditioned by (especially velar) NC sequences (*[teŋg-] > *tinguere* 'dip', *[peŋkwe] > *quinque* 'five'), but by no other type of consonant cluster,[19] was also triggered by ⟨gn⟩: *[dek-n-] > *dignus* 'worthy' (scil. via *[deŋn-]).

[17] It goes without saying that postulating an empty consonantal position or some other representational device in these two verbs could, in theory, give the same result. Since, however, the same empty position would not be required anywhere else in the phonology of Latin, I refrain from including it in the description and stay with [h] in a conservative manner. Nominal stems and other verb stems categorically do not end in [h].

[18] Word-initial ⟨gn⟩, which occurs in the name *Gnaeus*, may have retained or regained the archaic pronunciation [gn]. The same spelling-pronunciation cannot be excluded word-internally either. This cluster will be discussed at some length in 3.6.

[19] More precisely, a preconsonantal [ŋ] always triggered the change, preconsonantal [m] triggered it is some cases but not in others (e.g. *simplex* 'simple' vs. *semper* 'always', both from the Proto-Indo-European root **sem-* 'one'), whereas preconsonantal [n] never triggered it (e.g. *sentire* 'feel'). Other consonant clusters did not trigger the change (cf. *negligere* 'neglect', *lectus* 'bed', *consecrare* 'consecrate'). There was an unrelated [e] > [i] change in non-initial open syllables (*miletes > *milites* 'soldiers', see 5.2.1).

(iv) The spelling of nasal-final prefixes provides additional evidence. For example, negative *in-* is optionally spelt ⟨im⟩ before the labial stops and [m] (as in ⟨im+politus⟩ 'unpolished', ⟨im+berbis⟩ 'beardless', ⟨im+mortalis⟩ 'immortal'), ⟨il⟩ before [l] (as in ⟨il+lepidus⟩ 'lacking refinement') and ⟨ir⟩ before [r] (as in ⟨ir+revocabilis⟩ 'unalterable'; for more details see Chapter 7). As one would expect, it is written ⟨in⟩ before the velar stops, there being no distinct spelling for [ŋ] (as in ⟨in+celebratus⟩ [iŋkele-braːtus] 'unrecorded'). Before other consonants as well as before vowels, it is consistently written ⟨in⟩ (as in ⟨in+ermis⟩ 'unarmed', ⟨in+decens⟩ 'unseemly'). Before an original ⟨gn⟩-initial stem, however, the spelling of nasal-final prefixes involves the apparent (unparalleled) loss of an ⟨n⟩ as in ⟨ignoscere⟩ 'forgive' from ⟨in⟩+⟨gnoscere⟩ 'know', but this is easily explained if this written form represents [iŋnoːskere].[20]

Thus [ŋ] was in almost complementary distribution with [n], scil. [ŋ] before velar stops, but note *annus* 'year' and *agnus* 'lamb' with contrast between [nn] vs. [ŋn]; at the same time, it was in almost complementary distribution also with [g], scil. [ŋ] before [n], but note *agger* 'heap' and *angor* 'constriction' with contrast between [gg] vs. [ŋg].[21] The persistent spelling of the velar nasal with ⟨g⟩ instead of some other symbol (including most inscriptions) is not surprising given this nearly complementary distribution with [g] as well as with [n]; furthermore, in Greek spelling also, the letter gamma was used for [ŋ], i.e. ⟨γγ⟩ = [ŋg], ⟨γκ⟩ = [ŋk] and ⟨γχ⟩ = [ŋkʰ] besides its standard value ⟨γ⟩ = [g].

There is further evidence that [l] displayed an allophony somewhat similar to that found in British English, viz. it was velarised before consonants, velar vowels and possibly [e], and unvelarised before [i] and in gemination. The evidence, summarily discussed in Allen (1978: 23–5), Leumann (1977: 85–7), Meiser (1998: 68–9) and more recently in Sen (2012: 472–3; 2015: 15 sqq.) among others comes from grammarians' remarks, sound changes conditioned by [l] as well as its Romance reflexes. The phonology of this alternation is discussed in detail in 4.9.

2.2.1. *General distributional regularities in simplex forms*

All the consonants except [h] and [w] occur as geminates, though some of them mostly or only at prefix–stem boundaries. In simplex forms geminates are found only intervocalically (except for the final [kk] of the pronouns *hic* and *hoc* 'this'),

[20] For a fuller discussion of such forms and the specific problem of word-initial ⟨gn⟩ see 3.6 and Cser (2011).

[21] It is because of its odd distribution that I consistently mark [ŋ] in my transcriptions, although, strictly speaking, it is not a surface-constrastive unit. Cf. also Zirin's (1970: 26) description of the velar nasal as 'a classic case of partial phonemic overlapping'.

and the vast majority of occurrences immediately follows the stressed vowel (Giannini & Marotta 1989: 231–2, Loporcaro 2015: 2). Gemination is marked in spelling for all consonants except [j], which is rendered invariably with a single ⟨i⟩ or sometimes ⟨j⟩ in modern editorial practice, as in ⟨eius/ejus⟩ [ejjus] 'his/her'. The practice of writing single ⟨i⟩ for [jj] is based on what appears to have been the majority practice in Antiquity (see Kent 1912; Allen 1978: 37–40)[22] and was definitely general usage in the Middle Ages. Phonologically this spelling can be seen as the reflection of a neutralisation, since intervocalic [j], alone of all consonants, is always a geminate in simplex forms, and thus there is no contrast between V[j]V vs. V[jj]V.[23]

All consonants occur word-initially and intervocalically. The fricative [h] occurs only in these two environments in simplex forms (*homo* 'man', *vehere* 'carry'). For [f] word-initial position is its almost exclusive environment (*ferre* 'carry', *fur* 'thief', *frangere* 'break', etc.; in simplex forms, non-initial [f] occurs only in a handful of words[24]). It appears that while intervocalic [f] and [h] are not particularly frequent lexically, there is a noticeable preference for [f] to follow a long vowel and for [h] to follow a short vowel.[25]

Word-final consonants are mostly inflectional suffixes or parts of inflectional suffixes; this follows from the morphological character of the language. Consonants that constitute or end suffixes are [t d s r j]. Word-final consonants that are not suffixal are found in the following cases:

1. Neuter nouns belonging to the third inflectional class (consonant/*i*-stem) usually show the pure stem with a zero-suffix in the NomAccSing, e.g. *opus* 'work', *os* 'bone', *pulvinar* 'pillow', *pecten* 'comb', *animal* 'animal'. Such nouns end in [s r n l], the only exceptions being *caput* 'head' and *lac* 'milk', whose stems end in stops.[26]

---

[22] A remark found in Quintilian's *Institutio oratoria* (1.4.11) indicates that Cicero preferred spelling intervocalic [jj] with ⟨ii⟩ (*Ciceroni placuisse* aiio Maiiam*que geminata i scribere* 'that Cicero preferred to write *aiio Maiia* with double *i*'). Note further that the sequence [ji] is also regularly rendered with a single ⟨i⟩ regardless of the length of either segment, thus ⟨abicere⟩ [abjikere] 'throw away', ⟨reicere⟩ [rejjikere] 'throw back', ⟨Pompei⟩ [pompejji:] Gen of proper name *Pompeius*, and so on. This spelling practice is presented and discussed in detail in Kent (1912).

[23] Many dictionaries of Latin erroneously indicate a long vowel before intervocalic [jj] on the basis of the fact that the syllables whose nucleus is constituted by that vowel always scan as metrically heavy in poetry (but this is because they are *positione longa* rather than *natura longa*).

[24] *Āfer* 'black', *būfō* 'toad', *offa* 'bite, lump (of food)', *rūfus* 'red', *tōfus* 'tufa', *vafer* 'cunning' and their derivatives.

[25] For non-initial [f] see the previous note. Non-initial [h] is found in *incohare* 'start', *mihi* 'to me', *nihil* 'nothing', *trahere* 'drag', *vehemens* 'vehement', *vehere* 'carry'; the interjections *eho* (virtually only in Plautus and Terence) and *ēheu*; *cohors* 'cohort' and *prehendere* 'grab' should perhaps be assigned to the prefixed class. The preference for short vowels before [h] is simply an extension of the regularity that bans long vowels in the first position of a hiatus, i.e. the [h] behaves as if it did not exist. On hiatus see 2.3.3.

[26] In fact, the stem of *lac* is *lact-*, but [t], which is only allowed finally after vowels and the coronal consonants [s n l r], is dropped in the unsuffixed form. The phonotactic motivation will be explained in more detail in Chapter 3.

2. Masculine and feminine nouns belonging to the third inflectional class also assume the zero-suffix instead of the usual NomSing suffix *-s* if their stems end in the same four consonants as in (i) ([s r n l]): *honos* 'honour, office', *consul* 'consul', *mulier* 'woman', *lien*[27] 'honeycomb'; some heteroclitic *o*-stem nouns also occur in the NomSing in a zero-suffixed [r]-final form (*puer* 'boy'), as do some [r]-final adjectives in both the *o*-stem class (e.g. *aeger* 'ill') and the consonant/*i*-stem class (e.g. *celer* 'quick'; more on nominal declensions in Chapter 6).

3. The majority of prepositions (*ab* 'from', *prae* [praj] 'for, before', *per* 'through', *penes* 'with, at') and conjunctions (*et* 'and', *ac* 'and', *seu* [sew] 'or').

4. Some interjections, such as *at(t)at, fafae, (ē)heu, vae.*

5. The four imperatives *dic* 'say', *duc* 'lead', *fac* 'do', *fer* 'carry'. The last of these is a generally irregular verb in that some of its personal endings in the present are not preceded by a vowel (e.g. *fert* Pres3Sing).

6. A family of deictics ending in [k] (*hic, haec, hoc* 'this', *illac* '(to) there', *hinc* 'from here', *illinc* 'from there', *nunc* 'now' and a handful of others).

The descriptive generalisation for word-final consonants appears to involve a marked preference for coronals. As was indicated above, suffixal final consonants include only [t d s r j], non-suffixal final consonants are mostly from the set [s r n l] with one noun ending in [t] (*caput* 'head') and one in [k] (*lac* 'milk'). It so happens that no stem ends in [h f j]; and stems ending in the consonants not listed above do not have zero-suffixed forms.

On non-coronal final consonants the following seem clear. Definitely no Classical Latin word ends in [p f h g m].[28] Word-final orthographic ⟨m⟩ merely indicates the nasalisation plus lengthening of the preceding vowel, rather than phonetic [m];[29] it is analysed here as a placeless nasal (see 2.2.3).

---

[27] Non-neuter *n*-final stems that retain the [n] in the NomSing are exceedingly rare (another example is *tibicen* 'flutist'). A large portion of feminine and masculine *n*-stems end in [oː] in the NomSing (*homo*, stem *homin-* 'man', *multitudo*, stem *multitudin-* 'crowd', etc.). Only one of the masculine *n*-stems, *sanguin-* 'blood', assumes the *-s* suffix (*sanguis*).

[28] The word *volup* 'pleasur(abl)e' occurs only in Plautus and Terence and is hence preclassical. Moreover, in almost all of its occurences it is followed by *est* 'is' and may thus have been part of a lexicalised expression rather than a lexical item in its own right by that time. At any rate, by the first century BC this word was not only out of use but demonstrably the object of scholarly explanations and antiquarian interest (as Festus's *Epitome* testifies, it was included and explained in Verrius Flaccus's *De Verborum significatu*, a now lost lexicographic work), hence clearly not part of Classical Latin.

[29] This has been established beyond doubt on the basis of ancient grammarians' remarks as well as metrical evidence (see Allen 1978: 30). It is believed that one or two monosyllables may have retained the final nasal consonant in some form; this is conjectured from a handful of reflexes like French *rien* [ʀjẽ] 'nothing' with a nasal vowel < CL *rem* 'thing' Acc (but cf. *jà* [ʒa] < CL *iam* 'already' without any trace of the nasal).

Final [b] only occurs in three prepositions (*ab* 'from', *sub* 'under', *ob* 'against, because of'), which are always proclitic, so this [b] is not at the end of a phonological word.

The token frequency of final [j] is very high, but its type frequency is extremely low, since it only occurs (apart from the preposition *prae* and a few interjections such as *vae* or *fafae*) in three inflected forms of *a*-stem nouns and adjectives. The genitive and dative singular and the nominative plural of such stems all end in [aj] (e.g. *puellae* 'girl' GenSing, DatSing, NomPlur).

Final [w] occurs in five words altogether (*seu* 'or', *neu* 'neither, and not', *ceu* 'as, like', *(e)heu* INTERJ, *hau* 'not'). *Seu* and *neu* are preconsonantal variants of the vowel-final (prevocalic) forms *sive* and *neve*, respectively. It is also a fact that *ceu* is almost never used prevocalically;[30] before vowels other, functionally overlapping, conjunctions are used in its stead (*ut, sicut, velut, quasi*). It was probably proclitic[31] and thus not much more harmful to the coronal generalisation than the three *b*-final prepositions. Surprisingly, the interjections *heu* and *eheu* are, at least in their attested use, also confined to preconsonantal position.[32] *Hau* is the optional preconsonantal variant of *haud* and is overwhelmingly found in pre- and postclassical literature. The almost exclusively preconsonantal environment shows that in the few extant cases of final V[w]-sequences there was a strong tendency to avoid resyllabification of this sound at word boundary, which prevocalic position would have entailed (see 3.5). But apart from this there does not seem to be any well-defined phonological motivation for the *neu* ~ *neve* and the *seu* ~ *sive* allomorphy.

---

[30] I established this from the Brepols corpus, which indicates that of its 493 occurrences in the entire volume 1 only three are prevocalic (0.6%), of which two are found in Pliny's *Nat. hist.* (10.182 *ceu Alpini*, 22.93 *ceu in ovo*), one in Paulinus Nolanus (26.255 hexameter-initial *ceu aliquando*), a Christian poet of the late fourth and early fifth centuries AD.

[31] In most of its occurrences it is followed by a noun, an adjective, occasionally an adverb or a verb; it is almost never followed by function words, which are likely to have been unstressed. This implies that *ceu* was probably much like a preposition prosodically.

[32] In the Brepols corpus *heu* occurs about 700 times, *eheu* 64 times. If one disregards listings in grammars and direct quotations (only a handful anyhow, e.g. Petronius *Sat.* 34.7 *complosit Trimalchio manus et 'eheu' inquit* 'Trimalchio clapped his hands and said 'alas'') as well as the not infrequent *heu heu* type repetitions, *heu* is found in prevocalic position about 20 times, *eheu* only in a handful of instances. Many of the prevocalic occurrences of *heu* are made up by Ovid's stock phrase *heu ubi* 'alas, where is/are ...?' (5 occurrences), which was imitated later by Statius (4 occurrences plus *heu ubinam* 'id.' once) and much later by Claudius Claudianus (once). Statius also has *heu iterum* 'alas, and again ...' once. All these poetic examples are hexameter-initial (which, I think, underscores the formulaic nature at least of *heu ubi(nam)*) and thus *heu* scans as a heavy syllable. It is an interesting question how an interjection could be so sensitive to phonological environment, but this particular case is perhaps a stylistic, rather than a properly linguistic, issue.

Final [k] is found in the three irregular imperatives *dic* 'say', *duc* 'lead', *fac* 'do', the noun *lac* 'milk', the conjunction *ac* 'and', plus the family of deictics illustrated above.[33]

2.2.2. *The question of the labiovelar(s)*

In this section I revisit, in a comprehensive manner, a classic question about which much has been written, but even more has been taken for granted without discussion, viz. the question of labiovelar stops in Latin.[34] The so-called labiovelars of Proto-Indo-European were partly preserved as *some sort of* labiovelars in Latin, Anatolian and Germanic. In the other languages they developed into various other sounds. The interesting fact about these segments is that their phonological status is variable both historically and cross-linguistically. There are compelling reasons (taken from phonotactics and from patterns of alternation, not to be discussed here in detail) for assuming that labiovelar stops were monosegmental in Proto-Indo-European. But there are equally compelling reasons to assume that e.g. in English, a descendant of Proto-Indo-European, the only remaining 'labiovelar' [kw] is not a segment but a sequence of two segments much like [pr] or [kl]. As for the reconstructed phonological system of Proto-Germanic, opinions differ. A look at the literature reveals that no consensus has been reached, though the monosegmental interpretation, parallel to that of Proto-Indo-European, appears to be somewhat more widespread (see Lehmann 1994: 22–3; Ringe 2006: 88 sqq.; Seebold 1967; Stausland Johnsen 2009 among others).

I will now critically review the arguments for the monosegmental vs. the cluster interpretation of 'labiovelar stops' in Classical Latin, an issue on which the literature has long been divided.[35] To anticipate the conclusion, the question cannot be settled definitively, which leads to two important problems, one practical, the other theoretical. The practical question is how one incorporates such information into phonological inventory databases. (Incorporating it into descriptions *qua* descriptions is no problem since explanations

---

[33] It may be surmised that – in view of the characteristic deictic ending [k] – it is not entirely accidental that three out of the four zero-suffixed imperatives in the so-called third verb class (traditionally called consonant- and *i*-stems) happen to end in [k]. In classical times, there were only four simplex verbs whose infectum stems ended in V[k(i)]. In addition to *dic*, *duc* and *fac*, the fourth is *iacere* 'throw', whose imperative is regularly *iace*. Preclassical *specere* 'look' is not attested in the imperative form; its prefixed forms are regular (*respice* 'look round', etc.), but the same is true of *facere* (*confice* 'accomplish', etc.). Perhaps some odd kind of analogical pull is at work here.

[34] Portions of this section first appeared, in somewhat different form, in Cser (2013).

[35] Devine & Stephens (1977: 13–104) is by far the most detailed discussion of the Latin labiovelars to date, followed by Ballester (1996: 53–107); both works look at the basic phonotactic patterns to be discussed below, and both take a close look at ancient testimonia. For a classic summary of some of the arguments, to which later 'phonemic' analyses hark back, see Sturtevant (1939). For a less thorough but astute survey see Zirin (1970: 29–40). Important observations are found in Allen (1978), another classic. The issue was picked up again in Touratier (2005) and Watbled (2005). Of course, if any of the above works had provided a definitive solution, I would not have written about the issue as extensively as I have done.

can always be added.) The theoretical question is whether it is possible for a phonological entity to play an ambiguous role (segment or cluster) in a language's phonological system. These two problems, to which the discussion leads, are left for future research to resolve.

In this section the entities in question will be written ⟨qu⟩ and ⟨gu⟩ in order not to prejudge either conclusion regarding their phonological status (though, of course, I have prejudged it already by not including them in Figure 1). Note that while the former spelling in the generally accepted form of writing Latin unequivocally corresponds to the voiceless labiovelar entity in question, the latter can correspond to its voiced counterpart but also to the sequences [gu] and [guː], as in *arguere* 'show' and *argutus* (PassPart of same), respectively.

The basic facts of distribution are the following. The voiceless labiovelar entity is found in word-initial and word-internal position, in all cases followed by a vowel. It can be preceded by [s] both initially (*squalor* 'dirt') and internally (*usque* 'until'). Internally it can also be preceded by [ŋ], [r] or [j] (*quinque* 'five', *torquere* 'turn', *aequus* 'flat', resp., though of these clusters only ⟨nqu⟩ occurs in more than one word). ⟨qu⟩ is never found in word-final or preconsonantal position and it is also not found in prefixes or suffixes.

The voiced labiovelar entity has an extremely restricted distribution phonologically and a correspondingly restricted lexical incidence. It is only found in the eleven words shown in (2) (and their derivatives), in all of them in the environment [ŋ]_V.

(2) Words including the voiced labiovelar entity
    anguis 'snake'
    inguen 'loin'
    languor 'languidity'
    lingua 'language/tongue'
    ninguit 'it snows' (or *ningit*)
    pinguis 'fat' ADJ
    sanguis 'blood'
    stinguere 'extinguish'
    tinguere 'dip' (or *tingere*)
    unguis 'nail (on hand and foot)'
    unguere 'smear' (or *ungere*)

To these one may add *urguere*, a rare by-form of the verb *urgere* 'urge' [urg(w)eːre]. As is indicated in the list, in some words ⟨gu⟩ is in free variation with [g], e.g. *ninguit ~ ningit*. What these facts, viz. the very limited distribution and the very low lexical incidence mean for the phonological status of ⟨gu⟩ is discussed below.

2.2.2.1. The issue of frequency

Devine & Stephens (1977) claim that the textual frequency of ⟨qu⟩ and [k]C is much higher than that of either [k] or [w].[36] This means, they argue, that it is better analysed as a single segment. But they also admit that the markedly high textual frequency of ⟨qu⟩ simply follows from the fact that it occurs in many of the interrogative and relative pronouns *quis* 'who', *quid* 'what', *qui/ quae/quod* 'which, who', *quo* 'where', etc., as well as the clitic conjunction -*que* 'and' (Devine & Stephens 1977: 94). My own calculations[37] bear out Devine and Stephens's generalisations only in part. In particular, the frequency of [w] is almost twice as high as that of [kw] (38,865 vs. 20,225 over the 191,025-word selective corpus), and it would be so even if one subtracted the number of tautosyllabic [aw] sequences (erroneously called diphthongs, see 2.3.2 and Cser 1999) from the number of [w] tokens (35,189 vs. 20,225). Thus their claim that '*kw* would be the only cluster which would be more frequent than all other occurrences of the second consonant of that cluster: f(kw) > f(w)' (Devine & Stephens 1977: 49) does not seem to be correct.

On the other hand, it is true that if [kw] is a cluster, [k] occurs in clusters more frequently than without an adjacent consonant. In my corpus [k] occurs in clusters (not including geminates but including [kw]) 39,062 times, in gemination 924 times, in neither clusters nor gemination 29,694 times. Furthermore, [kw] is more frequent than all the other [k]-clusters combined (20,225 vs. 18,837). By contrast, the stop [p], whose distribution is in other respects broadly similar to that of [k], occurs in clusters (not including geminates) 13,314 times, in gemination 703 times, in neither clusters nor gemination 16,364 times. The proportions will be similar if we analyse [kw] as a segment rather than a cluster, because in that case [k] occurs in clusters 18,837 times (vs. 29,694 times not in clusters). Whether other consonants are generally like [p] remains to be verified, but there is a likelihood that Devine and Stephens's claim is right on that count. In sum, however, the frequency arguments are not conclusive.

2.2.2.2. Phonetic issues

There is some indication that the vocalic element in ⟨qu⟩ was different, less 'noisy', than the [w] in other positions. Allen (1978: 17) points to direct evidence for this from the early second century AD grammarian Velius

---

[36] '[I]f *qu* and *gu* are biphonemic, then *k* would be the only consonant which would be more frequent in clusters than in single occurrences: f(kw) + f(kC) > f((V)k(V)) ... and *kw* would be the only cluster which would be more frequent than all other occurrences of the second consonant of that cluster: f(kw) > f(w)' Devine & Stephens (1977: 49).

[37] The textual frequency of consonants was calculated from the selective corpus described in Appendix 1.

Longus, and Modern Italian seems to have preserved precisely such a pattern. While ancient grammarians' and orthographers' remarks on phonetic details are often unreliable and hard to interpret, the passage cited by Allen (1978: 17) can, indeed, be plausibly understood as saying that the [w] element in ⟨qu⟩ was less consonant-like than other [w]s.[38] The conclusion Allen draws is that ⟨qu⟩ was a segment rather than a cluster. But even if there existed a phonetic difference between the two realisations of the labial element, and even if their distribution was [k]_ vs. elsewhere (which is not clear), it may mean no more for a phonological analysis than a simple case of allophony of some sort.

Allen (1978: 16–17) also makes the point that the spelling of words like *tamquam* 'just as', with ⟨m⟩ before the ⟨q⟩ instead of an assimilated ⟨n⟩=[ŋ], indicates that lip rounding was simultaneous with the closure and regards this as another piece of evidence in favour of the monosegmental interpretation. But in fact the ancient grammarians make it clear that the nasal before ⟨qu⟩ and ⟨gu⟩ was velar (see the relevant testimonia in Devine & Stephens 1977: 37). The spellings with ⟨m⟩ were etymological spellings used in compounds, not at all to the exclusion of ⟨n⟩ (*tanquam, nunquam* 'never', etc.).

Thus the meagre phonetic indications that we have certainly do not support the monosegmental interpretation – though they also do not contradict it. They simply do not add up to a critical amount of really relevant information and are thus inconclusive.

2.2.2.3. Geminates

Turning now to static phonotactic issues (more fully treated in Chapter 3), let us consider geminates first. While all stops occur as geminates in simplex forms, ⟨qu⟩ does not. Furthermore, it does not even occur in a [kkw]/[kkʷ] sequence (which could, in theory, be analysed as the phonetic representation of geminate [kʷ] but also as a [k]+[k]+[w] sequence). This squares neatly with the fact that geminates do not occur next to another consonant (in this case [kk] before [w]). It also squares neatly with the fact that [kkw] can emerge (though rarely does) at prefix–stem boundaries, as in *acquirere* 'get'

---

[38] *v litteram digamma esse...non tantum in his debemus animadvertere in quibus sonat cum aliqua adspiratione ut in valente et vitulo et primitivo et genetivo sed etiam in his ⟨in⟩ quibus ⟨cum q⟩ confusa haec littera est ⟨ut⟩ in eo quod est quis...* 'we need to be mindful that the letter v is digamma [i.e. [w] — A. Cs.] not only in those [words] in which it is accompanied by a certain noisiness, as in *valente* and *vitulo* and *primitivo* and *genetivo*, but also in those in which that letter merges ⟨with q⟩, as in *quis*' (Velii Longi *De Orthographia*, Keil 1855–78, vol. 8: 58, translation mine; the parts in ⟨ ⟩ are missing from the most important manuscript as well as the first printing of this work). The contrast the grammarian gives is between *adspiratio*, here probably best translated as 'noise', and *littera confusa*, the technical term for vocal forms that cannot be precisely rendered with letters, here probably meaning roughly a sound (scil. [w]) that is fused with the preceding stop ⟨q⟩, i.e. [k]. But note that the examples he gives for the 'noisy' ⟨v⟩ are initial and intervocalic, and he contrasts these with ⟨qu⟩ only; he is silent about postconsonantal [w] in general.

and *acquiescere* 'acquiesce' from *ad+⟨qu-⟩*. It is only at such boundaries that geminates can be adjacent to consonants. Note, however, that if this particular sequence was analysed as a [k]+[kʷ] cluster, the lack of [kkʷ] could be explained with reference to the fact that in two-stop clusters the second stop can only be [t] (i.e. only [pt] and [kt] are found, apart from geminates), and thus the gap in question would be compatible with a monosegmental interpretation too.

2.2.2.4. *Positional restrictions and stop + glide sequences*

Sequences of an obstruent and a glide are virtually non-existent in Classical Latin. In word-medial and word-final position no such clusters are found unless one regards ⟨qu⟩, which occurs medially in many words, and the few occurrences of ⟨gu⟩, all medial, as clusters. Apart from ⟨qu⟩ (and ⟨gu⟩), medial [w] can be preceded only by [l r j] (e.g. *silva* 'forest', *parvus* 'small', *laevus* 'left', respectively). In word-initial position [kw], [sw] and [skw] (as in *quis* 'who', *suavis* 'sweet' and *squalor* 'dirt', respectively) would be the only obstruent+glide clusters.[39] Furthermore, when occasional desyllabification in poetry produces a stop+glide cluster internally,[40] scansion shows that such a cluster is heterosyllabic, which indicates that a stop+glide cluster generally cannot be tautosyllabic.

This seems to tilt the balance towards the monosegmental interpretation. But the fact is that the phonotactic patterning of ⟨qu⟩ under a monosegmental interpretation is at least as irregular as under a cluster interpretation (and perhaps more irregular). In addition to the absence of gemination (see above), ⟨qu⟩ and ⟨gu⟩ cannot be followed by any consonant in any position, which would be most untypical for a stop in Latin (monophonemic in Proto-Indo-European, the labiovelars could be followed by sonorants without neutralisation[41]). Under a cluster interpretation this fact receives a very simple explanation. Since in Classical Latin the medial member of a three-consonant cluster can never have higher sonority than either of the flanking consonants,[42] a cluster [kw] could possibly only be followed by [j], nothing else. But since [j] never follows a consonant in Classical Latin, [w]-medial clusters are not found.

---

[39] The argument in Watbled (2005: 43 sqq.) is based on these considerations, and so is in part Ballester (1996: 53–107). One of the advantages Watbled sees in a monophonemic analysis for both labiovelars is that it makes it easier to establish the putative complementary distribution of [u] and [w]. But as the works devoted to this latter goal generally show, this feat can only be achieved through laboured and counterintuitive analyses anyhow (e.g. Touratier 2005: 70; on this, see also Zirin 1970: 80–7).

[40] Vergil's *abiete* 'fir' ABL scanned as three syllables, i.e. [abjete] instead of [abiete] in all of its four occurrences: *Aen.* 2.13, 5.662, 8.597, 11.665.

[41] E.g. **kʷjeh₁-* > La *quies* 'rest, repose', cf. Rix et al. (2001: 393), de Vaan (2008: 508–9).

[42] With the exception of [kst], [pst], in which the [s] is extrasyllabic, see chapter 3.

Note, however, that the restriction of ⟨qu⟩ to the environment _V again does not absolutely preclude a monosegmental analysis. Phonetically oriented (functional) approaches explain such phenomena with reference to the perceptual strength of cues that help identify segments, e.g. Boersma (1998), Steriade (1999), Côté (2000), Kiss (2007). A following consonant effectively masks such cues and so certain types of consonants, such as labiovelars, will be dispreferred in preconsonantal position. On this interpretation then Proto-Indo-European would be more untypical cross-linguistically than Latin.

The fact that ⟨qu⟩ and ⟨gu⟩ never occur word-finally can also be seen from two different perspectives and can be explained on the basis of both. Under a cluster interpretation it is because of sonority sequencing, to which Latin rather strictly adheres, that rising sonority clusters are never found in that position.[43] But it was also seen in 2.2.1 above that in Latin there is a marked preference for final coronal consonants. Of the non-coronal consonants some occur marginally and some not at all, so the lack of word-final labiovelars is also consistent with the monosegmental assumption and falls under a very simple segmental distributional generalisation. Furthermore, the weakness of stop place cues in final position can also be invoked just as in the case of preconsonantal position above.

As for the poetic license of the *abiete* → *abjete*-type, it is indeed true that it produces heterosyllabic clusters. It remains a question, however, to what extent this is informative with respect to the status of ⟨qu⟩ (and ⟨gu⟩). While natural classes are expected to display more or less uniform behaviour, the distribution of the two glides in Latin is different in at least three ways, independently of the labiovelar issue. In particular, while postconsonantal [j] does not exist at all, C[w] is found not only in the *sw*-initial words like *suāvis* 'sweet', but also in the clusters [lw], [rw] and [jw] (*silva* 'forest', *parvus* 'small', *laevus* 'left') irrespective of how one analyses ⟨qu⟩ and ⟨gu⟩. Furthermore, [w] is never geminated, while intervocalic [j] always is. Combination with the corresponding vowels also reveals two different patterns: **#[ji] vs. #[wu] (*vulgus* 'crowd', *vultus* 'face').

2.2.2.5. *The question of [sw]*

Another static structural argument impinges on [sw], the only other cluster including an obstruent + [w]. If ⟨qu⟩ and ⟨gu⟩ are taken to be segments rather than clusters, the environments of [w] shrink so radically that one is practically compelled to regard [sw] as a single segment (i.e. [sʷ]) rather than a cluster. This is because under such an analysis, [w] is never found in complex onsets (except initial [sw]) and, independently of this, [s] is never found before voiced consonants in simplex forms (again except for initial [sw]). That this logically follows was realised by Devine & Stephens (1977: 80): 'syllabification and system congruity ... point to /sʷ/', but they add a

---

[43] Again except for [ps], [ks], which include extrasyllabic [s].

disclaimer on the very next page: 'It might be thought that monophonemic assessment of Lat. *kw* almost compels the same for *sw*. But this is arguable' – importantly though, they give no arguments apart from the suggestion that the Tarascan language 'very likely' has monophonemic [k^w] and cluster [sw], and the somewhat more relevant point that Proto-Indo-European is usually analysed as having the same combination. Given that they do not recognise coda glides and analyse [aw(C)]-type sequences as diphthongs, it follows from their analysis that absolutely the only position in which [w] is found is as a solitary onset consonant, unless one still analyses initial [sw] as a cluster.[44] Thus the parallel of [sw] appears to be a solid argument for the cluster status of the labiovelars.

2.2.2.6. Verb root structure

A point Devine & Stephens make (1977: 48, where it is attributed to Robert Godel) is that verb roots do not end in three consonants, but they do end in ⟨Cqu⟩ at least in *linquere* 'leave' and *torquere* 'turn' (and to these one may add the [ŋgw]-final *tinguere* 'dip' and *ninguit* 'it snows').

This point is valid only diachronically, not structurally. How is one to make a principled distinction between what could be described as the root of *torquere* 'turn' and that of *monstrare* 'show', another verb with a heavy consonant cluster before the inflectional endings? It will not do to argue that *monstrare* has a more complex morphological structure than *linquere* or *torquere* (and derives from the primary root attested in *monere* 'warn') because this is more of a statement about the etymology than the structure of these forms. Historically, of course, the claim that verb stems do not end in three consonants makes perfect sense in view of two generally accepted details of reconstruction: (i) Proto-Indo-European *[k^w] as a single consonant, and (ii) the well known Proto-Indo-European root structure constraints on intramorphemic consonant clusters, viz. the maximal root being *s*CCVCC with CC portions that strictly adhere to sonority sequencing, e.g. **streŋg^h*- 'pull together'. But this only underscores the point that the argument would be valid only if roots and stems could be consistently distinguished in Classical Latin, and the statement is made about a linguistic unit (the root) which, strictly speaking, no longer exists in the language.

2.2.2.7. Voicing contrast in clusters

Consonant clusters including at least one obstruent are found relatively frequently in Latin. Since stops (but not fricatives or sonorants) are contrastive

---

[44] The structural parallelism between ⟨qu⟩ and [sw] was hinted at already in Brandenstein (1951), cited in Zirin (1970: 38). But there is an evident reluctance on the part of all the authors mentioned to take seriously the consistency of the analysis at this point and say that *if* ⟨qu⟩ is a single segment *then* so is the labialised fricative [s^w].

for voice, it is an interesting question how this contrast is present in consonant clusters. The data (listed in Tables 4 to 6 in Chapter 3) clearly show that the possibility for voice to be contrastive depends on the size of the cluster. Notably, voicing contrast for stops is found only in CC clusters, e.g. [VndV] $\neq$ [VntV], as in *quando* 'when' vs. *quantus* 'how much', or [VlbV] $\neq$ [VlpV], as in *albus* 'white' vs. *culpa* 'sin'; no voicing contrast is found in CCC clusters, e.g. [VntrV] as in *antrum* 'cave' but **[VndrV] and [VmplV] as in *simplex* 'simple' but **[VmblV].[45] If one analyses the clusters found in e.g. *linquam* 'I leave' SUBJ vs. *linguam* 'tongue' ACC as CCC rather than CC, these will be the only instances of CCC clusters with contrastive stop voicing ([VŋkwV] $\neq$ [VŋgwV]). If, however, one analyses these as CC clusters, they pattern as expected ([Vŋk^{w}V] $\neq$ [Vŋg^{w}V]). This is certainly a fact that points towards the greater plausibility of the monosegmental interpretation of labiovelars.

2.2.2.8. Alternations

The entity denoted by ⟨qu⟩ alternates with [k] just like [g] does, e.g. *coquere* ~ *coctus* 'cook' INF ~ PASSPART much like *agere* ~ *actus* 'do' INF ~ PASSPART. As Devine & Stephens (1977: 50) point out, the parallel alternation in identical environment suggests that ⟨qu⟩ is a single consonant just like [g], since both alternate with [k]. As for ⟨gu⟩, in some words it is in free variation with [g] (*ninguit* ~ *ningit* 'it snows'); in some verbs it seems to parallel the *coctus*-type alternation (*unguere* or *ungere* ~ *unctus* 'smear' INF ~ PASSPART). This seems to imply the same for the voiced as for the voiceless entity, i.e. monosegmental status. The issue of alternations, however, is a complicated one and the fuller picture is far from unambiguous with respect to the phonological status of the entities involved.

First, it is important to note that the apparent ⟨qu⟩ ~ [k] alternations are practically restricted, at least in inflectional morphology, to two environments. One is second declension (*o*-stem) nouns and adjectives (*ecus* ~ *equī* 'horse' NOMSING ~ NOMPLUR),[46] the other the environment exemplified above, where ⟨qu⟩ occurs in the infectum stem of a verb, while [k] in the third stem and its derivatives (such as the PASSPART). The voicing alternations like [g] ~ [k] are found in a somewhat broader range of forms, such as *rex* ~ *regis* 'king' NOMSING ~ GENSING, *fingere* 'shape' ~ *finxi* 'I shaped' ~ *fictus* 'feigned' (or the isolated *secare* 'cut' ~ *segmentum* 'slice'). In the second declension the closest parallel to the *ecus* ~ *equi* type alternations, so far as I can judge, is the apparently short-lived pattern of *dius* ~ *divi* 'godly' NOMSING ~ NOMPLUR, where

---

[45] The non-existent clusters occurred only in Greek loans and names, e.g. *cylindrus* 'cylinder', *emblema* 'relief'.

[46] The analogical levelling of the type *ecus* ~ *equi* > *equus* ~ *equi* became general only during the first century AD, and modern editorial practice on this particular point is based on a tradition that postdates even Augustan times (see Buck 1899).

a segment is clearly lost.[47] By contrast, the alternations in verb stems are rather varied and generally show little phonological regularity apart from *a*-stems such as *amare*:[48]

(3) Infectum (present infinitive) vs. third stem alternations
    amare ~ *amatus* 'love' (no alternation)
    facere ~ *factus* 'do' (no alternation)
    dīcere ~ *dictus* 'say' (vowel length)
    agere ~ *āctus* 'do' (voicing and vowel length[49])
    vincere ~ *victus* 'win' (presence vs. absence of nasal)
    fingere ~ *fictus* 'shape' (voicing and nasal)
    spernere ~ *sprētus* 'despise' (vowel length, nasal and [r]-metathesis)
    sternere ~ *strātus* 'lay down' (vowel length and quality,
      nasal, [r]-metathesis)
    solvere ~ *solūtus* 'solve' ([w] ~ [uː] alternation)
    fluere ~ *fluxus* 'flow' ([k] plus [s] instead of more usual [t])
    ferre ~ *latus* 'carry' (suppletion)

Those infectum stems that end in ⟨qu⟩ show two patterns. In the third stem either [k] or [kuː] appears:

(4) Infectum (present infinitive) vs. third stem alternations involving ⟨qu⟩
    relinquere ~ *relictus* 'leave'
    coquere ~ *coctus* 'cook'
    loqui ~ *locūtus* 'speak'[50]
    sequi ~ *secūtus* 'follow'

Given the great variety of formal differences between the two verb stems (infectum vs. third stem), which can perhaps best be captured as a continuum with no alternation at one extreme and suppletion at the other, how does one decide how these patterns (*coquere* vs. *loqui*) support the argument for either interpretation of ⟨qu⟩?

The tendency is for -*ūtus* to correspond to [Cw] or [Cu] in the infectum stem, as the examples in (5) show:

---

[47] The form *dius* replaced earlier *divos*, and was itself analogically replaced by *divus* already in the early first century AD (Buck 1899).

[48] These pairs are all INF (-*(e)re*) and PASSPART (-*tus*). Some details of such affixed forms are explained in Chapter 6. Apart from the first example, which is an *a*-stem (first conjugation), all the others are consonant- or *i*-stems (third conjugation), as are all the stems involving supposedly alternating ⟨qu⟩ except for *torquere* (second conjugation). In an informal sense, the list is meant to represent an increasing distance between the alternants.

[49] Note that the length alternation is just the other way round than for *dīcere*. The *agere* ~ *āctus* type exemplifies the lengthening rule discussed in detail in 5.4.2.

[50] *Loqui* and *sequi* are formally passive in almost all their forms. This is immaterial to the status of ⟨qu⟩.

(5) Infectum (present infinitive) vs. third stem alternations involving -*ūtus*
     solvere ~ *solūtus* 'solve'
     volvere ~ *volūtus* 'roll'
     acuere ~ *acūtus* 'sharpen'
     arguere ~ *argūtus* 'show'
     tribuere ~ *tribūtus* 'distribute'

On this basis it is reasonable to say that *loqui* and *sequi* point to ⟨qu⟩ being a cluster rather than a single segment, since it parallels the [lw] of *solvere* and *volvere*.[51] But then what does one do with the case of *relinquere* and *coquere*? The point here is that there is no way of telling, in a synchronic grammar of Latin, which of the types in (3) they should be seen as belonging to.[52] Is *coctus* parallel to *āctus*? If yes, then this would be an argument for ⟨qu⟩ being a single segment. But what if we say that *coctus* is parallel to *fictus* or *sprētus*, where a consonant is lost?

If we look at stems whose relevant portion ends specifically in [w], we see the following. The passive participle forms of the verbs *favēre* 'favour', *cavēre* 'be on one's guard', *movēre* 'move' and *vovēre* 'vow'[53] are *fautus, cautus, mōtus* and *vōtus*, respectively. This means no alternation in the first two (*fautus, cautus*),[54] and loss of [w] with vowel lengthening in the others (*mōtus, vōtus*). This shows that it is possible for [w] to alternate with zero (cf. also *bos* ~ *boves* ~ *boum* 'ox' NomSing, NomPlur, GenPlur) just as it is possible for it to alternate with a vowel, as in *solūtus*. The moral of this point is that the *loqui* ~ *locūtus* type points to a cluster interpretation rather than the opposite, whereas the *coquere* ~ *coctus* type does not point conclusively in either direction. Given this, plus the fact that these alternations are highly restricted anyhow, one cannot conclude from these facts that ⟨qu⟩ is a single consonant in Classical Latin rather than a cluster.

As for the alternations outside inflectional morphology (e.g. *inquilinus* 'tenant' ~ *incola* 'inhabitant'), they do not unequivocally support the monosegmental analysis for basically the same reason. Alternation of [w] with zero before consonants and round vowels is an attested phenomenon in Latin, as has been exemplified above.

---

[51] Clearly one could not argue that ⟨qu⟩ parallels – in the relevant sense – a CV sequence on account of the *arguere*-type.

[52] This is not to say that comparative linguistics has not established with a fair amount of certainty the original morphological composition and the phonological history of all the forms adduced here. Everyone with at least a little familiarity with Indo-European linguistics knows that the nasal in *relinquere* used to be an infectum infix and the [k] in *relictus* results from the neutralisation of PIE *[kʷ] and *[k] in preconsonantal position, the length difference in *dīcere* ~ *dictus* goes back to ablaut, and so on. But the point is that these pieces of information do not impinge on how Classical Latin verb forms are synchronically related or whether ⟨qu⟩ is a cluster or not.

[53] These verbs belong to the second conjugation, not the third, which means that in the infectum-based forms an [e:] is found before the endings.

[54] Note that these spellings stand for [fawtus] and [kawtus].

2.2.2.9. Ad-assimilation

As a minor point let me anticipate a fact discussed in 7.2.4.5. It is indicated in Prinz (1949–50: 91) and corroborated by my own corpus research that the [d] of the prefix *ad-* tends to assimilate to stem-initial stops if these are followed by vowels, but this tendency extends very weakly to forms in which the stem-initial stop is followed by a consonant (thus *ad+petere*, *ad+capere* → *appetere* 'try to reach', *accipere* 'receive', but more typically *adprehendere* 'grasp', *adclamare* 'shout'; this generalisation is most evidently true of stem-initial [k]).

My own counts show the following. The ratio of assimilation with [k]V-initial stems is 98 per cent; with [kl] it is 33 per cent, with [kr] 25 per cent, and with ⟨qu⟩ 16 per cent. Two points of comparison are particularly edifying: with [p]-initial stems the numbers are [p]V: 88 per cent, [pl]: 44 per cent, [pr]: 38 per cent; and with the only prefixed [sw]-initial stem (*adsuescere* 'get used to') the ratio of assimilation is 24 per cent. As can be seen, assimilation is rarely attested in ⟨qu⟩-initial stems (it is even rarer than with [kl]- and [kr]-initial stems), thus e.g. *adquirere* 'acquire' is much more frequent than *acquirere*, which means that *ad*-assimilation treats ⟨qu⟩ as a cluster rather than a stop.

2.2.2.10. Diachronic considerations

Both the prehistory and the later history of Latin arguably point to a single segment. In PIE *[k^w] can be reconstructed as a stop, which is, interestingly, in contrast with the cluster [kw]. This is clear from the phonotactic patterns that are reconstructed and also from the alternations involving these entities (primarily ablaut, see Rix et al. 2001 for the lemmata e.g. on pages 374–6 vs. 377 sqq.). In the Romance languages, the continuation of Classical Latin ⟨qu⟩ is frequently a single stop again, either [k] as in French (CL *qui* > Fr *qui* [ki] 'who') or [p] as in Rumanian (CL *aqua* > Rum *apă* [apə] 'water').

Note, however, that while these considerations certainly have diachronic interest, they are of no import in terms of a phonological analysis. Restructuring is possible with or without concomitant phonetic change. The history of English shows a parallel development of PIE *[k^w] > (Old) English [hw] and *[g^w] > English [kw], as in *which* and *queen*, respectively, where stops developed into what are analysed as clusters on phonological grounds independently of their provenance. Furthermore, the later history of Classical Latin ⟨qu⟩ is far from uniform: in Italian, for instance, it developed intervocalically into [kkw], as in *acqua* [akkwa] 'water', which can be seen as a diachronic reflection of its cluster nature (though, admittedly, in Vulgar rather than Classical Latin).

2.2.2.11. Poetic licence

In a very small number of cases the glide [w] scans as a full vowel [u] in poetry when following a consonant (Platnauer 1951: 70). This phenomenon appears to happen only when the glide follows [l] or initial [s] (e.g. *silvae* 'forests' in Hor. *Epodi* 13.2 or *suadent* 'they urge' in Lucr. *De rerum nat.* 4.1157, both scanned as three syllables instead of the usual two). The same never happens to the [w] involved in ⟨qu⟩ or ⟨gu⟩: a word like *aqua* or *inguen* is always two syllables. This could be seen as an argument for the monosegmental analysis of the labiovelar entities, but only as a weak one, since the phenomenon itself is so marginal and rare.

2.2.2.12. Further remarks on the voiced labiovelar

As was shown in (2) above, the voiced labiovelar entity ⟨gu⟩ is found only in eleven lexical items and their derivatives, in all of them internally, following a velar nasal. This does not make it easy to argue for either position. If ⟨gu⟩ is a single segment, it is odd that it should be restricted to this particular position and not be found elsewhere (though, of course, the same could be said of [f], which practically only occurs word-initially in Latin). If, on the other hand, it is regarded as a cluster, the phonotactic restrictions seem to pattern somewhat less surprisingly: [ŋg] is an attested word-internal cluster and postconsonantal [w] can occur in the internal clusters [lw], [rw], [jw], [kw], [ŋkw], [rkw], [jkw], [skw] and [ŋgw] (plus initial [sw]). Admittedly this is still far from a very good-looking generalisation, but it is perhaps less counterintuitive than having a single segment restricted to a very narrowly defined environment (*pace* Watbled 2005: 45 sqq.).

If one turns to other phonological regularities, there are not many of them involving ⟨gu⟩. As was again noted above, in some words it is in free variation with [g] (*ninguit ~ ningit* 'it snows'); in some verbs it seems to parallel the *coctus*-type alternation (*unguere* or *ungere ~ unctus* 'smear' INF ~ PASSPART). This entity does not take part in any other type of alternation.[55] With this free variation and this alternation the balance seems to be tilting towards the monosegmental interpretation. But bear in mind that the *coctus*-type of alternation was argued to be inconclusive (see 2.2.2.8) on account of the generally highly varied formal relations between infectum and third stems. Also note that the handful of examples of the ⟨gu⟩ ~ [g] free variation do not necessarily point to ⟨gu⟩ being a single segment. Free variation between [w] and zero is not unheard of in Classical Latin (again see 2.2.2.8): in the perfectum-based forms of many verbs stem-final [w] is optional (*scivit* or *sciit* 'he knew', etc., see Chapter 6), but also note forms like *antiquus* or *anticus* 'old'. Thus it appears that the patterns involving ⟨gu⟩ are also inconclusive, though perhaps they point very weakly towards a cluster with a relatively low incidence.

[55] If one disregards the totally idiosyncratic *ning(u)it* 'it snows' ~ *ni*[ks] 'snow' NOMSING ~ *nivis* 'snow' GENSING.

2.2.2.13. *Summary of the labiovelar question*

Many of the arguments I have surveyed proved to be inconclusive. One argument can be adduced quite clearly in favour of the monosegmental interpretation, and another one more weakly; two arguments can be adduced for the cluster interpretation, and another two arguments weakly also for the cluster interpretation. This is summarised in Table 1.

The upshot is that we have a balance that tilts slightly – but not very convincingly – towards the cluster interpretation, and at least half of the arguments reviewed are inconclusive. Indeterminacy of this kind is not untypical of the world's languages. It is a fact to bear in mind whenever data are collected from descriptions and are processed for higher-level use, as in databases or in theoretical argumentation. Many analytical decisions go into the description of any language. But the farther one moves away from the primary data the less accessible and the more consequential the empirical bases of these decisions are.

With that in mind, the present work assumes (as does Ballester 1996) that both ⟨qu⟩ and ⟨gu⟩ are clusters and Classical Latin does not have labiovelar stops.

2.2.3. *The placeless nasal*

An investigation of the distribution of, and the processes affecting, the nasal consonants and the nasal vowels (see 2.3.1) in Classical Latin reveals that a phonological analysis needs not only the consonants [m] and [n] plus the non-contrastive velar nasal [ŋ], whose distribution was explained above, but a further nasal segment that manifests itself sometimes as a nasal consonant ([m], [n] or [ŋ]), sometimes as nasalisation and length on a vowel, and is sometimes deleted, all depending on phonological environment. This segment is a placeless nasal consonant which is not interpretable in itself and thus needs to undergo either

Table 1. Summary of the labiovelar question

	C	CC	Inconclusive
Frequency (2.2.2.1)			X
Phonetics (2.2.2.2)			X
Geminates (2.2.2.3)		(X)	
Positional restrictions, stop + glide sequences (2.2.2.4)			X
[sw] (2.2.2.5)		X	
Verb root structure (2.2.2.6)			X
Voicing contrast (2.2.2.7)	X		
Alternations (2.2.2.8)		(X)	
Ad-assimilation (2.2.2.9)		X	
Poetic licence (2.2.2.11)	(X)		
⟨gu⟩ distribution, variation (2.2.2.12)			X

phonological modification via assimilation or merger with the preceding vowel, or deletion.[56] Details of processes involving the placeless nasal will be explained later at various points of the discussion (mainly 4.6, 4.8 and 5.4.4); here I exemplify the arguments with the help of two occurrences of the segment in question.

Word-finally many instances of the placeless nasal involve the accusative singular affix. On the surface it appears either as nasalisation and lengthening on the preceding vowel or as a place-assimilated nasal when certain clitics are attached to accusative singular pronouns of the appropriate kind:

(6) *eam* [eã:] 'she' AccSing
     eandem [eandẽ:] 'she, the same' AccSing (=*eam*+*dem*).

There is good reason to believe that the nasal in the [ã:] and [and] sequences here can be derived synchronically neither from [n] nor from [m]. It cannot be derived from [n] because that consonant freely occurs word-finally (as in *forsan* 'perhaps' or *pecten* 'comb') and V[n]# sequences are thus in contrast with nasal vowels. But it also cannot be derived from [m] because the labial nasal does not undergo synchronic place assimilation to coronals (e.g. *sum+tus* → *sumptus* and not **suntus* 'take' PassPart as opposed to *eandem*, see 4.7). We thus assume that this word-final nasal is a third kind of nasal consonant best described as a placeless segment, which explains both its readiness to merge with a preceding vowel and its capacity to assimilate to a following stop.

The other example is the final consonant of the prefix *con-* 'with'. It is clear that the behaviour of this segment cannot be explained on the assumption that it is either [n] or [m] for two reasons: (i) it is consistently deleted before vowels (*coarguere* 'prove', *coire* 'meet'), while both V[n]V and V[m]V sequences are well-formed; and (ii) it also appears to be deleted before [n]-initial stems (*con+nectere* → *cōnectere* 'join'), while V[nn]V and V[mn]V sequences are again well-formed. In both respects *con-* contrasts with the prefix *in-*, whose final nasal remains intact before vowels (*inest* 'is in') and forms a geminate with a following [n] (*innectere* 'weave'). To anticipate points to be made in more detail later, both aspects of the behaviour of *con-* can be explained if we assume that its nasal is placeless: consonants cannot normally acquire the place features of vowels for reasons of geometry (see 2.4), and the placeless nasal cannot assimilate to a coronal nasal because the specific conditions on place assimilation processes do not allow this (see 4.8); hence no nasal consonant surfaces in either environment.

---

[56] The placeless nasal is not entirely unlike the moraic nasal in Japanese (see Labrune 2012: 133–5, also called placeless nasal in Japanese linguistics, e.g. Benua 1995: 42; Itô & Mester 1993: 208–9), or the Hungarian placeless nasal (assumed by Siptár & Törkenczy 2000: 210 sqq.), though its distribution and behaviour in phonological processes differs from both that of its Japanese and its Hungarian counterpart in significant ways.

In the following I list where this segment is found in Classical Latin. The placeless nasal is:

- the suffix of the accusative singular after all masculine and feminine vowel-final nominal stems and after one class of neuter stems (see chapter 6);
- found in final position in a number of adverbs that developed historically from nominal accusatives (*statim* 'immediately', *palam* 'in public');
- the suffix of the first person singular after all vowel-final extended verb stems (see Chapter 6);
- the final segment of the prefix *con-* 'with' (see 7.2.3.2); and
- often found before the fricatives [s] and [f], where it results in many cases from [n] via loss of its place node (see 4.6), but in several words it is arguably lexically given (see 5.4.4).

The spelling for the placeless nasal is ⟨m⟩ word-finally, ⟨n⟩ word-internally and can be either ⟨m⟩ or ⟨n⟩ in *con-/com-*. When it merges with the preceding vowel, resulting in length and nasalisation, the spelling remains; when deleted without vowel nasalisation, the spelling does not retain any consonant letter (see *coarguere* 'prove', *coire* 'meet'). The phonological representation of the placeless nasal is shown in 2.4.

2.3. VOWELS

The surface-contrastive set of vowels and their usual spellings with examples are given in Figure 2.[57]

The Classical Latin vowel system consists on the surface of three parallel sets of five vowels. Minimal pairs or quasi-minimal pairs are not difficult to find, see (7) in addition to those given in Figure 2. Grammarians' remarks and Late Latin developments indicate that the short vowels (with the exception of [a]) may have been lower than their long counterparts, i.e. [ɪ ɛ ɔ ʊ]. This well-known phonetic detail will be disregarded in the representations throughout. Furthermore, vowel length will be indicated only where strictly relevant.

---

[57] Length distinctions were marked in three different ways: double letter (for ⟨a e o u⟩), the so called *I longa*, a tall ⟨i⟩, and a diacritic called *apex*, which resembles the modern acute, and which mostly replaced the previous two methods towards the middle of the first century BC. However, the use of all of these methods was somewhat restricted and inconsistent, and medieval manuscripts as well as modern editions systematically omit all marking of length. For further details see Flobert (1990); for a detailed discussion of the historical development of contrastive vowel length in Latin and Romance see Loporcaro (2015).

[58] The spelling ⟨o⟩ for [u] after [w] persisted into the first century AD (Buck 1899; Anderson 1909). It is possible that the ⟨uo⟩ spelling was merely an orthographic device to avoid ⟨uu⟩, as the grammarian Velius Longus surmises (Keil 1855–78, vol. 8: 58).

	short		long		nasal	
	front	back	front	back	front	back
high	i	u	iː	uː	ĩː	ũː
mid	e	o	eː	oː	ẽː	õː
low		a		aː		ãː

Segment	Spelling	Example
[i], [iː]	⟨i⟩ (⟨ei⟩)	*vir* 'man', *vīs* 'force'
[e], [eː]	⟨e⟩	*venit* 'he comes', *vēnit* 'he came'
[a], [aː]	⟨a⟩	*mane* 'stay' IMP, *māne* 'in the morning'
[o], [oː]	⟨o⟩	*fortis* 'brave', *fōrma* 'shape'
[u], [uː]	⟨u⟩ (⟨o⟩ / w_)	*furor* 'rage', *fūr* 'thief' (*volt* ~ *vult* 'he wants')[58]
nasal vowels	⟨Vn⟩ internally	*consul* 'consul', *amans* 'loving', *inferus* 'lower'
	⟨Vm⟩ finally	*puerum* 'boy' ACCSING, *palam* 'in public'

Figure 2. The Classical Latin vowels and their spellings

(7) Minimal pairs for vowel length and nasality
latrō 'robber' vs. *lātrō* 'I bark'
dēs 'you give' SUBJ vs. *dens* [dẽːs] 'tooth'
puella 'girl' NOMSING vs. *puellā* ABLSING vs. *puellam* -[ãː] ACCSING
leporēs 'rabbits' vs. *lepōrēs* 'niceness'
gemitus 'sigh' NOMSING vs. *gemitūs* GENSING
potes 'you are able' vs. *pōtēs* 'you drink' SUBJ

2.3.1. *The nasal vowels*

While nasal vowels contrast with oral vowels, their distribution is partly predictable with respect to the two nasal consonants [m n]. Nasal vowels occur in two environments, finally and before fricatives (certain other environments may be hypothesised for the prefix *con-*, see 7.2.3.2). Before fricatives no nasal consonant appears on the surface;[59] final [n] is found in many words (e.g. *pecten* 'comb', *forsan* 'perhaps', *lien* 'honeycomb', *non* 'no(t)'); final [m] is not expected, given the general ban on labial and velar consonants word-finally (see 2.2.1 above).

The overwhelming majority of the nasal vowel + [f] cases are prefixed forms consisting of *in-* or *con-* plus an *f*-initial stem (*conferre* 'collect', *infamis* 'disreputable'), but see also the simplex *inferus* [ĩːferus] 'lower' and its derivatives. Since the incidence of [s] is much higher than that of [f], nasal

[59] The only word that comes close to being an exception is *hiems* 'winter', a *m*-stem noun affixed with the nominative singular suffix *-s*, often found in manuscripts as *hiemps* with epenthetic [p]. Other cases of a stem ending in [m] combined with an *s*-suffix include perfectum-based verb forms like *sum+s+i → sumpsi* 'I took', where an epenthetic [p] consistently appears, thereby breaking up the [m] + fricative sequence (see 4.7). Other *m*-stem nominals are all heteroclitic *m-/mi*-stems, and their singular nominative forms end in *-mi-s*, e.g. *comis* 'affable'. On heteroclisy see Chapter 6.

vowels are also much more frequently found before [s] (*ensis* 'sword', *anser* 'goose', *quotiens* 'how many times', *monstrum* 'omen'). A large part of the nasal vowel + [s] cases are made up of two classes: (i) *in-* and *con-* plus an *s*-initial stem (*inscius* 'unaware', *conscius* 'privy'), and (ii) [Vnd] and [Vnt] sequences alternating with a long nasal vowel when followed by [s] across a morpheme boundary, as in *frons* [frõːs] 'foliage' NomSing ~ *frondis* [frondis] GenSing and *dens* [dẽːs] 'tooth' NomSing ~ *dentis* [dentis] GenSing. The [t] ~ ∅ and [d] ~ ∅ alternation before [s] is independent of the nasal and does not in itself involve compensatory lengthening (e.g. *milĕs* 'soldier' NomSing ~ *militis* GenSing, see the discussion in 4.3). Vice versa, the alternating nasal vowels in simplex forms generally alternate with [Vn] followed by a coronal stop. An exception is *manere* ~ *mansum* [mãːsũ] 'stay' Inf ~ Sup with alternation but no stop.[60] The third fricative, [h] does not occur postconsonantally or after nasal vowels in Classical Latin. There are [h]-initial stems that are prefixed with *in-* and *con-*, but these behave identically to vowel-initial stems (see Chapter 7) and no nasal vowel emerges.

The two rounded nasal vowels [ũː] and [õː] are in almost complemetary distribution in that the former tends to occur finally, the latter internally (neither occurs initially).[61] Examples are *pons* 'bridge', *consul* 'consul' vs. *manum* 'hand' AccSing, *nondum* 'not yet'. Since, however, there is one perfect minimal pair: *tonsus* [tõːsus] 'shear' PassPart vs. *tunsus* [tũːsus] 'shove' PassPart, strictly speaking they cannot be regarded as positional variants.

I assume that nasal vowels are not lexical; they can all be derived from a sequence of a non-nasal vowel and the placeless nasal consonant (see 5.4.4). This explains the invariable length of nasal vowels and a considerable part of their incidence. The placeless nasal can represent two different morphemes in itself (cf. 2.2.3 above), and these account for the vast majority of word-final nasal vowels: AccSing forms such as [puellãː] from the stem [puella-] 'girl' and 1Sing verb forms such as [fuerĩː] from the extended perfectum stem [fueri-] 'be' PerfSubj (see Chapter 6). Word-internally (*mansum* and *frons*-type) and at prefix–stem boundary (*inscius*-type) the placeless nasal consonant often results from the loss of place of [n] before fricatives (for detailed discussion see 4.6 and 5.4.4). Where, however, a word-internal nasal vowel never alternates with an oral vowel + [n] sequence (i.e. *ensis*-type), considerations of economy recommend postulating the same sequence of an oral vowel and a placeless

---

[60] The alternation in *sanguis* 'blood' NomSing ~ *sanguinis* GenSing is irregular on at least two counts: (i) it involves a short and, by all appearances, non-nasal vowel; and (ii) it is the only *n*-stem noun that takes the *-s* suffix, see above the discussion of final consonants and note 27. *Sanguis* also has a neuter by-form *sanguen*, without the *-s* suffix, mainly preclassical in its occurrences.

[61] The word-final spelling ⟨om⟩ (probably [õː]) does not occur in Classical Latin except as a deliberately archaising variant of ⟨um⟩ after [w] in some authors, e.g. Vergil (*aequom*, *divom* for *aequum* 'equal' AccSing, *divum* 'divine' AccSing).

nasal, but in these words – as in the prefix *con-* – the placeless nasal is possibly lexical, unlike in the *mansum/frons*-type.

It must be noted here that the realisation of the nasal vowels may well have been subject to a great deal of variation. It is possible that for many speakers they were not nasal at all by Classical Latin times (for these speakers *dens* and *dēs* would be homophonous). It is also possible that in educated circles a spelling pronunciation (or some analogy-based norm in the case of the alternating instances) gained some currency in which [n] was pronounced before [s], perhaps with the retention of the long vowel. The details will, in all likelihood, remain in the dark, and the evidence is far from unequivocal.

2.3.2. *The question of diphthongs*

Virtually all discussions of the Classical Latin vowel inventory include a number of complex entities referred to as diphthongs traditionally. These are ⟨ae⟩, [aj], ([ai̯], etc.), ⟨oe⟩, [oj], ([oi̯]), ⟨au⟩, [aw], ([au̯]), for some also ⟨ei⟩, [ej], ([ei̯]), ⟨eu⟩, [ew], ([eu̯]), ⟨ui⟩, [uj], ([ui̯]), even ⟨ou⟩, [ow] ([ou̯]). This practice goes back to a terminological and notational tradition in which a glide (in the Indo-European languages [w] and [j]) that is tautosyllabic with a preceding vowel is said to form a diphthong with it. Such an approach is not only dated now but was already inconsistent before the appearance of modern phonological analysis not least because it introduced an unwarranted distinction between prevocalic and postvocalic glides (see e.g. Marotta 1999: 290–1).

A consistent phonological analysis can hardly support a view of the Classical Latin vowel system that postulates diphthongs in the strong sense of the word, i.e. complex entities that are functionally equivalent to 'pure' vowels, or at least a significant subgroup of them, e.g. long vowels.[62] Functional equivalence involves two aspects: (i) the entity in question is phonotactically equivalent to a vowel, i.e. it only occupies the syllable nucleus; and (ii) it is equivalent to a vowel in terms of alternation patterns and generally in terms of triggering and undergoing phonological rules.

Before I embark on the arguments for and against diphthongs, the status of the entities ⟨ei⟩, ⟨eu⟩, ⟨ui⟩ and ⟨ou⟩ (not always listed as diphthongs in traditional descriptions) needs to be addressed. Of these four ⟨ou⟩ is found in the words *prout* 'accordingly', a compound, and *boum* 'ox' GENPLUR. The poetic corpus unequivocally and consistently indicates a disyllabic scansion for the latter in its more than 40 occurrences; *prout* has but a single occurrence in the poetic corpus

---

[62] If one is inclined to say that 'diphthong' is to be understood phonetically, i.e. a vocalic entity that involves movement along a trajectory in terms of articulation (and also in acoustic terms), then one also has to claim that entities like that at the beginning of *vafer* ([wa-]) 'cunning', the mirror image of the [aw] in *fauce* [fawke] 'throat' ABLSING, are also diphthongs. If a phonetic difference is found between [wa] and [aw], talking of a diphthong in one case may be warranted phonetically, but the phonological relevance of that difference does not follow.

(Hor. *Sat.* 2.6.67) and is a monosyllable there. Thus ⟨ou⟩ is at best a marginal candidate for diphthonghood.

The sequence ⟨ei⟩ is tautosyllabic in the word *deinde* and its shorter variant *dein* 'thereafter'.[63] This word, especially in the longer form, was fairly popular with the poets and the scansion unequivocally yields a single heavy syllable for *dein(-)* in spite of the transparent composition (*dē+inde* 'from here'; cf. 7.2.1.1 for *dē-* prefixed forms). This lexical item would then be one instance of a diphthong written ⟨ei⟩. The other one is a compound based on this word, *deinceps* 'consecutively', which occurs only twice in the poetic corpus, and it scans as two heavy syllables on both occasions (Lucr. *De rerum nat.* 2.333, Hor. *Sat.* 2.8.79).

The tautosyllabic sequence ⟨eu⟩ occurs in the four strictly preconsonantal words discussed earlier (*seu* 'or', *neu* 'neither, and not', *ceu* 'as, like', *(e)heu* INTERJ). While *(e)heu* could easily be dismissed as an interjection, a cross-linguistically not always well-behaved type of word, the remaining three words are still there. In Greek names ⟨eu⟩ is monosyllabic by rule in poetry (e.g. *Theseus* is a spondee), but in Latin words, apart from the four above, this spelling represents a hiatus (e.g. *purpureus* 'purple' is four syllables).[64]

The sequence ⟨ui⟩ [uj] occurs in three words altogether, *huic* 'to him' and *cui* 'to whom', and the interjection *hui*. Of these, only the first two are used by poets, and they are practically always monosyllabic.[65]

The arguments that can be adduced for a diphthongal interpretation are the following:

(i) The glides in postvocalic position may have been phonetically different from those in prevocalic position. The Classical Latin spelling of [aj] as ⟨ae⟩ instead of earlier ⟨ai⟩ indicates that the [j] in that position was replaced by a more open variant.[66]

---

[63] Note that here I am not talking about the archaising ⟨ei⟩ (=[i:]) or the ⟨ei⟩ involving geminate [j], as in ⟨eius⟩ 'his'.

[64] I see no compelling evidence that the word *neuter* includes the same phonological sequence as *neu*, *seu*, *ceu* and *heu*. Lehmann (2005: 177) asserts that *neuter* is always disyllabic, but the data do not unequivocally imply this. In the entire poetic corpus, this word (and all its inflected forms) occurs 14 times altogether (Ov. *Am.* 1.14.10, *Metam.* 5.91, *Trist.* 2.114, Hor. *Sat.* 2.2.66, Sil. It. *Pun.* 2.386, 14.109, Luc. *Phars.* 2.63, 2.231, 5.466, 5.794, Stat. *Theb.* 9.257, 10.408, Mart. *Epigr.* 3.38.6, 10.46.2). In each case, the first half of the word is the second half of a foot, which allows a heavy (i.e. [new.t-]) as well as a light–light (i.e. [ne.u.t-]) scansion. But the fact that the first syllable of *neuter* is never found in the first half of a foot, a position reserved for heavy syllables, makes it highly likely that it was not actually a heavy syllable, that is, the scansion [ne.u.t-] is implied more strongly by the metrical evidence, and thus *neuter* simply presents a case of hiatus just like *deus* or *purpureus*. This confirms Kent's (1932: 50) description of *něŭter* as a trisyllabic word.

[65] In theory, some occurrences of *huic* could also be scanned as two light syllables. When in the second half of a foot in a hexameter and followed by a vowel-initial word, metrically both a single heavy syllable and two light syllables are possible (see also the previous note on *neuter*). There are not many of these ambiguous cases and, significantly, this word never occurs in the second half of the fifth foot of a hexameter, where two light syllables would be the norm. Interestingly, not a single instance of *cui* is found in prevocalic position in the entire poetic corpus, though in prose this constellation was not avoided.

[66] Safarewicz (1974), for instance, claims that this lowering of [j] is the criterial point at which [aj] and [oj] diachronically became monophonemic – a clear case of *non sequitur*.

(ii) The point in (i) is underscored by the diachronic development of pre-vs. postvocalic glides. Classical Latin prevocalic glides tend to appear in Romance languages as strengthened consonants (basically [w] > [v] and [j] > [dʒ] /_V), while postvocalic glides tend to coalesce with the preceding vowel ([aj] > [ɛ], [oj] > [e] and [aw] > [o], the first quite early in some dialects of Latin[67]).

(iii) Word-final [aj] is elided in poetry just like any vowel (including the nasal vowels) before a vowel-initial word, thus *puellae etiam* 'girls also' is scanned [puelletiã:]. The sequence [oj] does not occur word-finally; [au] only occurs in *hau*, which is not found before vowel-initial words; [ew], whose behaviour was discussed earlier (*neu, seu, ceu, heu, eheu*), is studiously avoided before vowel-initial words, and *cui*, the only remaining word with a final glide is absolutely never found before vowel-initial words in poetry. This may in theory indicate that these glide-final words patterned differently than words ending in [aj], though perhaps a more natural explanation would refer to the morphological peculiarity of [aj]-final words and the highly improbable scenario of GENSING, DATSING and NOMPLUR *a*-stem nouns and adjectives being generally avoided in certain phonological positions.[68]

(iv) If one dismisses ⟨ei⟩, ⟨eu⟩, ⟨ou⟩ and ⟨ui⟩ as marginal, one can argue that postvocalic [w] can only follow [a], and [j] can only follow [a] and [o], thus their distribution is not independent of the preceding vowel. There is also no length contrast before postvocalic glides, unlike before postvocalic [r] or [l] (see *fortis* 'brave' vs. *fōrma* 'shape' above or *silva* 'forest' vs. *mīlvus* 'hawk', *ille* 'he/that' vs. *mīlle* 'thousand', etc.).

By contrast, the arguments in favour of a bisegmental interpretation are the following:[69]

(i) With respect to (i) under the diphthongal interpretation, while it may well be true that pre- and postvocalic glides were phonetically different in Classical Latin, this appears to have been a simple case of allophony with no obvious implications for a phonological analysis. A parallel that comes to mind is English [l], which has different pre- and postvocalic variants, the latter highly vocalic in many dialects, without this necessarily affecting the phonological status of [l] or that of the preceding vowel.

---

[67] It is believed by several scholars that ⟨ae⟩ represented a monophthong generally rather than dialectally already in the second century BC (see e.g. Deroy 1980 for the arguments, also Väänänen 1981, as opposed to e.g. Sturtevant 1916). The fullest and most recent treatment of the issue, which arrives at the opposite conclusion, and which I find much more convincing, is Adams (2007: 78–88).

[68] As Sturtevant and Kent (1915) convincingly argue, elision in general (not just of [aj] but of all vowels) was a feature of prose as well as of the spoken language, at least within phrases.

[69] For an earlier elaboration see Cser (1999).

(ii) With respect to (ii) under the diphthongal interpretation, these diachronic facts are beyond doubt, but their relevance for an analysis of Classical Latin is not self-explanatory. The fact that certain phonic entities developed in certain ways over time simply indicates that the phonological system of Classical Latin transformed into another system. An analysis of Middle English [r], for instance, cannot take into consideration the fact that pre- and postvocalic [r] developed differently in many dialects of (Early) Modern English; that is simply another phonological system (or systems).

(iii) With respect to (iv) under the diphthongal interpretation, it is undoubtedly true that single postvocalic glides mostly occur after [a] (plus [j] after [o] in a few words, after [u] in three, after [e] in two, and [w] after [e] in four). This is, however, no reason to analyse any or all of the set ⟨ae⟩, ⟨au⟩, ⟨oe⟩, ⟨ui⟩, ⟨ei⟩ and ⟨eu⟩ as phonological units in themselves. Segments with very restricted distribution are not unknown in many languages; Classical Latin [h], [f] or [g] are cases in point. Furthermore, geminate [j] occurs not only after [a] but after [e] and [u] as well: *maior* 'bigger', *eius* 'his', *cuius* 'whose'. The lack of a length contrast before postvocalic glides, including geminates, appears to be a fact, whose significance remains to be evaluated in view of the larger pattern (and vowel length in closed syllables is not always known for certain in Classical Latin). Note that if one analyses the entities in question as VC sequences rather than diphthongs, the fact that there are many instances of ⟨ae⟩ and ⟨au⟩ as opposed to the fewer including ⟨oe⟩ and the very few including ⟨eu⟩, ⟨ui⟩ and ⟨ei⟩ simply ceases to be a problem: these are all licit environments for glides with different lexical incidences.[70] Also, [VjjV] sequences will not need to be treated as something inherently different from sequences including ⟨ae⟩, etc.[71]

(iv) The glide [w], like all consonants, is syllabified as onset whenever immediately followed by a vowel. This is clear also in the three cases involving ⟨au⟩:[72] *cavere ~ cautus* 'be on one's guard' INF ~ PASSPART, *lavare ~ lautus* 'wash' INF ~ PASSPART and *favere ~ fautus* 'favour' INF ~ PASSPART. If one looks beyond the misleading modern spelling conventions (⟨v⟩ vs. ⟨u⟩), these forms are a perfect parallel to *facere ~ factus* 'do' INF ~ PASSPART. The case of [j] is complicated by the

---

[70] For some reason the issue of ⟨ui⟩ appears to have been especially vexing for a long time, see Husband (1910) and Sturtevant (1912), more recently Biville (1994) and Ballester (1996: 86–88) and the literature cited in the last reference.

[71] See, for instance, Hoenigswald (1949a), where an extremely complicated phoneme subsystem is set up simply in order to avoid having to analyse the different occurrences of [j] as representing the same phonological entity.

[72] As said earlier, the four *eu*-words *neu, seu, ceu, (e)heu* do not occur before vowel-initial words, and neither does *hau*.

fact that in simplex forms it is always a geminate intervocalically and hence immune to resyllabification, and it also never occurs stem-finally. But the [j] of *prae-*, the only glide-final prefix, is clearly resyllabified before vowel-intial stems (e.g. *praeacutae* 'sharpened to a point' beginning with two light syllables in Ovid's *Metam.* 7.131; for details of prefixed forms see 3.5 and Chapter 7). These facts certainly do not support a diphthongal analysis.

(v) The entities ⟨ae⟩, ⟨oe⟩, ⟨au⟩, ⟨eu⟩, ⟨ui⟩ and ⟨ei⟩ do not take part in alternations that simple vowels often enter into: *pecten ~ pectinis* 'comb' NOMSING ~ GENSING, *amor ~ amōris* 'love' NOMSING ~ GENSING, *agere ~ āctus* 'do' INF ~ PASSPART, *dīcere ~ dictus* 'say' INF ~ PASSPART, *cinis ~ cineris* 'ash' NOMSING ~ GENSING (see Chapter 5). The only alternations that involve two of them, ⟨ae⟩ and ⟨au⟩, are those encountered in prefixed forms, e.g. *caedere* 'cut' ~ *recīdere* 'cut back/up', *claudere* 'close' ~ *reclūdere* 'id.' For details of this alternation (called weakening), see 5.2.1; the immediately relevant points are the following. Given that short vowels tend to alternate in simplex vs. prefixed forms, e.g. *facere* 'do' ~ *reficere* 'do again', etc., one could, in theory, argue that the *caedere ~ recīdere* type alternation nicely parallels the *facere ~ reficere* type except that the former involves long vowels and the latter short vowels. But the fact is that long vowels absolutely never take part in this kind of alternation: *clāmāre* 'shout' ~ *reclāmāre* 'shout back', *cēdere* 'go' ~ *recēdere* 'withdraw', etc. What we see, then, is this: (i) short vowels alternate with short vowels; (ii) long vowels do not alternate at all; and (iii) ⟨ae⟩ and ⟨au⟩ alternate with long vowels and are thus unlike short vowels as well as unlike long vowels. Hence, even if one wishes to include prefix-induced stem-vowel alternations in the synchronic phonology of Classical Latin (which I explicitly do not), I see no way in which an argument for the diphthongal status of ⟨ae⟩ and ⟨au⟩, let alone the other candidates, could rest on these alternations.[73]

(vi) For the last (and, to my mind, strongest) point we need to anticipate a detail of phonotactics to be discussed at length later. It is an established fact of Classical Latin that a syllable coda can support at most one sonorant; sequences like [lm] and [rw], etc. are always heterosyllabic.[74] It is also abundantly clear from the data that ⟨ae,⟩ ⟨au⟩, ⟨oe⟩, (and, for that matter, ⟨ui⟩ and ⟨eu⟩) are never followed by a tautosyllabic sonorant; in Classical Latin there are no forms like

---

[73] I note it here that the historical emergence of prefix-induced alternations unequivocally points to, and is crucially dependent on, [aj], etc. being VC sequences in that (Old Latin) period. Since this is, strictly speaking, irrelevant to the phonological analysis of Classical Latin, I do not rehearse the explanation here, but see Cser (1999: 190–1) or the literature cited in 5.2.1.

[74] See Chapter 3, also Cser (1999, 2012a), Marotta (1999) and Lehmann (2005).

**poentor, **caelsum, **laur. This is evidence that the glide is itself the coda sonorant and hence not part of the nucleus.[75] The phonotactic structure involving the entities in question yields the following parallels:

(8) Phonotactic parallels involving coda glides
   caedit 'he cuts' ≈ pandit 'he extends' ([j.d] ≈ [n.d])
   auctus 'increased' ≈ emptus 'taken' ([wk.t] ≈ [mp.t])
   laus 'praise' ≈ pars 'part' ([ws] ≈ [rs])
   faex 'dregs' ≈ falx 'scythe' ([jks] ≈ [lks])
   poena 'punishment' ≈ pulmo 'lungs' ([j.n] ≈ [l.m]),etc.

This very strong generalisation is contradicted only by three items, proin(de) 'therefore', dein(de) 'thereafter' and deinceps 'consecutively', which are exceptional on several counts: (i) dein(de) and deinceps are the only words with a tautosyllabic sequence of [ej] apart from those with geminate [j]; (ii) they are the only instances of a tautosyllabic sequence of two sonorants ([jn]# or [jn].C); and (iii) proin(de) is the only instance of [oj] consistently spelled ⟨oi⟩ rather than ⟨oe⟩ (cf. poena 'punishment', coetus 'meeting', etc.).
The net result of the arguments is that there are no diphthongs in Classical Latin. The sequences ⟨ae⟩, ⟨au⟩, etc. are all VC sequences and do not represent phonological units.[76] Of the arguments in favour of a diphthongal interpretation (i, ii, iv) were shown to be irrelevant or at best of dubious value. The third argument is the only one that cannot be dismissed: word-final prevocalic elision in poetry indeed treats [aj] as if it were a vowel, whereas [ew] and the [uj] of cui are systematically avoided in the relevant position. Formally, however, this is not an intractable issue. Poetic elision may have operated on an asymmetrical basis:

[75] Another way of formulating the same observation is that a sonorant in Latin is always adjacent to at least one vowel, but no sonorant is ever found between ⟨ae⟩, ⟨oe⟩ and ⟨au⟩ and a consonant (in this order), hence ⟨ae⟩, ⟨oe⟩ and ⟨au⟩ are demonstrably not vowels.

[76] Zirin (1970) and in his wake Moralejo (1991) and Ballester (1996) appear to be saying something similar, but in fact they are not. While Zirin analyses the diphthongs as VC sequences, he analyses all long vowels in the same way. Ballester (1996: 108) draws a parallel between diphthongs and long vowels similarly to Zirin, but in a slightly different way: 'a long vowel is analysed as two adjacent short vocalic phonemes of the same timbre, with the second phoneme in a non-syllabic function, /ee/ → [eĕ]; two vowels of different timbre are, when adjacent, in principle syllabic, /eo/ → [eo], with three restrictions: (i) /ae au oe/ → [aĕ aŭ oĕ]; and (ii) /#iO/ → [#i̯O], and 3) /uO/ → [u̯O]' (translation mine). It is clear that Ballester's analysis boils down to a recapitulation of the traditional view, viz. that ⟨ae, oe, au⟩ are really just long vowels. While this analysis neatly predicts prevocalic shortness via 'resyllabification', it runs into a serious problem: to wit, it renders the general syllable template inconsistent with respect to those forms in which a long vowel is followed by a sonorant, such as forma, because in these one is practically forced to assume two sonorants in coda position (/foọr.ma/), which is impossible in Latin. I note it here that Eichner (1992) also claims that the 'diphthongs' are biphonemic, though he gives no arguments either for or against this position. Pulgram (1975: 91) says 'a diphthong, consisting of a vowel followed by a semi-vowel, like ae [ai̯], au [au̯], oe [oi̯], produces a closed syllable since it ends in a segment which, though phonetically related to a vowel, is functionally a consonant'. This seems to imply the same analysis as that presented above, but Pulgram's own analysis of the syllabification of diphthongs (1975: 155) blatantly contradicts what was said earlier, among others by denying the resyllabification of [j] and disregarding that of [w].

arities. The first **vowel** can be [u i e]; of the remaining two vowels, [o] is
r found on the left **of a** hiatus, [a] is found in *aeneus* [ae:neus] 'bronze' ADJ
ait 'he said'. **Vowels** separated by [h] show exactly the same regularities,
a single word, *trahere* 'drag' having [a] in hiatus, and the interjection *ēheu* a
vowel before ⟨h⟩.

anticipate things **that** will be seen in more detail later, hiatus rules largely
ail in prefixed **forms** and compounds too. Vowels are shortened, as in
vus 'forefather' (**vs.** *prōmittere* 'send forth'), *dĕhinc* 'from here' vs. *dēsinere*
se'.[81] As the **former** example shows, melodic restrictions are somewhat
er in prefixed **forms** (cf. the vowel [o] in the first position). Note further that
prefix (*re-*) has a **prevocalic** allomorph with a hiatus-filler (*red-ire* 'go back'
pposed to *re-mittere* 'send back'); a prevocalic *d*-variant is also found with
prefix *pro-* (*prōdire* 'go forward'). A detailed discussion of prefixed forms
phonological **processes** at prefix–stem boundaries will be the topic of 3.5
Chapter 7.

. THE PHONOLOGICAL REPRESENTATIONS

e representations I **assume** for the Classical Latin segmental inventory involve
features (in square **brackets**) and nodes (capitalised) in Tables 2 and 3.[82]

ble 2. Distinctive **features** for Classical Latin consonantal segments

		l	r	m	n	b	d	g	p	t	k	f	s	h
ce	Coronal	✓	✓		✓		✓			✓			✓	
	Dorsal							✓			✓			
	Labial			✓		✓			✓			✓		
nner	[son]	+	+	+	+	−	−	−	−	−	−	−	−	−
	Laryngeal	✓	✓	✓	✓	✓	✓	✓	✓	✓	✓	✓	✓	✓
	[voice]	+	+	+	+	+	+	+	−	−	−	−	−	+
	[nas]	−	−	+	+	−	−	−	−	−	−	−	−	−
	[cont]	+	+	−	−	−	−	−	−	−	−	+	+	+
	[lat]	+	−		−		−			−			−	

Vowels may also be **deleted** as in *cōgere* 'coerce' < *co+agere*, but this process is not
nchronically systematic. **The** realisation of the word *quoad* 'to what/that extent' must have involved
me sort of contraction or **desyllabification**, but the details will remain in the dark. Evidence shows
oidance of this word in **poetry**, and its three occurrences in the poetic corpus (Lucr. *De rerum nat.*
1213, 1433 and Hor. *Sat.* 2.3.91) are all monosyllabic.

The feature set is based **on** Hall (2006). While the system presented there is not without problems,
Hall duly points out, it **embodies** a fairly standard set of assumptions about feature inventories and
rtain aspects of subsegmental structure. I depart from Hall's system in the treatment of [j] as dorsal
ee next note). I also depart from it in treating [l] as [+continuant], though this is immaterial for the
gumentation presented here.

in what is informally called a two-vowel sequence acros
left half had to be a structurally vocalic segment (i.
Consonant Place node), whereas the right half had to be a
segment (i.e. a syllable nucleus) in order for elision to o

The other problem that remains is the set *proin(de)*, *dein*
this is, I think, precious little in the light of the counter
significant simplification of the entire vowel system: not o
the entities previously thought to be part of the inventory,
fake problems like whether ⟨ui⟩ or ⟨eu⟩ or ⟨ou⟩ are part of
marginally part of it, or exceptions, and so on.

2.3.3. *Hiatus*

Two heterosyllabic vowels may be adjacent in simplex
restricted circumstances. Two constraints are very genera
tionless: (i) the first vowel is short (and non-nasal); and (
alternates.[77] To the first constraint there are three sorts
involves the disyllabic forms of the verb *fieri* 'become, hap
fiunt 3PLUR, another the pronominal genitive suffix *-īus* (as
third a handful of genitive-dative forms belonging to the
stems), most notably *diēī* 'day'.[79] Exceptions to the second
a handful of words with [ie] and [ue] (*hiems* 'winter', *puer*
duellum 'war').[80] As for the melodic content of the vowels in
only apply to the first vowel, the second being governed mos

---

[77] The second restriction translates the traditional dictum that hiatus only o
boundaries. This is diachronically obviously true; as a synchronic statement
given above for reasons explained in the introduction, viz. that reference to mo
in many cases problematic.

[78] Godel (1953: 93) argues that the *fīo-* and *illīus*-type exceptions can be
assume a phonological representation involving [ijjV]. While this could work f
problem with the proposal is that the absence of the same [j] is unexplained
fieri. Safarewicz (1974: 231 sqq.) generalises differently: he argues that the [i
followed by a heavy syllable, which is true only if isolated forms are considere
form *fiat* can be a heavy–light sequence when followed by a vowel-initial word
line (*Epistulae ex Ponto* 3.1.97): *numen adorandum est, non ut mihi fiat ami
worshipped not in order that they be friendly to me'.

[79] The rule is that in these genitives the [e] is short if preceded by a consonant
long if preceded by a vowel (in fact always [i]), as in *diēī* 'day'. This phenomen
as a ban on the double application of the short-vowel-in-hiatus rule (viz. sho
following [iː], and then short [i] because of the following [e]). Note, howe
declension nouns apart from *res* and *dies* were few and far between, and in poetr
forms in *-iēī* were avoided in particular. The only such form used in poetry is a
used without reservation (11 occurrences), but apart from his work only two occu
the entire poetic corpus (Verg. *Aen.* 9.156, Hor. *Sat.* 1.9.35). All the thirteen oc
hexameter-final. The other *-iēī* forms (*faciei* 'face', *speciei* 'appearance', *pernic
'scab(ies)', *rabiei* 'ferocity', *aciei* 'edge') are used only in prose texts.

[80] In *abies* 'fir-tree' and two other words the vowel shows length alternatio
morpheme boundary: *abiēs* NOMSING ~ *abietis* GENSING. More on this in 5.4.5.

Table 3. Distinctive features for Classical Latin vowels and glides

		a	e	i/j	o	u/w
place	Dorsal	✔	✔	✔	✔	✔
	[high]	–	–	+	–	+
	[back]	+	–	–	+	+
	Labial				✔	✔

As regards manner, all vowels and glides are redundantly [+son], [+voice], [+cont], and underlyingly [–nas]. On the surface, however, there is a contrast between [–nas] and [+nas] vowels, as was explained in 2.3.1. The featural composition of the glides [j w] is the same as that of [i] and [u], respectively. The difference between glides and vowels is encoded in their syllabic position rather than their subsegmental structure.[83] The difference between short and long vowels is encoded in the association between the Root node and one vs. two skeletal nodes.

As regards place features, I follow the assumption embodied in recent work on feature geometry that the place features of consonants and the place features of vowels are organised under two different nodes. Generally speaking vowels and glides only have a V-place node, whereas consonants only have a C-place node.[84] Exceptions involve secondary place in consonants, which is found in Latin only in predictable environments (velarised [l] in preconsonantal position and before certain vowels, to be discussed in 4.9). Figures 3–6 illustrate the three basic configurations.

[83] While not uncontested, this assumption is fairly widespread among phonologists. For an excellent overview, counterarguments and an alternative proposal, see Padgett (2008). In contemporary phonology the idea seems to go back to the early 1980s (Clements & Keyser 1983; Steriade 1984; Levin 1985) though, of course, the idea of the structural correspondence between high vowels and glides was central already to ablaut theory in nineteenth century Indo-European linguistics.

[84] Arguments for such a model of feature geometry come mainly from cross-linguistic patterns of interactions between vocalic and consonantal place features, the distribution and behaviour of secondary place features in consonant systems and various phonological processes affecting place. Clements & Hume (1995) give a detailed exposition of such a model, though in their geometry only the intermediate nodes differ in consonants and vowels, the trees converge at the bottom on the same features on the same tiers. This makes their model extremely powerful since the interaction between vocalic and consonantal place features can be described with reference to the features, which are identical, but lack of interaction between vocalic and consonantal place features can be described just as well, scil. as long as reference is made to the intermediate nodes, which are not identical. Morén (2003) elaborates a more restricted model based on a very similar assumption, viz. that a V-Place node is subsumed under the C-Place node and dominates the place features of vowels which are identical to the secondary place features of consonants. In Cser (2003) I worked out a substantially simpler geometrical model of subsegmental structure in which vowel and consonant place elements are on different tiers and the former can also function as secondary place elements in consonants.

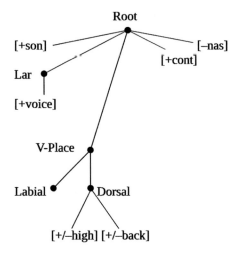

Figure 3. The structure of vowels and glides

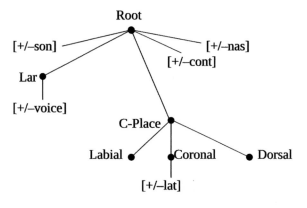

Figure 4. The structure of consonantal segments

2.5. CONCLUSION

This chapter has established the segmental inventory of Classical Latin that will be the basic point of reference throughout this work. One debated point has been settled (there are no diphthongs); another outstanding problem has been shown to be impossible to decide unequivocally, but for practical purposes a principled decision has been made (there are no labiovelar stop segments). This chapter also introduced a novel phonological segment, the placeless nasal.

regularities. The first vowel can be [u i e]; of the remaining two vowels, [o] is never found on the left of a hiatus, [a] is found in *aeneus* [aeːneus] 'bronze' ADJ and *ait* 'he said'. Vowels separated by [h] show exactly the same regularities, with a single word, *trahere* 'drag' having [a] in hiatus, and the interjection *ēheu* a long vowel before ⟨h⟩.

To anticipate things that will be seen in more detail later, hiatus rules largely prevail in prefixed forms and compounds too. Vowels are shortened, as in *prŏavus* 'forefather' (vs. *prōmittere* 'send forth'), *dĕhinc* 'from here' vs. *dēsinere* 'cease'.[81] As the former example shows, melodic restrictions are somewhat looser in prefixed forms (cf. the vowel [o] in the first position). Note further that one prefix (*re-*) has a prevocalic allomorph with a hiatus-filler (*red-ire* 'go back' as opposed to *re-mittere* 'send back'); a prevocalic *d*-variant is also found with the prefix *pro-* (*prōdire* 'go forward'). A detailed discussion of prefixed forms and phonological processes at prefix–stem boundaries will be the topic of 3.5 and Chapter 7.

2.4. THE PHONOLOGICAL REPRESENTATIONS

The representations I assume for the Classical Latin segmental inventory involve the features (in square brackets) and nodes (capitalised) in Tables 2 and 3.[82]

Table 2. Distinctive features for Classical Latin consonantal segments

		l	r	m	n	b	d	g	p	t	k	f	s	h
place	Coronal	✔	✔		✔		✔			✔			✔	
	Dorsal							✔			✔			
	Labial			✔		✔			✔			✔		
manner	[son]	+	+	+	+	−	−	−	−	−	−	−	−	−
	Laryngeal	✔	✔	✔	✔	✔	✔	✔	✔	✔	✔	✔	✔	✔
	[voice]	+	+	+	+	+	+	+	−	−	−	−	−	+
	[nas]	−	−	+	+	−	−	−	−	−	−	−	−	−
	[cont]	+	+	−	−	−	−	−	−	−	−	+	+	+
	[lat]	+	−		−					−				

---

[81] Vowels may also be deleted as in *cōgere* 'coerce' < *co+agere*, but this process is not synchronically systematic. The realisation of the word *quoad* 'to what/that extent' must have involved some sort of contraction or desyllabification, but the details will remain in the dark. Evidence shows avoidance of this word in poetry, and its three occurrences in the poetic corpus (Lucr. *De rerum nat.* 5.1213, 1433 and Hor. *Sat.* 2.3.91) are all monosyllabic.

[82] The feature set is based on Hall (2006). While the system presented there is not without problems, as Hall duly points out, it embodies a fairly standard set of assumptions about feature inventories and certain aspects of subsegmental structure. I depart from Hall's system in the treatment of [j] as dorsal (see next note). I also depart from it in treating [l] as [+continuant], though this is immaterial for the argumentation presented here.

in what is informally called a two-vowel sequence across a word boundary, the left half had to be a structurally vocalic segment (i.e. a segment with no Consonant Place node), whereas the right half had to be a 'prosodically vocalic' segment (i.e. a syllable nucleus) in order for elision to operate.

The other problem that remains is the set *proin(de)*, *dein(de)* and *deinceps*. But this is, I think, precious little in the light of the counterarguments and of the significant simplification of the entire vowel system: not only have we got rid of the entities previously thought to be part of the inventory, we have also got rid of fake problems like whether ⟨ui⟩ or ⟨eu⟩ or ⟨ou⟩ are part of the vowel system, or marginally part of it, or exceptions, and so on.

2.3.3. *Hiatus*

Two heterosyllabic vowels may be adjacent in simplex forms under certain restricted circumstances. Two constraints are very general and almost exceptionless: (i) the first vowel is short (and non-nasal); and (ii) the second vowel alternates.[77] To the first constraint there are three sorts of exceptions: one involves the disyllabic forms of the verb *fieri* 'become, happen', e.g. *fīō* 1SING, *fīunt* 3PLUR, another the pronominal genitive suffix *-īus* (as in *illīus* 'his'),[78] the third a handful of genitive-dative forms belonging to the fifth declension (*ē*-stems), most notably *diēī* 'day'.[79] Exceptions to the second restriction consist in a handful of words with [ie] and [ue] (*hiems* 'winter', *puer* 'boy', *puella* 'girl', *duellum* 'war').[80] As for the melodic content of the vowels in hiatus, restrictions only apply to the first vowel, the second being governed mostly by paradigmatic

---

[77] The second restriction translates the traditional dictum that hiatus only occurs across morpheme boundaries. This is diachronically obviously true; as a synchronic statement I prefer the formulation given above for reasons explained in the introduction, viz. that reference to morphological structure is in many cases problematic.

[78] Godel (1953: 93) argues that the *fīō*- and *illīus*-type exceptions can be explained away if we assume a phonological representation involving [ijjV]. While this could work for the second type, the problem with the proposal is that the absence of the same [j] is unexplained in the longer forms of *fieri*. Safarewicz (1974: 231 sqq.) generalises differently: he argues that the [i] of *fieri* is long when followed by a heavy syllable, which is true only if isolated forms are considered, since the SUBJ3SING form *fiat* can be a heavy–light sequence when followed by a vowel-initial word, cf. Ovid's hexameter line (*Epistulae ex Ponto* 3.1.97): *numen adorandum est, non ut mihi fiat amicum* 'a deity is to be worshipped not in order that they be friendly to me'.

[79] The rule is that in these genitives the [e] is short if preceded by a consonant, as in *rēī* 'thing', but long if preceded by a vowel (in fact always [i]), as in *diēī* 'day'. This phenomenon may be thought of as a ban on the double application of the short-vowel-in-hiatus rule (viz. short [e] because of the following [iː], and then short [i] because of the following [e]). Note, however, that Latin fifth-declension nouns apart from *res* and *dies* were few and far between, and in poetry the genitive-dative forms in *-iēī* were avoided in particular. The only such form used in poetry is *diei*, which Lucretius used without reservation (11 occurrences), but apart from his work only two occurrences are found in the entire poetic corpus (Verg. *Aen.* 9.156, Hor. *Sat.* 1.9.35). All the thirteen occurrences of *diei* are hexameter-final. The other *-iēī* forms (*faciei* 'face', *speciei* 'appearance', *perniciei* 'danger', *scabiei* 'scab(ies)', *rabiei* 'ferocity', *aciei* 'edge') are used only in prose texts.

[80] In *abies* 'fir-tree' and two other words the vowel shows length alternation, but there is no morpheme boundary: *abiēs* NOMSING ~ *abietis* GENSING. More on this in 5.4.5.

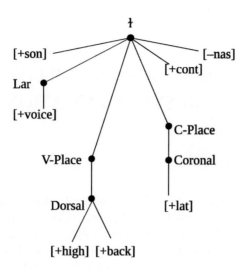

Figure 5. The structure of a consonant with secondary articulation (velarised [l])

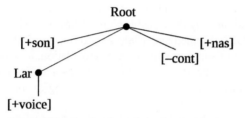

Figure 6. The structure of the placeless nasal

The framework for the analysis of Classical Latin segmental phonology includes a specific set of features arranged into a specific geometry. Having thus laid the foundations, as it were, I now proceed to a discussion of consonantal phonotactics in chapter 3.

3

THE PHONOTACTICS OF SIMPLEX FORMS
AND RESYLLABIFICATION

3.1. INTRODUCTION

In this chapter the consonantal phonotactics of simplex forms and the regularities of resyllabification are presented in detail and analysed in a framework organised around sonority, a scalar property, and the syllable, a structural unit.[85] The four focal points are: (i) syllable structure, especially with respect to the non-nuclear constituents (onset and coda), where consonants are found, and the way the Sonority Sequencing Principle (see Hooper 1976; Steriade 1982; Selkirk 1984; Clements 1990; Zec 2007; Parker 2011 among others) manifests itself; (ii) the regularities governing the distribution of consonants in heterosyllabic clusters in simplex forms and the way the Syllable Contact Law (see Hooper 1976; Murray & Vennemann 1983; Vennemann 1988; Zec 2007; Seo 2011) manifests itself; (iii) the interaction of sonority with place of articulation, to which I give a semi-formal expression in the Place Condition and its ramifications; and (iv) the realignment of consonants in the case of morphological or syntactic concatenation.

I assume what may be called a traditional constituent-based notion of the syllable (a hierarchical structure consisting of onset, nucleus and coda, the latter subsumed under rhyme), including the possibility of certain segments being extrasyllabic (e.g. [s] in *stare* 'stand'). In being syllable-based, my analysis departs from some current theories of phonotactic analysis which are based on the assumption that the phonological properties of a higher-than-segmental order, such as syllables, are epiphenomenal and can be derived from the low-level phonetic properties and syntagmatic relations of segments. On this latter approach, phonotactic regularities reflect articulatory and perceptual constraints and do not presuppose higher phonological constituents like the syllable.[86]

As I see it, there are at least three practical reasons for presenting an account of Latin phonotactics in the former, more strictly structural way, in which the syllable is the organising principle.

---

[85] Portions of this chapter first appeared, in somewhat different form, in Cser (2012a).

[86] For arguments and exemplary analyses, see e.g. Steriade (1999), Côté (2000), Kiss (2007) or Hayes et al. (2004).

THE PHONOTACTICS OF SIMPLEX FORMS AND RESYLLABIFICATION 49

(i) The alternative – non-syllable-based – approach hinges crucially on a detailed phonetic investigation of the language in both its articulatory and its perceptual aspects. Needless to say this is unfeasible for a dead language like Latin. While it is true that much can be conjectured with certainty about the phonetic details of Latin as it was spoken in Antiquity, the fine-grained empirical evidence that has to be accumulated in order to build up a serious phonetically based argument (the precise nature of formant transitions, the timing relations of articulatory gestures, the amount of overlap, etc.) is, and will be, lacking. Admittedly, however, a general typological knowledge of phonetic processes can bridge this gap to a certain extent (see Sen 2015 for several analyses of this kind).

(ii) Much of what we know about the phonology, and specifically the phonotactics, of Latin comes from analyses of the vast amount of poetry produced in Antiquity. The formal nature of classical poetry has always been understood in terms of the syllable as a basic unit of prosody. If an analysis assumes the syllable as a phonological unit, it will, in some sense, be closer to the data as we have them,[87] and will also be more readily comparable to previous analyses.

(iii) A phonotactic analysis couched in terms of the syllable can be fairly easily reinterpreted in other frameworks, whereas the opposite is not necessarily true.

Sonority will be made use of here as a classificatory notion, a scalar property of segments. I assume without discussion, and in line with much of the relevant literature,[88] that (i) sonority is a property based on some physical characteristics of speech sounds, most probably intensity (loudness or the amount of acoustic energy), the openness of the vocal tract, formant structure (resonance) and voicing; and (ii) there exists a scale along which segments or segment types can be arranged as a function of their particular sonority value. While there is no a priori reason for the sonority scale to be linear, i.e. non-branching, I will work

---

[87] Naturally I do not claim that syllables as such are a given in the data. What I mean is that the data *as we have them* include strict metrical patterns that impinge on some native intuition concerning the structure of the language, which can be conveniently described as a distinction between light and heavy syllables, but the same data do not include a lot of phonetic detail, which would be self-explanatory for a living language.

[88] See Parker (2002; 2003; 2008; 2011), Clements (2009), Lodge (2009: 77–9), Clements and Hume (1995), Blevins (1995: 210–12), Cser (2003: 28–43), Jany et al. (2007), Szigetvári (2008). In Parker (2011) and (2008) a very detailed scale is given with flaps higher, and trills lower, in rank than laterals (see also Parker 2002: 255–7). It will be seen later that there may be some reason to assume that in Latin [r] had higher sonority than [l] (as Steriade 1982 also claims), although it is uncertain whether it was a flap or a trill. Another aspect of the scale in Parker's works is the ranking of voiced obstruents above voiceless ones in general, thus the ranking of voiced stops higher than voiceless fricatives, though the author admits that 'the ranking of voiced stops over voiceless fricatives is harder to justify than most aspects of this hierarchy' (Parker 2011: 1179). Here I assume that stops are generally less sonorous than fricatives.

with a traditional linear scale, viz. Vowels >> Glides >> Liquids >> Nasals >> Fricatives >> Stops. What will be examined here is to what extent such a scale is helpful in making generalisations about syllable structure and the distribution of consonants in Classical Latin.

The role of sonority will be taken up again at two points. In section 6.5 the sonority of vowels is taken under scrutiny in the context of its role in conditioning allomorphy. In Chapter 7 prefixed forms are discussed and the phonological processes affecting consonants are analysed. It is shown there that sonority plays a crucial role in when and how these processes operate; it is also shown that the interaction between sonority and place of articulation follows the same general pattern as in simplex forms, albeit differently in certain respects.

In what follows, after a brief excursus on the basics of metrical evidence, I first give a descriptive taxonomy of the consonant clusters attested in Latin; then I extract the observable patterns and relate them to syllable structure, arriving at the general syllable template, which is organised around the Sonority Sequencing Principle. The details of the operation of the Syllable Contact Law and the Place Condition are then presented, followed by a discussion of resyllabification and a brief excursus on ⟨gn⟩-initial stems, a phonologically peculiar set of lexemes.

3.1.1. *Excursus on metrical evidence*

A brief note on metrical evidence is in order here, since much of this chapter is concerned with syllable structure and syllabification, for which evidence comes mainly from scansion. The poetic metres used in the Classical Latin period have been researched for centuries and are well known at the empirical level (see e.g. Raven 1965; Halporn et al. 1963 or Boldrini 2004; see further Allen 1973), and they have also been the object of theoretical inquiry (e.g. Fabb & Halle 2008). Everything I presuppose here in terms of metrical interpretation can be found even in introductory textbooks; the outlines are the following.

Latin metre is based on systematic alternations of heavy (-V:., -VC(C)., -V:C(C).) and light (-V.) syllables. There were many patterns in use in the Classical period, all modelled on Greek precursors (for which see West 1982 and Devine & Stephens 1994). The metrical patterns reveal unambiguously in most cases which syllables are heavy and which are light (the exceptions include e.g. line-final syllables, which are not strictly delimited by the metre). In the overwhelming majority of cases the length of vowels is known too on independent grounds. Thus in many configurations the syllabic affiliation of consonants can be detected on the basis of the relation between vowel length and syllable weight.

For example, the last foot in a hexameter always consists of two syllables, the first of which is heavy, the second indeterminate. If such a foot includes the word *pŏntēs* 'bridges', the only possible syllabification of the cluster is [n.t] with a syllable boundary between the two consonants, because the first syllable of the word is heavy, although its vowel is short, thus the [n] has to be its coda. If a word like *impĕtrō* 'I achieve' is found to constitute a heavy–light–heavy sequence, this shows that the cluster [m.p] is heterosyllabic but [.tr] is a complex onset to the third syllable because the second syllable of the word, being metrically light, cannot have a coda.[89]

3.2. THE PRESENTATION OF THE CONSONANT CLUSTERS

In Tables 4–6 all attested consonant clusters are shown and exemplified, arranged according to the three basic positions, i.e. word-initial, medial and word-final. For each cluster I indicate whether the list of examples is exhaustive or not. If the list is not marked as exhaustive, it is to be understood that there are at least five derivationally unrelated lexemes containing the cluster. In the last column of the tables I indicate if a certain cluster also occurs in either of the other two positions. Note that clusters occurring at prefix–stem boundaries are not included in the list that follows; the discussion of such forms is found in Chapter 7.

3.3. THE ANALYSIS OF THE CONSONANT CLUSTERS

The picture that first emerges does not seem to offer intuitively obvious generalisations. The phonological classes apparently cross-classify elementary distributional categories, as is shown in Figure 7.

What we see is the following:

- Obstruent + sonorant clusters belong to the intersection of initial and medial clusters except for [fl] and [sw], which are only found initially, and for [gm], which is only found medially.
- CCC clusters belong to the exclusively medial class if they neither begin nor end in [s] (in the chart this is the 'all other CCC' field); [s]-initial clusters are found initially, some of them also medially; [s]-final clusters are found finally, some of them also medially.
- Of the two-obstruent clusters, [s]-initials are found both initially and medially, [s]-finals are found both finally and medially. Two-stop clusters are only found medially. The only cluster in the language that occurs initially, finally as well as medially is [st].
- Sonorant + voiceless obstruent clusters are evenly distributed between the medial and the medial–final classes with the marginal [ms] of *hiems/ hiemps* spilling over into the final class.

---

[89] For summary descriptions of Latin syllable structure, which differ from my analysis on several points, see Marotta (1999) and Lehmann (2005).

Table 4. Initial clusters

Cluster type			Example + gloss	exh	Remark
1.1.	**#CC-**				
	1.1.1.	**s+stop**			
		[sp]	*spirare* 'breathe', *spargere* 'strew', *spondere* 'promise'		Medially 3.1.1
		[st]	*stare* 'stand', *studium* 'assiduity', *stipendium* 'tribute'		Medially 3.1.1 Finally 2.1.1
		[sk]	*scire* 'know', *scalpellum* 'knife', *scelus* 'sin'		Medially 3.1.3
	1.1.2.	**obs+son**			
		[pr]	*primus* 'first', *premere* 'press', *prurire* 'stick out'		Medially 3.1.3
		[br]	*brutus* 'inert', *bruma* 'winter solstice', *brevis* 'short'		Medially 3.1.3
		[fr]	*frater* 'brother', *frigidus* 'chilling', *fructus* 'fruit'		Medially 3.1.3
		[tr]	*trahere* 'drag', *tristis* 'sad', *truncus* 'mutilated'		Medially 3.1.3
		[dr]	*Drusus*	yes	only in one proper name; Medially 3.1.3
		[kr]	*crines* 'hair', *cruor* 'blood', *crescere* 'grow'		Medially 3.1.3
		[gr]	*gravis* 'heavy', *grex* 'flock', *gradus* 'step'		Medially 3.1.3
		[pl]	*plenus* 'full', *plus* 'more', *planta* 'sprout'		Medially 3.1.3
		[bl]	*blandus* 'cajoling', *blatta* 'cockroach', *blaterare* 'babble'	yes	Medially 3.1.3
		[fl]	*flamma* 'flame', *fluere* 'flow', *flos* 'flower'		
		[kl]	*claudere* 'close', *cliens* 'personal dependant', *clemens* 'gentle'		Medially 3.1.3
		[gl]	*gladius* 'sword', *globus* 'sphere', *gliscere* 'swell'		Medially 3.1.3
		[kw]	*quantus* 'how large', *querela* 'altercation', *quies* 'repose'		Medially 3.1.3
		[sw]	*suadere* 'persuade', *suescere* 'be/get accustomed', *suavis* 'sweet'	yes	
1.2.	**#CCC-**				
		[spr]	*spretus* 'disdained'	yes	Medially 3.2.1
		[str]	*stridor* 'hissing noise'		Medially 3.2.1
		[skr]	*scribere* 'write'		
		[spl]	*splendor* 'shining'	yes	
		[skw]	*squalor* 'dirt', *squama* 'scales (of fish)', *squilla* 'lobster'	yes	Medially 3.2.1

Table 5. Final clusters

Cluster type		Example + gloss	exh	Remark
2.1.	**-CC#**			
2.1.1.	**obs+obs**			
	[ps]	*ops* 'help', *trabs* 'beam', *plebs* 'people'		Medially 3.1.1; *s* always NomSing suffix
	[ks]	*rex* 'king', *grex* 'herd', *audax* 'daring'		Medially 3.1.1; *s* always NomSing suffix
	[st]	*est* 'is', *ēst* 'eats', *ast* 'but', *post* 'after'	yes	Initially 1.1.1 Medially 3.1.1
2.1.2.	**son+obs**			
	[nt]	*ferunt* 'they carry'	(yes)	Medially 3.1.5; *nt* = 3Plur suffix
	[lt]	*vult* 'he wants'	yes	Medially 3.1.5; *t* = 3Sing suffix
	[rt]	*fert* 'he carries'	yes	Medially 3.1.5; *t* = 3Sing suffix
	[wt]	*aut* 'or'	yes	Medially 3.1.5
	[wd]	*haud* 'not'	yes	Medially 3.1.4
	[ŋk]	*hinc* 'from here'		Medially 3.1.5; only [k]-final deictics
	[jk]	*istaec* 'this', *haec* 'this', *illaec* 'those', *huic* 'to this'	yes	Medially 3.1.5; only [k]-final deictics
	[ms]	(*hiems* = *hiemps* 'winter')	yes	*s* = NomSing suffix; the only non-heteroclitic *m*-stem noun, also frequently *hiemps*
	[ls]	*puls* 'porridge', *uls* 'beyond'	yes	Medially 3.1.5
	[rs]	*pars* 'part', *misericors* 'merciful', *iners* 'incompetent'		Medially 3.1.5; *s* always NomSing suffix; all *t*- or *d*-stem nouns/adjectives
	[js]	*aes* 'bronze', *praes* 'guarantor'	yes	Medially 3.1.5
	[ws]	*laus* 'praise', *fraus* 'deceit'	yes	Medially 3.1.5; *s* = NomSing suffix; both *d*-stem nouns
2.1.3.	**son+son**			
	[jn]	*dein* 'thereafter', *proin* 'therefore'	yes	Medially 3.1.2
2.2.	**-CCC#** (*s* always NomSing suffix)			
	[mps]	*siremps* 'same', *hiemps* (=*hiems*) 'winter'	yes	Medially 3.2.2
	[rps]	*urbs* 'city', *stirps* 'root'	yes	Medially 3.2.2
	[jps]	(*saeps* 'enclosure' by-form of more frequent *saepes*)	yes	Medially 3.2.2
	[ŋks]	*coniunx* 'spouse', *lanx* 'dish', *quincunx* '5/12', *septunx* '7/12', *deunx* '11/12'	yes	Medially 3.2.2
	[rks]	*arx* 'fortress', *merx* 'price'	yes	
	[lks]	*falx* 'scythe', *calx₁* 'heel', *calx₂* 'lime'	yes	
	[jks]	*faex* 'dregs'	yes	cf. plural *faeces* in 3.1.5
	[wks]	*faux* 'throat'	yes	Medially 3.2.2

Table 6. Medial clusters

Cluster type		Example + gloss	exh	Remark
3.1.	**-CC-**			
	3.1.1.	**obs+obs**		
	[pt]	*aptus* 'fit(ted)', *optare* 'choose', *scriptus* 'written'		
	[kt]	*actus* 'done', *octo* 'eight'		
	[ps]	*ipse* 'himself', *lapsus* 'fallen'		Finally 2.1.1
	[ks]	*vexi* 'I carried', *fluxus* 'flown'		Finally 2.1.1
	[sp]	*hospes* 'host', *crispus* 'having curled hair'		Initially 1.1.1
	[st]	*hostis* 'enemy', *crista* 'crest', *honestus* 'respectable'		Finally 2.1.1 Initially 1.1.1
	[sk]	*crescere* 'grow', *fiscus* 'basket', *musca* 'fly'		Initially 1.1.1
	3.1.2.	**son+son**		
	[mn]	*amnis* 'river', *somnus* 'dream', *temnere* 'despise'		
	[ŋn]	*agnus* 'lamb', *dignus* 'worthy', *pugna* 'battle'		
	[lm]	*ulmus* 'elm-tree', *almus* 'nourishing', *pulmo* 'lung(s)'		
	[rm]	*forma* 'shape', *sermo* 'speech', *arma* 'arms'		
	[ln]	*ulna* 'elbow', *vulnus* 'wound', *alnus* 'alder'		
	[rn]	*cernere* 'see', *lucerna* 'oil-lamp', *aeternus* 'enduring'		
	[lw]	*silva* 'forest', *alvus* 'belly', *solvere* 'solve'		
	[rw]	*parvus* 'small', *larva* 'mask', *servus* 'slave'		
	[jm]	*aemulus* 'rival', *caementum* 'quarry-stone'	yes	
	[wn]	*Faunus*	yes	only in one proper name
	[jn]	*poena* 'punishment', *paene* 'almost', *moenia* 'walls'		Finally 2.1.3
	[wl]	*aula* 'court', *paulum* 'small'	yes	
	[jl]	*caelum* 'sky', *caelebs* 'unmarried', *proelium* 'battle', *paelex* 'concubine'	yes	
	[wr]	*aura* 'air', *aurum* 'gold', *laurus* 'laurel', *taurus* 'bull'	yes	
	[jr]	*quaerere* 'ask, search', *maeror* 'grief', *aereus* 'bronze'		
	[jw]	*aevum* 'age', *saevus* 'raging', *laevus* 'left', *scaevus* 'left', *naevus* 'birth-mark'	yes	
	3.1.3.	**obs+son**		
	[pr]	*capra* 'she-goat'		Initially 1.1.2
	[br]	*febris* 'fever'		Initially 1.1.2
	[fr]	*afra* 'black', *vafra* 'cunning', *infra* 'below', *mufrius* (term of abuse, hapax)	yes	Initially 1.1.2
	[tr]	*patres* 'fathers', *impetrare* 'achieve'		Initially 1.1.2
	[dr]	*dodrans* '3/4', *quadratus* 'rectangular'	yes	Initially 1.1.2
	[kr]	*acris* 'sharp'		Initially 1.1.2
	[gr]	*agrum* 'field'		Initially 1.1.2
	[pl]	*poples* 'knee'		Initially 1.1.2

(continued)

Table 6. (continued)

Cluster type		Example + gloss	exh	Remark
	[bl]	*publicus* 'public', *scriblita* 'cake', *tablinum* 'balcony'	yes	Initially 1.1.2
	[kl]	*periclitari* 'try'	yes	Initially 1.1.2
	[gl]	*figlina* 'pottery', *iuglans* 'walnut', *fraglare* 'emit a smell' (variant *fragrare*)	yes	Initially 1.1.2
	[kw]	*sequi* 'follow'		Initially 1.1.2
	[gm]	*agmen* 'train'		only with deriv. suffix -*men(tum)*
3.1.4.	**son+voiced obs**			
	[mb]	*cumbere* 'lie'		
	[nd]	*quando* 'when'		
	[ŋg]	*pungere* 'punch'		
	[lb]	*albus* 'white', *balbus* 'stutterer', *galbeus* 'armbend'	yes	
	[rb]	*verbum* 'word'		
	[ld]	*valde* 'very'	yes	
	[rd]	*tardus* 'slow'		
	[lg]	*vulgus* 'crowd'		
	[rg]	*mergere* 'sink', *largus* 'abundant', *ergo* 'on account of'		
	[jb]	*glaeba* 'clod'	yes	
	[wd]	*audire* 'hear', *claudere* 'close'		Finally 2.1.2
	[jd]	*caedere* 'cut'		
	[wg]	*augere* 'grow', *augur* 'bird-watching oracle'	yes	
	[jg]	*aeger* 'ill'	yes	
3.1.5.	**son + voiceless obs**			
	[mp]	*rumpere* 'break'		
	[nt]	*ante* 'before'		Finally 2.1.2
	[ŋk]	*mancus* 'lacking'		Finally 2.1.2
	[lp]	*culpa* 'sin'		
	[rp]	*carpere* 'pick'		
	[lt]	*vultus* 'face'		Finally 2.1.2
	[rt]	*parte* 'part' ABL		Finally 2.1.2
	[lk]	*sulcus* 'furrow'		
	[rk]	*parcere* 'mercy'		
	[ls]	*pulsus* 'beaten'		Finally 2.1.2
	[rs]	*arsit* 'burned'		Finally 2.1.2
	[wp]	*pauper* 'poor'	yes	
	[jp]	*saepe* 'often', *coepi* 'I began'	yes	
	[wt]	*autem* 'however'		Finally 2.1.2
	[jt]	*taeter* 'ugly'		
	[wk]	*paucus* 'few'		
	[jk]	*saeculum* 'age', *caecus* 'blind', *faeces* 'dregs' PLUR	yes	Finally 2.1.2
	[ws]	*causa* 'cause'		Finally 2.1.2
	[js]	*caesus* 'cut'		Finally 2.1.2

(continued)

Table 6. (continued)

Cluster type		Example + gloss	exh	Remark
3.2.	**-CCC-**			
3.2.1	**sonorant-final**			
	[spr]	*aspritudo* 'harshness'	yes	Initially 1.2
	[lpr]	*scalprum* 'chisel'	yes	
	[mbr]	*umbra* 'shadow'		
	[mpr]	*Sempronius*	yes	only in one proper name
	[ptr]	*receptrix* 'who receives'		almost all with deriv. suffix *-trix*
	[ktr]	*victrix* 'winner'		almost all with deriv. suffix *-trix*
	[str]	*castrum* 'camp', *monstrum* 'omen'		Initially 1.2
	[ntr]	*antrum* 'cave'		
	[ltr]	*ultro* 'by own will'		
	[jtr]	*taetra* 'ugly' FEM, *caetra* 'shield'	yes	
	[wtr]	*fautrix* 'who favours'	yes	deriv. suffix *-trix*
	[ŋkr]	*cancri* 'crabs'	yes	
	[lkr]	*sepulcrum* 'grave', *pulcrum* 'beautiful', *fulcrum* 'post of couch'		
	[jgr]	*aegra* 'ill'	yes	
	[mpl]	*amplus* 'large', *templum* 'temple', *exemplum* 'example'		
	[ŋkl]	*vinclum* 'bond'	yes	*vinculum* more frequent
	[ŋkw]	*quinque* 'five'		
	[rkw]	*torquere* 'turn'	yes	
	[jkw]	*aequus* 'flat'	yes	
	[skw]	*usque* 'until', *usquam* 'somewhere', *sesqui-* '1½'	yes	Initially 1.2
	[ŋgw]	*inguen* 'loin', *lingua* 'tongue'		
	[wgm]	*augmen(tum)* 'increase'	yes	
3.2.2	**sonorant + 2 obstruents**			
	[mpt]	*emptus* 'taken'		
	[ŋkt]	*cinctus* 'girdled'		
	[mps]	*sumpsi* 'I took'		Finally 2.2
	[ŋks]	*iunxi* 'I joined'		Finally 2.2
	[rpt]	*carptus* 'picked', *absorptus* 'swallowed'	yes	
	[lpt]	*sculptus* 'shaped', *scalptus* 'cut'	yes	
	[jpt]	*saeptus* 'hedged', *coeptus* 'begun'	yes	
	[rkt]	*herctum* 'inheritance', *ferctum* 'cookie'	yes	
	[lkt]	*mulctus* 'milked'	yes	
	[wkt]	*auctus* 'increased'	yes	
	[jst]	*maestus* 'grieving', *quaestus* 'asked', *aestus* 'summer', *caestus* 'boxing gloves'	yes	

(continued)

Table 6. (continued)

Cluster type		Example + gloss	exh	Remark
	[wst]	*faustus* 'favourable', *haustus* 'swallowed', *Auster* 'southerly wind'	yes	
	[wsk]	*auscultare* 'listen'	yes	
	[jsp]	*caespes* 'lawn'	yes	
	[wsp]	*auspicium* 'divination'	yes	
	[lps]	*sculpsi* 'I shaped', *scalpsi* 'I cut'	yes	
	[jps]	*saepsi* 'I hedged'	yes	Finally 2.2
	[rps]	*carpsi* 'I picked', *serpsi* 'I crawled', *absorpsi* 'swallowed'	yes	Finally 2.2
	[wks]	*auxi* 'I increased', *auxilium* 'help', *pauxillum* 'little'	yes	Finally 2.2
3.2.3	**three obstruents**			
	[pst]	*depstum* 'pastry', *subrepsti* 'you crawled'	yes	*subrepsti* short PERF[90]
	[kst]	*dexter* 'right', *duxti* 'you led'		*duxti* short PERF
3.3. **-CCCC-**				
3.3.1.	**including two sonorants**			
	[lktr]	*mulctra* 'milking bucket'	yes	
	[wstr]	*plaustrum* 'waggon', *Austrum* 'southerly wind', *claustrum* 'latch'	yes	
	[mptr]	*contemptrix* 'who contempts'		all with deriv. suffix *-trix*; preclassical *amptruare* 'dance'
	[ŋktr]	*coniunctrix* 'who joins', *expunctrix* 'who deletes'	yes	both words postclassical (St Augustine), with deriv. suffix *-trix*
3.3.2.	**including one sonorant**			
	[kstr]	*extra* 'outside', *textrix* 'seamstress', *dextra* 'right', *commixtrix* 'who mixes'	yes	postclassical *commixtrix* (St Augustine)
	[mpst]	*consumpsti* 'you consumed'	yes	short PERF
	[ŋkst]	*extinxti* 'you extinguished', *depinxti* 'you painted'	yes	preclassical *adiunxti* 'you joined', *intinxti* 'you dipped', *emunxti* 'you blew (nose)'; all short PERF-s

---

[90]On short perfect verb forms of this kind see 6.2.3.3.

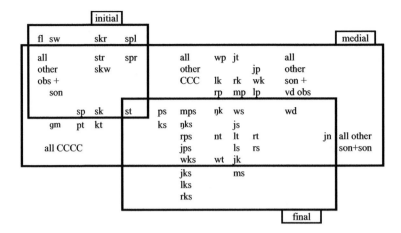

Figure 7. First classification of clusters

- Sonorant + voiced obstruent clusters consistently belong to the medial class except for [wd], which marginally occurs in final position.
- Sonorant + sonorant clusters consistently belong to the medial class except for [jn], which marginally occurs in final position.
- All CCCC clusters are medial.

The first step in a more thorough analysis of the consonant clusters will be the assignment of syllable boundaries. The initial heuristic that I use relies on the identification of syllable onsets word-internally. Since it is well known that word edges often show irregular phonotactic effects,[91] word-initial or word-final position cannot be taken as a safe indication of syllabic constituency. Word-internally, however, onsets can be identified when they follow a short vowel since the weight of the preceding syllable is evidenced by poetry.[92] Thus, if one contrasts the two words in (9) with vowel length and usual scansion indicated, one sees that two clusters that occur both initially and medially may behave differently:

---

[91] For a classic discussion see Piggott (1999) or Lowenstamm (1981), more recently Gussmann (2002: 91 sqq.), specifically for Latin e.g. Pulgram (1975: 137) but note that even such a well-informed discussion as Devine & Stephens (1977: 125) misses this point.

[92] I will not be concerned with syllable weight as a phonological category in general; I will simply assume the well-documented binary disctinction between heavy and light syllables, which distinction manifests itself in poetic metrics, stress assignment as well as a handful of minor morphophonological phenomena (diachronic rather than synchronic). The standard reference for the general phonological and phonetic aspects of syllable weight is now Gordon (2006) as well as two shorter discussions by the same author (Gordon 2002; 2004). For a survey of earlier literature, specifically with an eye to Latin, see Zirin (1970: 42–80). I will also not be concerned with the metrical phonology of Latin as such (see Mester 1994; Parsons 1999).

(9) Scansion of *patres* vs. *hostes*

$\quad\quad$ pắtrēs $\quad$ hŏ́stēs

scansion: $\cup$ — $\quad$ — —

On the basis of metrical evidence, [tr] thus turns out to be an onset cluster, whereas [st] turns out to be – at least internally – a heterosyllabic cluster, since the metrical difference between the two words can only be explained with the syllabification *pă.trēs* vs. *hŏs.tēs*. More generally, the following points have long been beyond dispute:[93]

- CCC (and *a fortiori* CCCC) clusters are always heterosyllabic medially (though where the syllable boundary falls may be a matter of debate).
- The so-called stop + liquid clusters are overwhelmingly tautosyllabic.[94]
- The cluster [kw] is always tautosyllabic (but is regarded as a single consonant by many Latinists, see 2.2.2).
- All other CC clusters are heterosyllabic.

This yields unequivocal results for most CC clusters. For CCC clusters the rule of thumb I apply here will be that, starting from the right, the longest sequence of consonants (i.e. either one or two consonants) that is evidenced to be tautosyllabic in the environment V_V will be assigned as onset to the following syllable.

In terms of the taxonomy set out in 3.2 above, the evidence shows the following in detail. The numbers in this list all refer to sections of Table 6:

- In the two-obstruent clusters in 3.1.1 the syllable boundary falls between the two consonants, thus [Vp.tV], [Vk.tV], [Vp.sV], [Vk.sV], [Vs.pV], [Vs.tV] and [Vs.kV]. The fact that [sp st sk] also occur initially does not seem to affect their medial syllabification.
- In the two-sonorant clusters in 3.1.2 the syllable boundary again falls between the two consonants, thus [Vm.nV], [Vŋ.nV], [Vl.mV], [Vr.mV], [Vl.nV], [Vr.nV], [Vl.wV], [Vr.wV], [Vj.mV], [Vw.nV], [Vj.nV], [Vw.lV], [Vj.lV], [Vw.rV], [Vj.rV] and [Vj.wV].
- In the obstruent+sonorant clusters in 3.1.3 the syllable boundary is usually before the cluster, thus [V.prV], [V.brV] or [Vb.rV], [V.trV],

---

[93] Note that these points are valid for simplex forms only. The basic patterns of syllable division presented here are corroborated by ancient inscriptions too, a kind of evidence I will not present in detail, but see Dennison (1906).

[94] The qualification *overwhelmingly* refers to token-level variation in poetic practice rather than type-level differences, though it is true that clusters including a voiced stop are more prone to heterosyllabic scansion than clusters including a voiceless stop. The history of this variation has been well researched and the consensus is that the heterosyllabic scansion of stop+liquid clusters was introduced in the wake of Greek models (for a good summary see Corte 1984–1991 s.v. *Muta cum liquida*; in a different context, see Hoenigswald 1992, who argues that morphological structure played a part in the syllabification of such clusters at least in early Latin; Sen 2006; 2015: 87–120 presents an excellent summary, with a focus on Archaic Latin and historical development). See below for further discussion.

[V.drV] or [Vd.rV],[95] [V.krV], [V.grV], [V.frV] or [Vf.rV],[96] [V.plV], [V.blV], [V.klV],[97] [V.glV] and [V.kwV]. The only truly heterosyllabic cluster in this category is [gm], thus [Vg.mV].[98]

- All the sonorant+obstruent clusters in 3.1.4 and 3.1.5, irrespective of the voicing value of the obstruent, are heterosyllabic in all cases, thus [Vm.bV], [Vn.dV], [Vŋ.gV], [Vl.bV], [Vr.bV], [Vl.dV], [Vr.dV], [Vl.gV], [Vr.gV], [Vj.bV], [Vw.dV], [Vj.dV], [Vw.gV], [Vj.gV] and [Vm.pV], [Vn.pV], [Vŋ.kV], [Vl.pV], [Vr.pV], [Vl.tV], [Vr.tV],

---

[95] The evidence for the syllabification of [dr] is, in fact, controversial. This cluster was exceedingly rare in simplex forms, the diachronic reason being the devoicing of [d] to [t] before [r] (i.e. [dr] > [tr], see Weiss 2009: 163). Actually, the only Latin words containing medial [dr] attested in poetry are derivatives and compounds based on *quădr-* (e.g. *quadratus* 'divided into four parts', *quadrupes* 'four-legged', *quadriiuga* 'drawn by four horses'). Such words occur 127 times in the entire poetic corpus. Out of the 127, 113 (= 89%) scan with a heavy first syllable, indicating a heterosyllabic cluster (e.g. Cat. 58.4, Verg. *Aen.* 3.541 vs. Verg. *Aen.* 8.642, Verg. *Ecl.* 5.24, Juv. *Sat.* 14.326). This may result from the fact that apart from the *quadr-* family the vast majority of words including [dr] are either Greek names/loans (e.g. *Hadria*, *cedrus* 'cedar', *hydrus* 'water serpent'), where heterosyllabicity of any stop+liquid cluster is the (borrowed) norm, or prefixed forms (e.g. *adripere* 'grasp'), where heterosyllabicity is a phonological rule of Latin (see 3.5 and Chapter 7). The rarity of [dr] in simplex forms, its absence from word-initial position coupled with the pull of the Greek pattern and the syllabification of prefixed forms apparently led to a preference for a heterosyllabic analysis of this cluster even in simplex native words.

[96] The cluster [fr] is only attested medially after a short vowel in a small number of proper names and the word *vafra/-um* 'cunning' and its derivative noun *vafritia*. The shortness of the stem vowel in *vafra/-um* is evidenced by the masculine form *vafer*, invariably scanned with a light first syllable (e.g. Hor. *Sat.* 1.3.128 or Ovid. *Her.* 20.27). In the case of the proper names *Rufrae* and *Safronius* a tautosyllabic cluster is evidenced in poetry (Verg. *Aen.* 7.739 and Mart. *Epigr.* 11.103 respectively, cf. Allen 1978: 90). The word *vafritia* is not attested in poetry; *vafra/-um* is attested only four times in classical poetry, all of which show a heavy first syllable and thus a syllabification [waf.rV-] (Ovid. *Ars Am.* 3.329; Hor. *Sat.* 2.2.130; Mart. *Epigr.* 6.64.24 and 12.66.3). The two preclassical occurrences of the word are indecisive (Pomponius Bononiensis fragments 87 and 139). There is a later occurrence in poetry (Prudentius *Liber Peristefanon* 5.265), which also suggests a light first syllable, but since it was composed around 400 AD and in an altogether different metrical system, it should not be taken as strong evidence for the syllabification of the cluster [fr]. It thus seems that we have to do with an indeterminacy similar to that of [dr] (see previous note). In Bakkum (1989: 26) it is said that the heterosyllabic scansion of [f.r] 'may reflect the fact that metrical conventions did not provide for /fR/ groups [i.e. [fr] and [fl] — A. Cs.], which were *Fremdkörper* in Latin and absent from Greek at the time metrical conventions were established'. I think something like this stands for [dr], as I explained above, but [fr] and [fl] actually occurred word-initially in several words, so their *Fremdkörper* status is dubious. (Note further that Bakkum demonstrates the heterosyllabic scansion of [fr] with the heavy initial syllable of *Africa* – a word that proves nothing because of its initial long vowel.)

[97] The only word with medial [kl], *periclitari* 'try' does not actually occur in classical poetry. Clusters of the form C[l] appear to be generally rare, and are somewhat problematic because of the widespread diachronic vacillation between CV[l] and C[l] forms (e.g. *periculum* ~ *periclum* 'danger'), which resulted from the conflict between the early tendency to insert a short vowel in the environment C_[l] and the somewhat later tendency to syncopate unstressed vowels in internal open syllables. For a good discussion see Ward (1951) and Sen (2006; 2015: 121–71) and the references above in note 94.

[98] The cluster [gm] is (i) the only consistently heterosyllabic *and* rising sonority cluster, (ii) the only instance of a coda voiced stop apart from the word-final [d] of neuter pronouns and (iii) the only instance of post-obstruent nasal.

[Vl.kV], [Vr.kV], [Vl.sV], [Vr.sV], [Vw.pV], [Vj.pV], [Vw.tV], [Vj.tV], [Vw.kV], [Vj.kV], [Vw.sV] and [Vj.sV].

- Most of the sonorant-final CCC clusters in 3.2.1 end in a stop+liquid sequence or [kw], which are evidenced to be tautosyllabic (i.e. complex onsets). Thus the syllabification of these is [Vs.prV], [Vl.prV], [Vm.brV], [Vp.trV], [Vk.trV], [Vs.trV], [Vn.trV], [Vl.trV], [Vj.trV], [Vw.trV], [Vŋ.krV], [Vl.krV], [Vj.grV], [Vm.plV], [Vŋ.klV], [Vŋ.kwV], [Vr.kwV], [Vj.kwV], [Vs.kwV]. The cluster [ŋgw] includes the sequence [gw], which only occurs in this particular cluster, so its tautosyllabic nature is not evidenced in the same way as it is for other stop+liquid sequences and for [kw]. However, on the analogy of [Vŋ.kwV] I will assume the syllabification [Vŋ.gwV] without further ado. The marginal, lexically and phonologically *hapax* cluster [wgm] is problematic under any analysis. Since I began by identifying possible onsets, I will assume [Vwg.mV]. This cluster will then be the only sonorant-final CCC-cluster where the syllable boundary falls between C_2 and C_3 rather than C_1 and C_2.
- In 3.2.2 all the clusters have the syllable boundary between the two obstruents. This is simply because no CC sequence is ever evidenced to be an onset if both consonants are obstruents. Thus we have [Vmp.tV], [Vŋk.tV], [Vmp.sV], [Vŋk.sV], [Vrp.tV], [Vlp.tV], [Vjp.tV], [Vrk.tV], [Vlk.tV], [Vwk.tV], [Vjs.tV], [Vws.tV], [Vws.kV], [Vjs.pV], [Vws.pV], [Vlp.sV], [Vjp.sV], [Vrp.sV] and [Vwk.sV].
- Those CCCC-clusters which include two sonorants in 3.3.1 end in the sequence [tr], which is unproblematic as an onset, thus [Vlk.trV], [Vws.trV], [Vmp.trV] and [Vŋk.trV].

To arrive at a more precise characterisation of syllable constituents we have to focus now on clusters consisting of [s] and another obstruent. The problematic status of such clusters, especially at word edges, has long been noticed in the general phonological literature (e.g. Lowenstamm 1981). Specifically in Latin, the problematic clusters are initial [s] + stop (+ sonorant), i.e. 1.1.1 and 1.2 in Table 4, final (sonorant +) stop + [s], i.e. 2.1.1 and 2.2 in Table 5, and medial (sonorant +) stop + [s] + stop (+ sonorant), i.e. 3.2.3 and 3.3.2 in Table 6. These clusters show the following peculiarities:

- They are the only clusters that do not conform to the Sonority Sequencing Principle. The [s] represents a relative sonority peak between two stops as well as between a stop and a word boundary in any order.
- Final (sonorant +) stop + [s] clusters are highly restricted in that they only appear when a specific inflectional suffix (nominative singular -*s*) is added to stop-final stems.
- Initial [s] + stop (+ sonorant) clusters are paralleled by medial clusters of the same segmental composition which are clearly heterosyllabic (*stare* 'stand' vs. *hos.tes* 'enemies').

- If a vowel-final prefix is added to a simplex form with initial [s] + stop (+ sonorant), apparent leftward resyllabification takes place and the [s] becomes the coda of the preceding syllable. This never happens when obstruent + sonorant initial simplex forms are prefixed (e.g. *re+stare* → *res.tare* 'remain' but *re+trahere* → *re.trahere* 'pull back'). Unambiguous evidence for this comes from poetic metre, e.g. *restant* 'they remain' always scans as two heavy syllables, while *retrahunt* 'they pull back' as light–light–heavy.
- Three verbs with initial [s] + stop have a reduplicated perfectum stem, which other CC-initial verbs never have. The three verbs are *stare* ~ *steti* 'stand', *spondere* ~ *spopondi* 'promise' and *scindere* ~ preclassical *scicidi* 'cleave'. Notice that reduplication only copies the stop portion of the cluster, not the [s], i.e. the forms are not **stesti, etc., although the fricative is still placed at the left edge of the word forms.[99]
- When the prefixes *ex-* and *sus-* are added to stems beginning with [s] and [s]+stop, respectively, the resulting geminate [ss] is degeminated (*ex+salire* → *exilire* 'jump out', *sus+spirare* → *suspirare* 'sigh', see Chapter 7). This is in line with the general rule that mandates degemination whenever the consonants cannot be syllabified (see 4.5), and thus proves that the syllabifications [eks.si-] and [sus.spi-] are impossible.

The evidence is, I believe, compelling enough to regard these (but only these) occurrences of [s] as extrasyllabic, a solution I suggested earlier (Cser 1999: 178 sqq.).[100] What this means for the specific types of clusters involved is the following:

- For those in 1.1.1 (Table 4) the syllabification is #[*s*.pV], i.e. [*s*[$_{Ons}$p]], etc.
- For those in 1.2 (Table 4) the syllabification is #[*s*.prV], i.e. [*s*[$_{Ons}$pr]], etc.
- For those in 2.1.1 (Table 5) the syllabification is [Vp.*s*]#, i.e. [[$_{Co}$p]*s*], etc.
- For those in 2.2 (Table 5) the syllabification is [Vmp.*s*]#, i.e. [[$_{Co}$mp]*s*], etc.
- For those in 3.2.3 (Table 6) the syllabification is [Vp.*s*.tV], i.e. [[$_{Co}$p]*s*[$_{Ons}$t]], etc.

---

[99] Also note the historical infectum reduplication *sistere* 'stop' from the same root as *stare*.

[100] In Lehmann (2005: 168 and passim) the same positions are called pre-initial and post-coda. An advantage of referring to them as extrasyllabic is that in internal [pst], [kst] one does not have to decide whether the trapped [s] is pre-initial or post-coda, which would be possible only on an ad hoc basis. Word-initial (but not final or internal) [s] of the same distribution was called extrasyllabic in Jacobs (1992: 57). Steriade (1982; 1988) analyses the same initial [s] with the help of stray adjunction, which means practically the same. Marotta (1999: 301) tentatively considers such clusters 'tautosyllabic, at least at some level of representation'.

- For those in 3.3.2 (Table 6) the syllabification is either of the kind [Vk.*s*.trV], i.e. [[$_{Co}$k]*s*[$_{Ons}$tr]], or of the kind [Vmp.*s*.tV], i.e. [[$_{Co}$mp]*s*[$_{Ons}$t]].

The final analysis is thus the following. Everything except extrasyllabic [s] is syllabified as coda or onset (and vowels as nucleus, obviously). Codas as well as onsets can consist of at most two consonants, an obstruent and a sonorant in the linear order dictated by the Sonority Sequencing Principle. The classification of consonant clusters is therefore significantly simplified, as is shown in Figure 8.

The generalisations captured in Figure 8 are the following:

- All CCC and CCCC clusters are now exclusively heterosyllabic clusters. Note that at this stage these labels no longer subsume the clusters in 1.2 (Table 4), 2.2 (Table 5), 3.2.3 and 3.3.2 (Table 6), that is, the long clusters including an extrasyllabic [s]. As has already been explained, the remaining CCC clusters are syllabified as C.CC if they end in a (non-nasal) sonorant and CC.C if they end in an obstruent (plus [wg.m]).
- The set of onsets is totally disjunct from all the other cluster types. Since onset clusters are all rising sonority clusters, whereas coda and heterosyllabic clusters tend to be equal or falling sonority clusters

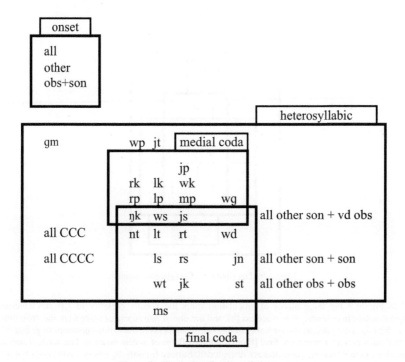

Figure 8. Final classification of clusters

(see section 3.4), the intersection of onsets and other clusters is indeed expected to be empty.

- Medial coda clusters are generally of the shape sonorant + non-coronal voiceless obstruent. Exceptions are [ws js], which end in a coronal, and [wg], which ends in a voiced obstruent.
- Apart from the exceptions listed in the previous points, obstruent + obstruent clusters cannot be onsets or codas, neither can clusters consisting of two sonorants or a sonorant followed by a voiced obstruent.
- Both medial coda clusters and final coda clusters are proper subsets of the heterosyllabic clusters (but for the isolated final [ms] of *hiems/hiemps* 'winter').
- The set of medial coda clusters and final coda clusters is almost completely disjunct.

This last point perhaps deserves more than passing mention. In a syllable-based framework it is not immediately obvious why coda clusters should not be more alike in different positions within the word. The criterion appears to be the place of articulation of C_2; and this, in fact, squares well with the distribution of single consonants in different syllabic positions (Figure 9):[101]

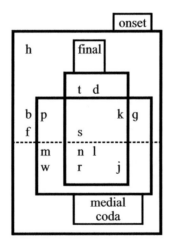

Figure 9. Distribution of single consonants

[101] In Figure 9 the three places of articulation (plus the vocalic dorsality of [j]) are indicated approximately in columns, as is placeless [h], and the dotted line separates obstruents and sonorants. The chart does not indicate the typicality of individual segments in the various positions (e.g. final [d] only figures in neuter pronouns, final [j] only in three affixes of *a*-stem nouns and adjectives) and, as elsewhere in this chapter, geminates are disregarded. Surface [ŋ] only figures as medial coda but is a positional variant of [n] or [g].

As was explained in detail elsewhere (2.2.1), final consonants are coronal (except for the deictic and imperative [k], and for [j], which has no consonantal place and is always a morphological marker). We can now add that medial codas are either voiceless and non-coronal (except for the marginal [g]), or sonorant (except for [s]). And as a perusal of the consonant clusters in 3.1 and 3.2 above quickly shows, post-consonantal onsets show a preference for coronality: if a post-consonantal consonant is an obstruent, it is often [t] or [s]. What this means is that final clusters bear more resemblance to heterosyllabic clusters than to medial coda clusters, which is equivalent to saying that final consonants bear more resemblance to onset consonants than to coda consonants.[102]

The general syllable template that can be distilled from the above considerations is shown in Figure 10. The following points need to be added to flesh out the template:

- Coda obstruents are voiceless stops or [s].
- The peripheral[103] fricative [h] is not found in any cluster. The other peripheral fricative [f] is only found in the onset clusters [fr] and [fl].
- Coda consonants and clusters are mostly coronal finally.
- Internal codas prefer sonorants, non-coronal and voiceless obstruents. More specifically, all seven sonorants [m n ŋ l r j w] are found as single coda consonants word-internally, but of the obstruents systematically only [p k s]. The voiced obstruents, the coronal stops, [f] and [h] are generally incompatible with the coda position.

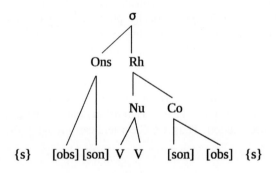

Figure 10. The general syllable template

---

[102] This point has been made with respect to other languages, see Harris (1994: 73–4) on English as well as French. In Goverment Phonology and some other models it is explicitly argued that final consonants *are* onsets. For a survey of these arguments see Gussmann (2002: 91 sqq.). Note that in Latin final [t] cannot follow stops, whereas internally it can (**[pt]# **[kt]#).

[103] Throughout this work the term *peripheral* refers to non-coronal consonants, i.e. labials and velars, and occasionally to the 'virtual' consonant [h]. In 6.5, where vowel sonority is discussed, peripheral is the opposite of central (with respect to vowels).

- Complex internal codas are sequences of a sonorant and [p] or [k] (e.g. *carp.tus* 'picked', *mulc.tus* 'milked', *emp.tus* 'taken', *sculp.si* 'I shaped'), but [js] and [ws] are also found (*caes.pes* 'lawn', *faus.tus* 'favourable') and the badly irregular hapax cluster [wg.m] of *aug.men(tum)* 'growth' includes the single occurrence of coda [wg].

- The only exception to the sonorant+obstruent structure (but not to the Sonority Sequencing Principle) is the final coda [st] found in four words altogether (e.g. *est* 'is').

- A complex onset always consists of an obstruent and a non-nasal sonorant; more specifically, these clusters include stop+liquid sequences (*plenus* 'full', *a.cris* 'sharp', but note that stop+[l] is much rarer than stop+[r][104]), [fr] and [fl] (*frater* 'brother', *a.fra* 'black', *flamma* 'flame' the latter only initially), [sw] (*suadere* 'persuade', only initially), [kw] (*quis* 'who', *a.qua* 'water') and [gw] (*san.guis* 'blood', only internally after [ŋ]). Nasals are not found in complex onsets at all.

- Extrasyllabic [s] may not be adjacent to any segment except a voiceless stop in the same word, which can only be non-coronal to the left, coronal to the right medially and any of the three initially.

- Two adjacent obstruents are always voiceless (regardless of syllabic constituency) and at least one of the two has to be coronal.

- Coda [s] is never followed by a voiced consonant. Initial [s] can only be followed by [w] of all voiced consonants.

- Out of the 182 hypothetically possible[105] CC clusters fifty (= 27.5%) are attested in at least five words each.

- In CCC clusters no two consonants may be the same.

- Out of the 2,184 hypothetically possible[106] CCC clusters fifteen (= 0.68%) are attested in at least five words each ([mbr], [ptr], [ktr], [str], [ntr], [ltr], [lkr], [mpl], [ŋkw], [ŋgw], [mpt], [ŋkt], [mps], [ŋks] and [kst]). In these clusters redundancy is very high. It is not a gross oversimplification to say that in C_3 virtually only manner is contrastive ([w] vs. [r] vs. [s] vs. [t]), in C_2 virtually only place ([p] vs. [t] vs. [k]),[107] in C_1 neither, since it is almost invariably a nasal with redundant place specification. Thus, CCC clusters carry roughly the same amount

---

[104] The asymmetry between [l]-final and [r]-final clusters may be due to a difference in the respective sonority values of the two liquids combined with the Minimal Sonority Distance effect, which is suggested in Steriade (1982), and also in Parker (2008; 2011), though in Parker's sonority scale this would only work if [r] was a flap rather than a trill since trills have a lower sonority value than [l].

[105] I.e. 14 × 13, not counting geminates.

[106] I.e. 14 × 13 × 12.

[107] The cluster [mbr] is among the frequent ones, but there is no [mpr] (except for the proper name *Sempronius*). Note, however, [ŋgw] vs. [ŋkw] (cf. 2.2.2.7).

of information as single segments, but distribute it over a span of three segments.[108] For instance, the structure of the cluster [ŋks] with the contrastive features highlighted is shown in Figure 11. As can be seen, in terms of contrastivity, this cluster carries exactly the same amount of information as a voiceless velar fricative [x].

3.4. SYLLABLE CONTACT AND THE INTERACTION BETWEEN PLACE OF ARTICULATION AND SONORITY

Heterosyllabic, i.e. coda–onset, clusters in Latin simplex forms are overwhelmingly in conformity with the Syllable Contact Law; that is, the last segment of the syllable on the left has higher sonority than the first segment of the syllable on the right.[109] The asymmetry of most permitted heterosyllabic cluster types is clear. For instance, [s] can only be followed by voiceless stops (*hos.pes* 'host', *hos.tis* 'enemy', *cres.cere* 'grow'); nasals can be followed by stops (*an.te*

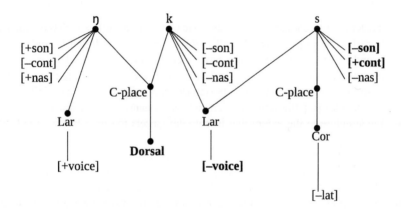

Figure 11. The structure of the cluster [ŋks]

[108] Admittedly, though, contrastivity and redundancy in CCC clusters is a more complicated issue. For instance, while there are two fairly frequent [l]-initial CCC clusters ([ltr], [lkr]), these are in almost perfect complementary distribution with NC[r] clusters in that the former occur after [u], where the latter never do (*ultra* 'beyond' vs. *antrum* 'cave'). The only counterexample is *altrix* 'nourisher' (vs. *ultrix* 'avenger'). Note furthermore that altogether five [Ctr] clusters are among the most frequent ones, though of these [ptr], [ktr] almost only emerge in the case of suffixation with *-trix*.

[109] The most important references for what came to be known as the Syllable Contact Law, repeated here from 3.1 are Hooper (1976), Murray & Vennemann (1983), Vennemann (1988), Zec (2007) and Seo (2011). Of these, Vennemann (1988) discusses some of the Latin data too. More recently, the role of sonority in the development of consonant clusters in Late Latin was analysed in Gess (2004), where the validity of essentially the same generalisation is demonstrated in an Optimality Theoretic framework.

'before') but never by liquids; stops can never be followed by nasals or glides ([kw] and [gw] are not heterosyllabic and [gm] is exceptional); liquids can be followed by stops, nasals and [s] (*al.bus* 'white', *pul.sus* 'beaten', *cer.nere* 'see', *ul.mus* 'elm-tree') but not by another liquid (**[rl lr]) or the glide [j] (**[lj rj]).

At the same time, there is an interesting interplay between sonority and place of articulation. In a sequence of a non-coronal and a coronal consonant (in this order, and excluding glides, which do not have consonantal place), C_1 does not have to be of higher sonority. Four of the five permitted equal-sonority clusters are of this kind (*ap.tus* 'fit', *ac.tus* 'done', *am.nis* 'river', *di[ŋ].nus* 'worthy') as are the two permitted stop+fricative clusters (*ip.se* 'himself', *ve[k.s]i* 'I carried'). This may be formalised in the following way:[110]

(11) The Place Condition
      Heterosyllabic clusters of two segments with consonantal place nodes and of equal or near-equal sonority are well-formed irrespective of the sonority relations if C_1 is non-coronal and C_2 is coronal (i.e. [pt kt ps ks mn ŋn] are well-formed). In all other cases, only sonority relations are decisive (i.e. [sp sk], all liquid+stop, liquid+[s], liquid+nasal and homorganic nasal+ stop clusters are well-formed, **[tk tp pk kp mŋ ŋm nm nŋ lr rl] are not).

The clusters not in conformity with the Place Condition (or the Syllable Contact Law) are [rw lw jw] (*par.vus* 'small', *sil.va* 'forest', *ae.vi* [aj.wiː] 'age' GEN). These end in [w], which does not have a consonantal place node. There is a conspicuous asymmetry between [w] and [j] in clusters: the regularity boils down to a categorical ban on postconsonantal [j] vs. the possibility of postconsonantal [w] (though not after any consonant). This is independent of syllable structure to the extent that in complex onsets too only [w] is found, [j] never (cf. 2.2.2.4).

The list of attested clusters shows that the Place Condition needs to be supplemented with a minor regularity, viz. a nasal cannot be followed by any [+continuant] segment. This means a ban on all nasal + fricative, nasal + liquid and nasal + glide sequences – the inclusion of the last of these is warranted since the continuancy of glides is the same as that of other consonants (as opposed to the place nodes and place features). The absence of the clusters **[pn bn kn gn] shows that the first clause of the Place Condition cannot override a sonority distance greater than that between stops and [s], hence the qualification included ('two segments of equal or near-equal sonority').

Recapitulating another pertinent point from the presentation of consonant clusters above, the clusters [fr] and [br] appear to be variably hetero- or tautosyllabic (see note 96); when heterosyllabic, they comply with the Place Condition in being non-coronal + coronal sequences, though the sonority

---

[110] Note that in this particular section the focus is on CC sections spanning a syllable boundary, thus e.g. [pt] here represents [pt], [mpt], [ptr], [mptr], and so on.

distance between [f]/[b] and [r] is comparable to that between a stop and a nasal. The other fricative [s] is never found before voiced consonants (at least internally; initial [sw] is attested in three stems and their derivatives). The odd behaviour of the rare cluster [dr] was remarked upon in note 95.

The Place Condition encapsulates an empirical observation that has been made in the literature earlier about a variety of languages; for Latin see Sen (2015: 177–80). Bailey (1970) briefly discusses metathesis as a diachronic change and generalises that it preferably results in non-coronal+coronal clusters. Clements (1990: 311–14) discusses the issue and the proposals made earlier to explain such effects by assigning lower sonority to coronals than to non-coronals of identical manner of articulation. He rejects such a solution because it leads to conflicting generalisations and opts instead for an explanation based on markedness, i.e. [t] being simpler than other voiceless stops, it is freer to occur in a variety of positions (see also de Lacy 2006 on markedness in general and place of articulation markedness in particular). This, however, does not in itself necessarily explain preferred sequential orderings (in other words, it explains why [pt] and [tp] are preferred to [kp] or [pk] but does not explain why [pt] is preferred to [tp]). The same is true of Booij's (1995: 44–6) analysis of a similar preference in Dutch clusters, which is based at this point on Yip (1991).

If coronals had lower sonority than labials and velars within the same manner class, cases like [pt] and [kt] could be accounted for, since these would be falling-sonority clusters, but the possibility of [ks] and [ps] would be left unexplained. Furthermore, as Steriade (1982) points out, the lack of complex onsets **[tl] and **[dl] can actually be an argument for the higher, rather than lower, sonority of [t] and [d] because the smaller sonority distance between coronal stops and [l] makes these clusters worse than e.g. [pl] and [kl].

Figure 12 summarises the distribution of heterosyllabic clusters in simplex forms as a function of sonority. As in the discussion so far, geminates are disregarded (e.g. the liquid+liquid box is left empty in spite of legitimate and numerous geminate liquids). Cluster types that only admit non-coronal+coronal

C_1	C_2	stop	fricative	nasal	liquid	glide
stop			1		([dr] [br])	
fricative					([fr])	
nasal				1		
liquid			2			3
glide						

Legend: 1 – Place Condition
           2 – Syllable Contact Law
           3 – Glide clusters
           empty box – no cluster attested

Figure 12. Heterosyllabic cluster types in simplex forms

sequences (i.e. comply with the Place Condition) are marked with (1) and a darker grey. Other well-formed cluster types are marked with (2) and a lighter grey. Cluster types that are not covered by the Place Condition are marked with (3) and the lightest grey. The marginally heterosyllabic clusters [fr], [dr] and [br] are in parentheses. The empty top right-hand half of the chart vs. the full bottom left-hand half (marked 2) shows the validity of the Syllable Contact Law.[111]

3.5. RESYLLABIFICATION AND EXTRASYLLABIC [s]

This chapter so far has been concerned with syllable structure in simplex forms. Now I briefly look at what happens to syllable structure in complex forms and at word boundaries.[112]

When a prefix is added to a stem, the assignment of the segments at the boundary to syllabic positions shows the following very general regularities in those cases where segmental or featural change can be factored out:

- A prefix-final consonant is syllabified as onset to the first syllable of the stem if and only if without it there would be no onset to that syllable: *ab+ire* → *a.bi.re* 'go away' vs. *ob+ruere* → *ob.ru.e.re* 'bury' in spite of simplex *fu.ne.bris* 'funeral', etc.[113]
- A stem-initial [s] that would be extrasyllabic in an unprefixed form is syllabified leftwards as coda if a well-formed coda results: *re+stare* → *res.ta.re* 'remain' (but *ob+stare* → *ob.{s}.ta.re* 'obstruct' with the [s] remaining extrasyllabic).
- There is no leftward syllabification of other stem-initial consonants: *re+fractus* → *re.frac.tus* 'broken'.[114]

What this shows is that syllabification cannot override the syllable structure that is created within morphological boundaries except if onsetless syllables would result following a closed syllable (as in *a.b+i.re*). The assignment of stem-initial extrasyllabic [s] to the prefix-syllable (as in *re+s.ta.re*) does not contradict this,

---

[111] In Cser (2012a) I proposed two conditions, the Place Condition covering only obstruents and nasals, and the Inverse Place Condition, a mirror image to the Place Condition, which covered the non-nasal sonorants. That analysis was based on a simpler conception of infrasegmental structure and assumed that [j] was one of the coronal consonants. On that assumption, the analysis was that the clusters not in conformity with the (narrower) Place Condition were all coronal+non-coronal sequences ([lw rw jw]) and thus showed the opposite distribution of place (e.g. a good parallel to the [mn]-type would be the non-existent cluster **[wj]). While descriptively adequate, that analysis is incompatible with the infrasegmental structures given here in 2.4.

[112] Portions of this section first appeared, in somewhat different form, in Cser (2012b).

[113] *Pace* Pulgram (1975: 138). Harris (1983) demonstrated the workings of this principle, generally referred to as Onset Satisfaction, in Spanish at word boundaries. For the different scansions involving [br] see the pentametre line Ovid *Epist.*2.2.60: *posse velim cineres obruere ipse meos* 'I wish I could bury my own ashes' vs. Horace's hexameter ending *Epist.* 1.19.49: *funebre bellum* 'grievous war'.

[114] Despite appearances, the prefixation of ⟨gn⟩-initial stems (e.g. *ignoscere* 'forgive' from *in+gnoscere*) does not involve leftward resyllabification. For discussion see 3.6.

since that [s] is not incorporated into the syllable structure of the stem.[115] In a cyclical derivation of syllable structure the resyllabification process can be represented as in Figure 13.

Resyllabification at word boundaries is subject to the same rules:[116]

(12) Resyllabification at word boundary
    videt ille 'he sees' → *vi.de.til.le* (like *a.bi.re*)
    videt rem 'he sees (a/the) thing' → *vi.det.rem* (like *ob.ru.e.re*)

There is, however, one significant difference. As we have just seen, extrasyllabic [s] is resyllabified as coda to the preceding syllable within a word unless an ill-formed syllable would result. At word boundary, the treatment of extrasyllabic [s] is more complicated. The poetic corpus shows the following.

Words beginning with an [s]+stop cluster[117] are most often found after consonant-final or long-vowel-final words or in line-initial position, where the syllabification of the extrasyllabic [s] is impossible (for the researcher) to determine and irrelevant (for the ancient poet) from the point of view of the metrical composition of the poem. These I call neutral positions. The only non-

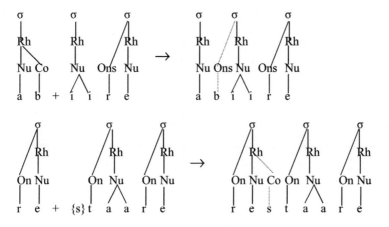

Figure 13. Resyllabification

---

[115] Note that this account of the interaction between syllable boundaries and morphological boundaries is considerably simpler than that presented in Devine & Stephens (1977: 136–8).

[116] A handful of examples of the leftward resyllabification of onset consonants are known in poetry (like *impotentia freta* 'unbridled waves' syllabified as *im.po.ten.ti.af.re.ta* in Catullus *Carm.* 4.18). These isolated manifestations of poetic licence are not regarded here as having any bearing on the phonological regularities of syllabification.

[117] In the classicist tradition the [s] in such clusters is referred to as *s impurum* ('impure *s*'). A number of initial clusters only found in Greek loans and names (viz. *sm, ps, x* [ks], *z* [dz] or [zd]) are also regarded as instantiations of *s impurum* because of their behaviour in poetry. With this latter group I will not be concerned although there is a certain degree of overlap. For an excellent discussion of their relation and their relevance to poetics see Hoenigswald (1949b); in that paper most of the data listed here can be found, and the earlier discussions are given thorough, if terse, critical treatment.

neutral position is following a short-vowel-final word within the same line. The incidence of [s]+stop-initial words in non-neutral position is very low: of the 10,217 occurrences of all such words in the poetic corpus only 48 (= 0.47%) are found in non-neutral position.[118]

The treatment of this configuration shows interesting differences between the individual poets, shown in Table 7. The proportion of [s]+stop-initial words in non-neutral position is relatively high for Catullus, lower but still not very low for Lucretius and the Golden Age poets Horace, Propertius and Tibullus. Vergil is strongly aversive to this configuration, and so are all the later Golden and Silver Age poets beginning with Ovid.[119]

Catullus applies leftward resyllabification in five out of the six cases; his contemporary, Lucretius never does (0 out of ten cases; his prosodic choice

Table 7. Extrasyllabic [s] in non-neutral position in poetry

	Total no. of [s]+stop-initial words	No. of [s]+stop-initial words in non-neutral position	Percentage of [s]+stop-initial words in non-neutral position	Resyllabified	Not resyllabified
Lucretius	445	10	2.25		10
Catullus	101	6	6	5	1
Vergil	1,112	2	0.18	1	1
Horace	620	9	1.45		9
Propertius	255	7	2.75		7
Tibullus	86	2	2.33	2	
Ovid	2,587	4	0.15		4
Silius Italicus	1,301	2	0.15	2	
Persius	59	0	0		
Lucanus	815	1	0.14	1	
Martialis	701	2	0.35	2	
Statius	1,308	2	0.15	1	1
Valerius Flaccus	530	0	0		
Juvenal	297	1	0.33	1	
	10,217	48			

[118] As Hoenigswald (1949b: 272) points out, 'in post-scenic verse, words ending in short vowel are not permitted before words beginning with s impure'. The term *post-scenic* refers to literature after Plautus and Terence, that is, roughly from the mid-second century BC on.

[119] Because of the fragmentary nature of what remains of their works I have not included Ennius and Lucilius here. But note the former's *auspicio regni stabilita scamna solumque* 'the chair and throne [of royalty], established firm by the watching of birds' (1.96, translation by E. H. Warmington, source: http: //www.attalus.org/poetry/ennius1.html) with resyllabification, and the latter's *inmutasse statumque* 'to have changed the condition' (fragm. 292), *atque accurrere scribas* approx. 'and that the scribes run' (*Sat.* 375, a hexameter ending), *deducere scalis* approx. 'to lead down the stairs' (*Sat.* 392, also a hexameter ending), perhaps *Albesia scuta* 'the Albenses' shields' (*Sat.* 1150, probably a hexameter ending) and *Pyrgensia scorta* 'Pyrgan whores' (*Sat.* 1271, perhaps a hexameter ending) without resyllabification (like in Plautus and Terence).

resembles that of Plautine comedy, where the configuration in question was not avoided and the [s] was not resyllabified). Horace, Propertius and Ovid never resyllabify, Vergil is indecisive; the first century AD poets Silius Italicus, Martialis and Lucanus resyllabify their [s]+stop words in non-neutral position, their contemporary, Statius, is again indecisive. Persius and Valerius Flaccus do not have a single instance of the configuration in question.[120]

What this very clearly shows is that the resyllabification of initial extrasyllabic [s] was not phonologically determined. In particular, the early contemporaries Catullus and Lucretius contrast sharply in their treatment of these segments, as illustrated by the scansion of the two hexameter lines in (13).

(13) Contrasting scansions of extrasyllabic [s]

Catullus *Carm.* 64.186
nulla fugae ratio nulla spes omnia muta[121]
(—UU— UU— — — — — —UU—U)

Lucretius *De rerum nat.* 4.475
unde sciat quid sit scir(e) et nescire vicissim[122]
(—UU— — — — — — —UU— —)

The later poets tend to simply avoid putting [s]+stop-initial words in non-neutral position (Vergil, Ovid, Silius Italicus, Lucanus, Statius, Martialis, Persius, Valerius Flaccus, Juvenal); those who do not, tend in the Lucretian way not to resyllabify (Horace, Propertius); Catullus' practice of not avoiding this configuration *and* resyllabifying is not followed by anyone except maybe Tibullus (but in his small corpus there are only two occurrences anyway). Although it is clear that poetic practice was shaped by a number of factors, among them the influence of the Greek models,[123] and that poetry was, in all likelihood, not actually recited metrically, I do suspect that the marked avoidance and/or

---

[120] Note, however, that two Valerius Flaccus-loci are open to such an interpretation. They are *Arg.* 5.602: *atque ubi Rhipaea stupuerunt flumina bruma* 'and when the rivers were frozen in the Rhipean winter' and 6.229: *vadit eques densa spargens hastilia dextra* 'the mounted warrior strides, frequently throwing (his) javelins with his right hand' (translations mine). While there is a tradition of interpreting *Rhipaea* and *densa* as feminine ablative singular forms, i.e. ending in a long *ā*, and thus irrelevant metrically from the point of view of the [s] + stop sequence, semantic and syntactic considerations make a neuter nominative and accusative plural interpretation (i.e. with short *a*) possible, respectively; in that case the former locus would have 'Rhipean rivers' rather than 'Rhipean winter', in the latter the adjective *densa* 'frequent' would refer to the javelins and not the warrior's right hand. However, I do not specifically argue for either interpretation, I merely point out that they are theoretically conceivable.

[121] 'Nowhere is path for flight: none hope shows: all things are silent' translation from Burton (1894).

[122] 'whence he knows what 'tis to know and not-to-know in turn', translation from Leonard (1921).

[123] Among others, Hoenigswald (1949b) and Zirin (1970) make the point that [s]+stop clusters were avoided in non-neutral positions because they presented a conflict between the Greek scansion (where leftward resyllabification was the practice) and the natural prosody of Latin (where leftward resyllabification did not apply across word boundaries). But the treatment of stop+liquid clusters also differed between the two languages and yet there was no tendency to avoid these in Roman poetry.

indeterminacy of the configuration exemplified here has a phonological basis and results from the conflict of two principles:

(14)   Principles constraining resyllabification
      (14/i) Resyllabification can only be rightwards.[124]
      (14/ii) An extrasyllabic segment may not be adjacent to a nucleus.

Within words (i.e. at prefix–stem boundaries) the second principle clearly has precedence over the first, and so leftward resyllabification always takes place (*re+s.ta.re*; see also *nescire* as opposed to *unde sciat* in the above line by Lucretius in 13). But between words this order of precedence seems to apply only for Catullus; for Lucretius, Horace and Propertius it is the opposite; and all the other poets are at pains to avoid having to take sides.[125]

To conclude this section the actual loci[126] are exhaustively listed in Tables 8 and 9.[127]

3.6. A NOTE ON WORDS WRITTEN WITH INITIAL ⟨GN⟩

There is a small set of words in Latin whose stem is variably written with initial ⟨gn⟩ or ⟨n⟩.[178] It is generally agreed that by the Classical Latin period they represented a spelling archaism rather than actual phonological [gn], and by this

---

[124] Since rightward resyllabification is subject to the constraint that it may only apply if a syllable would remain onsetless without it, this principle can actually be seen as an amalgamation of two principles: (14/ia) A coda cannot be followed by a nucleus; (14/ib) Resyllabification is not allowed, where (14/ia) always has precedence over (14/ib) in Latin, and consonantal epenthesis is generally disallowed, thus the only way to remedy coda+nucleus sequences is by rightward resyllabification.

[125] I note in passing that the proportion of the only remaining initial [s]C cluster [sw] in neutral vs. non-neutral position is three to one in the poetic corpus, which shows that there was no tendency to avoid [sw] in non-neutral position (cf. also Zirin 1970: 39; Ballester 1996: 78).

[126] Verg. *Georg.* 1. 84., not included here, appears to involve a data problem. The textual variant found in the Brepols corpus is *saepe etiam incendere sterilis profuit agros* 'Oft, too, 'twill boot to fire the naked fields' (translation from Greenough 1900); the memento to the text says it was adopted from the Teubner edition (Ribbeck 1894). However, that edition (as well as other editions I checked, e.g. Greenough's 1900 or Mynors's 1972 edition), has *saepe etiam steriles* (or *sterilis*) *incendere profuit agros*. In this variant the extrasyllabic [s] is in a neutral position and hence irrelevant. The source of the Brepols variant, which is problematic with the long [e:] of *incendere* and the long [i:] of *sterilis* is unclear to me, but it is certainly not the edition referred to. If it was an existing and authentic text, it would show extrasyllabic [s] in a non-neutral position, with no resyllabification.

[127] The word *mihi*, whose second vowel is variably short or long, even for the same poet, presents a minor difficulty here. If the second syllable scans light, resyllabification of [s] has obviously not taken place (and the vowel is short); see the last item in Table 9. (Note, however, that in this case a contracted pronunciation *mī* is not out of the question, and then, of course, resyllabification remains undetectable and metrically irrelevant.) By contrast, if the second syllable scans heavy, there are three possible explanations: (i) the vowel is long and the [s] was not resyllabified; (ii) the vowel is short and the [s] was resyllabified; and (iii) the vowel is long and the [s] was resyllabified. Since I see no way of deciding in the seven extant instances which of the three is the case, I simply disregard them. I do not think this distorts the data in any harmful way.

[178] The section includes material, in condensed and updated form, that appeared in Cser (2011).

Table 8. Extrasyllabic [s] resyllabified

Locus	Line	Syllabification of relevant portion
Catullus *Carm.* 17.24	si pote stolidum repente excitare veternum[128]	po.tes.to.li.dum
Catullus *Carm.* 22.12	hoc quid putemus esse qui modo scurra[129]	mo.dos.cur.ra
Catullus *Carm.* 44.18	nec deprecor iam si nefaria scripta[130]	ne.fa.ri.as.crip.ta
Catullus *Carm.* 63.53	ut aput nivem et ferarum gelida stabula forem[131]	ge.li.das.ta.bu.la
Catullus *Carm.* 64.186	nulla fugae ratio nulla spes omnia muta[132]	nul.las.pe.(s-)
Vergil *Aen.* 8.425	Brontesque Steropesque et nudus membra Pyracmon[133]	bron.tes.ques.te. ro.pes.(qu-)[134]
Tibullus *El.* 1.5.28	pro segete spicas pro grege ferre dapem[135]	se.ge.tes.pi.cas
Tibullus *El.* 1.5.53	ipsa fame stimulante furens herbasque sepulcris[136 316]	fa.mes.ti.mu.lan.te
Silius Italicus *Pun.* 9.575	immane stridens agitur crebroque coacta[137]	im.ma.nes.tri.den.(s-)
Silius Italicus *Pun.* 17.546	diversa spatio procul a certamine pugnae[138]	di.ver.sas.pa.ti.o
Lucanus *Phars.* 5.118	aut pretium; quippe stimulo fluctuque furoris[139]	quip.pes.ti.mu.lo
Martialis *Epigr.* 2.66.8	ut digna speculo fiat imago tua[140]	dig.nas.pe.cu.lo
Martialis *Epigr.* 5.69.3	quid gladium demens Romana stringis in ora[141]	ro.ma.nas.trin.gi.(s-)
Statius *Theb.* 6.551	praeceleres agile studium et tenuissima virtus[142]	a.gi.les.tu.di.(-)
Juvenal *Sat.* 8.107	occulta spolia et plures de pace triumphos[143]	oc.cul.tas.po.li.(-)

[128] 'Better a-sudden t'arouse that numskull's stolid old senses' translation from Burton (1894). Since the verse lines listed here for the sake of illustrating prosodic patterns do not necessarily constitute self-contained sense units, the translations are to be taken merely as indicative. Unless otherwise indicated, they were all taken from the Perseus database (http://www.perseus.tufts.edu/hopper/).

[129] 'What must we wot thereof? a Droll erst while' translation from Burton (1894).

[130] 'Nor do I now object if noisome writs [I hear]' translation from Burton (1894).

[131] '[that I] tarry 'mid the snows and where lurk beasts in antres frore' translation from Burton (1894).

[132] 'Nowhere is path for flight: none hope shows: all things are silent' translation from Burton (1894).

[133] 'naked Pyracmon and ... Brontes and Steropes' translation from Williams (1910).

[134] Though Hoenigswald (1949b: 277) claims that the heavy scansion of -*que* is a different issue altogether.

[135] '[to offer] for a field of corn wheat in the ear, or for the sheep-fold's health some frugal feast' translation by Theodore C. Williams (source: http://www.gutenberg.org/ebooks/9610).

[136] 'Made hunger-mad, [may she devour] the grass that grows on graves' translation by Theodore C. Williams (source: http://www.gutenberg.org/ebooks/9610).

[137] 'Trumpeting wildly and compelled by many [a stab]' translation from Duff (1927).

[138] 'a spot far removed from the strife of battle' translation from Duff (1927).

[139] '[receives death] as prize...surges with frenzy and the soul divine' translation from Ridley (1905).

[140] 'that the image may be worthy of your mirror' from the anonymous Bohn translation (source: http://www.tertullian.org/fathers/martial_epigrams_book02.htm).

[141] 'why did you draw the sword, madman, against the mouth of Rome?' from the anonymous Bohn translation (source: http://www.tertullian.org/fathers/martial_epigrams_book05.htm).

[142] 'the runners ... in a test of agility where valour plays little part' translation by A. S. Kline (source: http://www.poetryintranslation.com/klineasstatiusthebaid.htm).

[143] 'secret spoils, peace-trophies more numerous than those of war' translation from Ramsay (1918).

Table 9. Extrasyllabic [s] not resyllabified

Locus	Line	Syllabification of relevant portion
Lucretius *De rerum nat.* 1.372	cedere squamigeris latices nitentibus aiunt[144]	ce.de.re.{s}.qua.mi.ge.ris
Lucretius *De rerum nat.* 4.475	unde sciat quid sit scire et nescire vicissim[145]	un.de.{s}.ci.at
Lucretius *De rerum nat.* 4.772	inde statu prior hic gestum mutasse videtur[146]	in.de.{s}.ta.tu
Lucretius *De rerum nat.* 4.801	inde statu prior hic gestum mutasse videtur[147]	in.de.{s}.ta.tu
Lucretius *De rerum nat.* 4.849	multo antiquius est quam lecti mollia strata[148]	mol.li.a.{s}.tra.ta
Lucretius *De rerum nat.* 5.47	quidve superbia spurcitia ac petulantia quantas[149]	su.per.bi.a.{s}.pur.ci.ti.(-)
Lucretius *De rerum nat.* 5.79	libera sponte sua cursus lustrare perennis[150]	li.be.ra.{s}.pon.te
Lucretius *De rerum nat.* 6.195	speluncasque vel ut saxis pendentibus structas[151]	pen.den.ti.bu.{s}.truc.tas[152]
Lucretius *De rerum nat.* 6.943	sudent umore et guttis manantibus stillent[153]	ma.nan.ti.bu.{s}.til.lent
Lucretius *De rerum nat.* 6.1188	tenvia sputa minuta, croci contacta colore[154]	ten.vi.a.{s}.pu.ta
Catullus *Carm.* 64.357	testis erit magnis virtutibus unda Scamandri[155]	un.da.{s}.ca.man.dri
Vergil *Aen.* 11.309	ponite: spes sibi quisque. sed haec quam angusta videtis[156]	po.ni.te.{s}.pes
Horace *Epodi* 17.26	levare tenta spiritu praecordia[157]	ten.ta.{s}.pi.ri.tu
Horace *Sat.* 1.2.30	contra alius nullam nisi olenti in fornice stantem[158]	for.ni.ce.{s}.tan.tem
Horace *Sat.* 1.2.71	velatumque stola mea cum conferbuit ira[159]	ve.la.tum.que.{s}.to.la
Horace *Sat.* 1.3.44	si quod sit vitium non fastidire. Strabonem[160]	fas.ti.di.re.{s}.tra.bo.nem
Horace *Sat.* 1.5.35	linquimus, insani ridentes praemia scribae[161]	prae.mi.a.{s}.cri.bae
Horace *Sat.* 1.10.72	saepe stilum vertas iterum quae digna legi sint[162]	sae.pe.{s}.ti.lum
Horace *Sat.* 2.2.36	proceros odisse lupos quia scilicet illis[163]	qui.a.{s}.ci.li.ce.(t-)
Horace *Sat.* 2.3.43	quem mala stultitia et quemcumque inscitia veri[164]	ma.la.{s}.tul.ti.ti.(-)
Horace *Sat.* 2.3.296	Haec mihi Stertinius sapientum octavus amico[165]	mi.hi.{s}.ter.ti.ni.us
Propertius *El.* 3.1.27	Idaeum Simoenta Iovis cum prole Scamandro[166]	pro.le.{s}.ca.man.dro
Propertius *El.* 3.11.53	bracchia spectavi sacris admorsa colubris[167]	brac.chi.a.{s}.pec.ta.vi
Propertius *El.* 3.11.67	nunc ubi Scipiadae classes ubi signa Camilli[168]	u.bi.{s}.ci.pi.a.dae
Propertius *El.* 3.19.21	tuque o Minoa venumdata Scylla figura[169]	ve.num.da.ta.{s}.cyl.la
Propertius *El.* 4.1.41	iam bene spondebant tunc omina quod nihil illam[170]	be.ne.{s}.pon.de.bant

(continued)

Table 9. (continued)

Locus	Line	Syllabification of relevant portion
Propertius *El.* 4.4.48	tu cape spinosi rorida terga iugi[171]	ca.pe.{s}.pi.no.si
Propertius *El.* 4.5.17	consuluitque striges nostro de sanguine et in me[172]	con.su.lu.it.que.{s}.tri.ges
Ovid *Ars am.* 1.332	Altera Scylla novum Circes medicamine monstrum[173]	al.te.ra.{s}.cyl.la
Ovid *Her.* 10.106	Strataque Creteam belua stravit humum[174]	be.lu.a.{s}.tra.vi.(t-)
Ovid *Metam.* 4.45	Derceti quam versa squamis velantibus artus[175]	ver.sa.{s}.qua.mis
Ovid *Metam.* 12.438	manat et exprimitur per densa foramina spissus[176]	fo.ra.mi.na.{s}.pis.sus
Statius *Theb.* 7.733	quercus alumna vadi fas et mihi spernere Phoebum[177]	mi.hi.{s}.per.ne.re

---

[144] 'waters (they say) before the shining ... scaly creatures somehow give', translation from Leonard (1921).

[145] 'whence he knows what 'tis to know and not-to-know in turn', translation from Leonard (1921).

[146] 'That former [image] seemeth to have changed its gestures', translation from Leonard (1921).

[147] See previous note.

[148] 'Far ancienter than cushions of soft beds', translation from Leonard (1921).

[149] 'And lo, the pride, grim greed, and wantonness — how great [the slaughters]', translation from Leonard (1921).

[150] 'of own free will they circle their perennial courses round', translation from Leonard (1921).

[151] '[thou...canst view] their caverns, as if builded there of beetling crags', translation from Leonard (1921).

[152] Word-final [s] is often dropped in Lucretius and those before him.

[153] '[rocks] sweat moisture and distil the oozy drops', translation from Leonard (1921).

[154] 'the spittle in fine gouts tainted with colour of crocus', translation from Leonard (1921).

[155] 'to his valorous worth attest shall wave of Scamander' translation from Burton (1894).

[156] 'dismiss it! For what hope ye have is found in your own bosoms only. But ye know how slight it is' translation from Williams (1910).

[157] 'no breath...can ease my straining breast' translation by A. S. Kline (source: http://www.poetryintranslation.com/PITBR/Latin/HoraceEpodesAndCarmenSaeculare.htm).

[158] 'Another, again, will only have such as take their station in a filthy brothel.' translation from Smart and Buckley (1863).

[159] '[A woman]... covered with robes...when my ardor was at its highest' translation from Smart and Buckley (1863).

[160] 'if he has any defect, we ought not to contemn [our friend]; a cross-eyed person' translation from Smart and Buckley (1863).

[161] 'we passed ... laughing at the honors of that crazy scribe' translation from Smart and Buckley (1863).

[162] 'You that intend to write what is worthy to be read more than once, blot frequently' translation from Smart and Buckley (1863).

[163] 'dislike a large pike ... because truly [pikes are]' translation from Smart and Buckley (1863).

time the language did not have initial stop+nasal clusters at all. The exhaustive list of attested lexemes is the following:

(15) ⟨gn⟩-initial words
      Gnaeus proper name
      gnarus (overwhelmingly) ~ *narus* 'expert'
      gnatus (esp. preclass.) ~ *natus* (overwhelmingly)[179] 'born, son'
      gnavus ~ *navus* (more frequently) 'diligent'
      gnoscere (sporadically) ~ *noscere* 'know'
      gnobilis (2 preclassical occurrences) ~ *nobilis* 'noble'

Etymologically, all these words apart from *Gnaeus*[180] go back to two Proto-Indo-European stems, **genh₃-* (> *gnarus, gnavus, gnobilis*, cf. English *can, know*) and **genh₁-* (> *gnatus*, cf. English *kin*). It is clear that the gross diachronic process that affected them began with PIE **[gn-]* and finished at some point in the literary period with [n-]. In Cser (2011) it is argued in detail that the loss of the initial stop was not a one-step process but involved an intermediate stage at which a floating C-Place node lingered for some time before the nasal (that is,

---

[164] 'whom vicious folly or the ignorance of truth [drives]', translation from Smart and Buckley (1863).

[165] 'Stertinius, the eighth of the wise men, gave to me, as to a friend', translation from Smart and Buckley (1863).

[166] 'Idaean Simois and Scamander sprung from Jove', translation from Butler (1912).

[167] 'I saw her arms bitten by the sacred asps', translation from Butler (1912).

[168] 'Now where are Scipio's fleets, where the standards of Camillus?', translation from Butler (1912).

[169] 'And thou, Scylla, that didst sell thyself for the beauty of Minos', translation from Butler (1912).

[170] 'even then the omens boded her well, since ... [the horse ... had done] her no [hurt]', translation from Butler (1912).

[171] 'do thou take the dewy ridge of the thorn-clad hill', translation from Butler (1912).

[172] 'she consulted owls how she might have my blood, and [gathered...] for my [destruction]', translation from Butler (1912).

[173] 'the other one, Scylla, has been turned into a wonder [of the sea] by Circe's witchcraft', my translation; a textually problematic line, not included in many editions and hence usually untranslated.

[174] 'the prostrate monster tinged with its blood the Cretan ground', translation from Davidson (1813).

[175] 'Derceto...her body changed, and scales upon her limbs', translation from More (1922).

[176] 'liquors...thick squeeze out through numerous holes', translation from More (1922).

[177] 'this oak-spear, foster child of your stream. I can scorn Phoebus now', translation by A. S. Kline (source: http://www.poetryintranslation.com/klineasstatiusthebaid.htm).

[179] Zirin (1970: 27–8) cites data that show a distinction between the noun 'son' and the participle 'born' in manuscripts of Plautus in that the former is always written with ⟨gn⟩, the latter variably.

[180] Though note that a remark found in Paulus' epitome of Festus' dictionary referred to as *De verborum significatu* (second c. AD?) implies that this name was related to the common noun *naevus* (< **gnaevus*?) 'birth-mark' (*gneus et corporis insigne et praenomen a generando dicta... apparet* 'it is clear that [the word] gn[a]eus, 'mark on the body' as well as a first name, derives from engendering (*generare*)', here cited from the *Oxford Latin Dictionary* s.v. *Gnaeus*, translation mine).

the Root node and all the manner features of the velar stop were deleted and its C-Place node was left unattached).

The evidence for such a structure is furnished by the prefixed forms of these stems. Prefixed words based on ⟨gn⟩-initial stems appear to fall into two distinct groups, an older and a more recent one (Cser 2011: 74–7). Overall, the older group includes forms that exhibit the following properties:

- earlier attestation;
- higher frequency in the corpus;
- more complete paradigms;
- written with ⟨gn⟩ rather than ⟨n⟩; and
- sometimes less transparent meaning.

Although these criteria do not pattern together in all cases, they quite clearly distinguish between many of the prefixed ⟨gn⟩-words (e.g. *ignoscere* 'forgive' vs. *praenoscere* 'know in advance' or *cognatus* 'relative' vs. *internatus* 'growing between'). In general, prefixation with *ad-*, *con-* and negative *in-* appears to be more archaic in the set of ⟨gn-⟩ words than all other cases of prefixation. The common feature of these three prefixes is that they end in the consonants that are most prone to assimilation: [d], [n] and the placeless nasal (on place assimilation see 4.8 and 7.3.1.2).

Assuming that the phonological representations given in 2.4 are correct it is possible to give a principled explanation for why only these prefixes would combine with these stems at the stage when the latter began with a floating C-Place node. The argument crucially involves the following assumptions: (i) a defective structure (in this case a floating C-Place node) cannot surface unchanged, it needs to attach to an appropriate host node; (ii) a C-Place node cannot attach to a vowel; and (iii) a C-Place node also cannot attach to consonants that disallow the resulting configuration for any reason. Of these, (i) explains why the set of prefixes that combined with ⟨gn⟩-initial stems was restricted at that stage in general; (ii) explains why forms such as **regnoscere*, with vowel-final prefixes, were banned; and (iii) explains why forms such as **pergnatus* were banned (scil. the C-Place node would have attached to the [r], resulting in a velar rhotic, a non-existent segment in Latin). In other words, with prefixes ending in non-assimilating consonants and vowels, to which the place node of consonants could not spread for structural reasons, the resulting form would have included a stranded floating C-Place node and would thus have been ill-formed.

Figures 14 to 16 show assimilation in *in-* and *con-* and lack of assimilation with *re-*, repsectively.

By the Classical period the floating C-Place node was dropped, and these stems were now indistinguishable from original [n]-initial stems. Hence prefixes began to combine with them freely (see *praenoscere*, *internatus* above). The only remaining oddity about this set of stems was the curious prefix-allomorphy that they display: *i*[ŋ]*noscere* rather than **innoscere*, *co*[ŋ]*natus* rather than

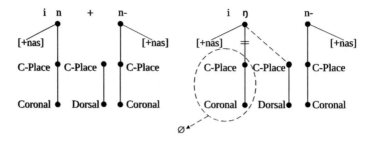

Figure 14. Assimilation in *in*+⟨gn⟩ (irrelevant details omitted)

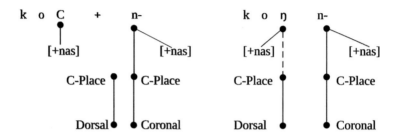

Figure 15. Assimilation in *con*+⟨gn⟩ (irrelevant details omitted)

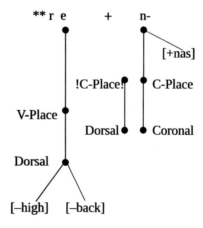

Figure 16. No assimilation in *re*+⟨gn⟩ (irrelevant details omitted)

**cōnatus*, and so on. But phonotactically the [ŋn] nasal clusters at the morpheme boundary were no longer different from those found in simplex forms (e.g. *dignus* 'worthy', *agnus* 'lamb').

3.7. Conclusion

This chapter has demonstrated in detail the phonotactic regularities that prevail in Classical Latin simplex forms. Sonority plays a central role both in intra-syllabic organisation and in syllable contact phenomena but it can be overridden to a certain extent by place of articulation, an observation I encapsulated here in the Place Condition.

The processes that take part in complex (prefixed) forms and the phonotactic regularities that prevail in them, including a generalised variant of the Place Condition, will be discussed in Chapter 7. Nevertheless, the present chapter has also looked at the resyllabification of consonants (especially extrasyllabic [s]) in prefixed forms and at word boundary, and its consequences for poetic practice. It has furthermore briefly presented the issue of ⟨gn⟩-initial stems, where the proper analysis of the data crucially relies on the geometric representations assumed throughout this work.

4

PROCESSES AFFECTING CONSONANTS

4.1. INTRODUCTION

In this chapter the segmental phonological processes affecting consonants are presented. The discussion will not be confined entirely to simplex forms; although the detailed presentation of prefixed forms is relegated to chapter 7, such forms will be mentioned in this chapter as well, since the consonantal processes in simplex and in prefixed forms show a great deal of overlap, and the discussion will be more coherent if the similarities are pointed out right at the first mention of the relevant phenomena.

Most phonological processes in the present chapter involve segments that are adjacent. This is because there are no systematic, phonologically general processes working at a distance in Classical Latin. The liquids appear to display a certain tendency for distance dissimilation, but these phenomena are not phonologically general, and are probably best analysed synchronically as allomorphic patterns rather than phonological processes. Nevertheless these patterns can be described in terms of the phonological shape of words, hence the decision to include them here in 4.11.

4.2. CONTACT VOICE ASSIMILATION

Adjacent obstruents are always voiceless in simplex forms, as a static phonotactic rule mandates (see 3.3), and when two obstruents come into contact in a derived environment, regressive voicing assimilation takes place. Only a Laryngeal node dominating [−voice] is able to spread, partly because of the static rule, partly because in simplexes no environment can emerge at all in which the second obstruent would be voiced.[181] The assimilation is nearly always indicated in writing:

(16) Regressive devoicing in simplexes
   scribere 'write' ~ *scripsi* PERF1SING ~ *scriptus* PASSPART
   regem ~ *rex* 'king' ACCSING ~ NOMSING
   plebem ~ *plebs* / (rarely) *pleps* 'people' ACCSING ~ NOMSING

---

[181] Etymologically, of course, there are numerous cases, e.g. **pezd- > pēdere* 'fart'. In Classical Latin, however, only regressive voiceless assimilation is in evidence synchronically; this is why Álvarez Huerta (2005: 146–7) is able to describe the process as coda neutralisation rather than assimilation (spreading).

At prefix–stem boundaries voicing assimilation is usually not indicated unless it produces a geminate, and it varies in certain cases with total assimilation:

(17) Regressive assimilation at prefix–stem boundary
   obtinere ~ (rarely) *optinere* 'preserve', probably [opt-][182]
   (rarely) *obpetere* ~ *oppetere* 'encounter' [opp-]
   adsistere ~ *assistere* 'stand near', probably [ats-] ~ [ass-]

In the phonological interpretation of non-simplex forms there is some uncertainty. While in simplexes active spreading of a Laryngeal node dominating [+voice] rather than [–voice] is not attested, and eligible forms simply do not emerge for morphological reasons, the same cannot necessarily be said of prefixed or cliticised forms. It is impossible to tell exactly how a prefixed form like *trans+gredi* 'step over' or *post+genitus* 'born later' sounded, and we also do not know how the cliticised pronouns of the type *eius+dem* 'he, the same' GENSING were pronounced. It is not entirely inconceivable that there was regressive voicing assimilation, but we have no evidence of it as Latin had no distinct way of spelling [z]. Apart from *trans*-prefixed words, *post*-prefixed words and *-dem*-cliticised and *-dam*-cliticised [s]-final inflected pronouns no other environments emerge in which a voiceless obstruent would be followed by a voiced obstruent (trivially apart from environments emerging across word boundaries).

The contact devoicing of obstruents is formalised in Figure 17. As can be seen, this assumes full featural specification for both voiced and voiceless obstruents. If the spreading of a Laryngeal node dominating [+voice] could be categorically excluded, one could argue (as Álvarez Huerta 2005 does) that the asymmetrical pattern warrants an asymmetrical representation. Since, however, the asymmetry is not unequivocal, I will stay with the symmetrical representation, leaving this question on a note of some uncertainty.

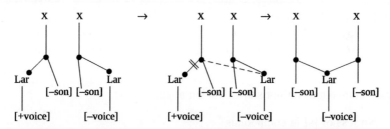

Figure 17. Contact devoicing of obstruents (irrelevant details omitted)

---

[182] Cf. Quintilian's remark in *Inst.* 1.7.7: 'Quaeri solet, in scribendo praepositiones sonum quem iunctae efficiunt an quem separatae observare conveniat, ut cum dico *optinuit* (secundam enim *b* litteram ratio poscit, aures magis audiunt *p*)', 'It is often debated whether in our spelling of prepositions we should be guided by their sound when compounded, or separate. For instance when I say *optinuit*, logic demands that the second letter should be a *b*, while to the ear the sound is rather that of *p*' (translation from Butler 1920).

In some lexically determined cases the delinked Laryngeal node is not deleted but projects a Root node and a skeletal slot, to which the preceding short vowel links and this results in surface lengthening on the vowel following on the devoicing. This process is described and formalised in 5.4.2.

4.2.1. *Excursus: loss of [s] before voiced consonants*

In a diachronically related process[183] the segment [s] was lost before voiced consonants – sonorants as well as obstruents – in all positions in the early history of the language, most probably through a voiced [z] stage. When it was immediately preceded by a short vowel, that vowel underwent compensatory lengthening. This can be seen, among others, in the allomorphy displayed by the prefix *dis-* (see 7.2.4.3):

(18) Loss of [s] in *dis-*
       distendere 'stretch', *discurrere* 'run away', *disponere* 'distribute'
       vs. *dīgerere* 'disperse', *dīmittere* 'send away', *dīluere* 'wash away'

Another *s*-final prefix, *ex-* shows the same regularity with loss of the entire cluster (see 7.2.4.2), which is also visible in compounds of *sex* '6':

(19) Loss of [ks] in *ex-* and *sex*
       extendere 'extend', *excellere* 'excel' vs. *ēmanere* 'stay away'; *sex* '6' vs.
       sēdecim '16'

On the other hand, the prefix *trans-* does not display the same regularity. Before non-coronal voiced consonants its [s] remains intact (or is not lost, at least), and before coronals it variably remains (though the tendency is for it to be lost, see 7.2.4.4):

(20) Loss of [s] in *trans-*
       transvolare 'fly across, *transmittere* 'send over', *transgredi* 'step over',
       translatus 'taken across'; *transnare* ~ *trānare* 'swim across', *trādere* 'hand
       over'

Certain compounds do not show deletion at all:

(21) No loss of [s] in compounds
       huiusmodi, eiusmodi 'of that kind'

The very frequent cliticised pronouns provide evidence that deletion of [s] was no longer a generally active rule in Classical Latin. The clitics *-dem, -dam, -nam,*

---

[183] This change is discussed in all treatments of the history of Latin, such as Leumann (1977: 112), Baldi (2002: 285), Weiss (2009: 165 and elsewhere), Niedermann (1953: 130), Meiser (1998: 118), Sen (2015: 69, 189). For a phonological discussion see Cser (2020).

-vis, *-met* and *-libet* can be attached to certain fully inflected pronouns to provide various pragmatic and semantic modifications of them (much like *-ever*, *-soever* in English).[184] Of the several [s]-final inflected forms only the NomSing forms of some of these pronouns lose the [s] before the clitic; all the others show the [s] (perhaps phonetically [z]?) intact:

(22) Loss and retention of [s] in cliticised pronouns
   īdem 'he, the same' (< **is+dem*), but *eiusdem* GenSing, *eosdem*
        MascAccPlur, *easdem* FemAccPlur, *īsdem* DatAblPlur
   quīvis 'whoever' (< **quis+vis*), but *cuiusvis* GenSing, *quibusvis*
        DatAblPlur...
   quisnam 'who then', *vosmet* 'yourselves', *nosmet* 'ourselves', *nobismet*
        DatAbl...

If one attempted to incorporate [s]-deletion in the phonology of Classical Latin,[185] the case of cliticised pronouns could, in theory, be explained with reference to the different levels of the morphology and of the lexical component of phonology. However, that would only be possible on the assumption that either the NomSing is affixed at a different level than all other case forms, or that the clitic is attached to NomSing forms at a different level than to all other case forms. Neither of these assumptions seems eminently plausible, and even in this way extra machinery would be needed to describe the *dis-* vs. *trans-* discrepancy. Very little would be gained anyhow since there are otherwise no alternations whose description would necessitate the [s]-deletion rule. While as a descriptive statement it is true that voiced consonants are not preceded by [s] in simplex forms, this generalisation is definable on much broader natural classes and is not specific to [s] (it follows from the Syllable Contact Law and from the ban on adjacent obstruents that are not both voiceless, see 3.3). The upshot of this is that we do not have sufficient grounds to assume that [s]-deletion is a phonological rule in Latin. What one could say at most is that this rule is specific to prefixes (with variable effect in compounds, see *sēdecim* vs. *huiusmodi*), but even in that domain it affects only *ex-* and *dis-* systematically; its effect on *trans-* is much more restricted.

4.3 TOTAL ASSIMILATION OF [t] TO [s]

The cluster [ts] does not exist in simplex surface forms. Word-internally this is explained by the Syllable Contact Law (not mitigated by the Place Condition,

---

[184] Here I only list the clitics beginning with a voiced consonant. The remaining clitics *-que*, *-quam*, *-piam*, *-cumque* are irrelevant to [s]-deletion. I do not discuss pronominal inflection at all in this book; at this point, the only important difference vis-à-vis noun and adjective inflection (cf. Chapter 6) is the existence of *-ius*-suffixed GenSing forms for pronouns in general.

[185] As Touratier (2005: 117–18) does, who describes and formalises [s]-deletion as a rule on the basis of the behaviour of *dis-*, but leaves all the *transgredi*, *eosdem* and *huiusmodi*-type problems unmentioned.

both consonants being coronal); word-finally by the constraint on extrasyllabic [s], which can only be preceded by the non-coronal stops [p] and [k]. When affixation results in a [ts] sequence, the [t] assimilates to the [s] and a geminate [ss] results[186] (subject to later processes of degemination, see 4.5). This rule is fed by voicing assimilation, so underlying [d]s undergo it as well. All the three [s] suffixes (perfectum, third stem and animate[187] nominative singular) trigger this process without exception:

(23) Examples of assimilation
   quat- 'shake' → *quassi* PERF1SING
                     quassus PASSPART
   ced- 'depart' → *cessi* PERF1SING
                     cessus PASSPART
   milet- 'soldier' → *miles* NOMSING (with degemination)

The transparent compound conjunctions *etsi* 'although' (from *et* 'and' and *si* 'if') and *tametsi* (for full *tamen etsi*) 'notwithstanding' include the cluster [ts] at what can be seen as word boundary. At prefix–stem boundaries this process is also found with the prefix *ad-*, but it is optional. With the two *post*-prefixed words *postsignani* 'soldiers stationed behind the standards' and *postscribere* 'add in writing' the assimilation is not attested.

The assimilation in a proper formalisation involves copying the Root node, as shown in Figure 18.

4.4. RHOTACISM

Intervocalic [s] is replaced by [r] in derived environments.[188] Typically, this is seen at the end of stems when a vowel-initial affix creates an intervocalic environment:

(24) Rhotacism
   [s] → [r] / V__V
   mus ~ *muris* 'mouse' NOMSING ~ GENSING
   ges- → *gero* 'carry' 1SING, cf. *gessi* PERF1SING, *gestus* PASSPART

---

[186] Such a rule is postulated by Touratier (2005: 120) as well.

[187] Throughout this work the term *animate* refers to the masculine and the feminine grammatical genders collectively.

[188] Rhotacism is a much discussed diachronic change in the prehistory of Latin (Leumann 1977: 178; Baldi 2002: 285; Clackson & Horrocks 2007: 96; Weiss 2009: 81). The more immediately pertinent question whether it was still a synchronic phonological rule in Classical Latin was touched upon already by de Saussure (1916: 202); the slate of papers from the past few years that discuss the synchronic status of rhotacism testify that it continues to be an intriguing issue, see e.g. Albright (2005), Gruber (2006), Embick (2010), Roberts (2012), Kiparsky (2017), Gorman (2012). Several of these authors (de Saussure 1916, Baldi 1994; Gorman 2012; Roberts 2012) deny that rhotacism was still operative in the Classical period but they either do not acknowledge the derived environment condition or give a different morphological analysis of the relevant forms.

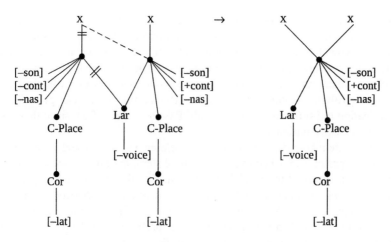

Figure 18. Total assimilation of [t] to [s]

Since rhotacism also occurs after glides, the V in the environment of the process clearly refers to the presence of a V-Place node in the immediately adjacent segments rather than nuclear position in the syllable (though this is relevant only for the segment on the left, since there are no postconsonantal instances of [j] and [w] does not occur after word-internal [s]). Witness the alternation between [ajs]C, [ajs]# ~ [ajr]V, and between [aws]C ~ [awr]V in the following examples:

(25) Rhotacism after glides
       maestus 'sad' ~ *maeror* 'sadness'
       quaestus ~ *quaerere* 'inquire' PassPart ~ Inf
       aes ~ *aeris* 'bronze' NomSing ~ GenSing
       haustus 'drawing (of water)' ~ *haurire* 'draw (water)'

Rhotacism is clearly absent from non-derived environments, as is pointed out already in McCarthy (2003); the derived environment condition is explicitly mentioned in Gorman (2012) too:

(26) Lack of rhotacism in non-derived environments
       miser 'miserable', *nisi* 'unless', *pisum* 'pea', *basis* 'base', *causa* 'matter'

Rhotacism also does not occur after nasal vowels even in derived environments:

(27) Lack of rhotacism after nasal vowels
       mansi 'remain' Perf1Sing, *ensis* 'sword', *mensis* 'month'

What this means is that rhotacism must precede the coalescence of the placeless nasal with the preceding vowel, which produces a long nasal vowel (on this process see 5.4.4). This is a clear example of counterfeeding relationship. In theory, one could also narrow down the environment of rhotacism so that the preceding vowel has to be non-nasal, but since nasal place loss as well as coalescence are independently needed because of the *manere* ~ *mansi* type and the *dens* ~ *dentis* type alternations, the more economical solution will clearly be the one involving counterfeeding order. Rhotacism must also precede the degemination of [s] (*cāssus* → *cāsus* 'fall' PASSPART, see 4.5.2), since these [s]s are systematically unrhotacised.

At prefix–stem boundary two different developments are attested. One is when a V[s]-final prefix is attached to a vowel-initial stem; the other is when a vowel-final prefix is attached to an [s]V-initial stem. The first is attested only in two lexicalised, highly opaque verbs and their derivatives: *dirimere* 'separate' (< *dis+emere*) and *diribere* 'sort (votes)' (< *dis+habere* with historical loss of the stem-initial [h]). Apart from *dis-* no other prefix ends in V[s],[189] and apart from these two words there is no instance of *dis-* combining with a vowel-initial stem; apparently in Classical Latin the combinations of vowel-initial stems with this prefix were avoided.

The other configuration, i.e. vowel-final prefix attached to an [s]V-initial stem, is formed apparently with great freedom. Rhotacism does not apply in any of these words (*pro+silire* 'jump forth', *de+sinere* 'desist', *re+secare* 'cut off' and many others). This may imply that rhotacism was relegated to a derivational level preceding prefixation, *dirimere* and *diribere* are lexicalised remnants from an earlier diachronic stage and are not synchronically rhotacised.[190] It may also imply that rhotacism operates at a later derivational level at which a prefix–stem boundary is no longer derived environment. In theory, it might also imply that preserving a stem consonant had some kind of priority over preserving a prefix consonant, but since this is evidently not true with respect to stem vs. suffix consonants (see the examples in 4.3), and is also not true with respect to stem vs. prefix vowels (see chapter 5), it is unlikely to be a general principle in the language.

A formalisation of rhotacism (Figure 19) may represent it as an assimilation in voicing to the two neighbouring vocalic segments. Since this would produce a segment with incompatible feature specifications, viz. [+voice], [+cont] and [–son], a further readjustment is forced by the change from [–voice] to [+voice]. The readjustment is the change in the feature [–son] to [+son], thus producing [r].[191]

---

[189] *Trans-*, as in *transire* 'cross', contains a nasal vowel, after which rhotacism is not expected.

[190] Roberts (2012) gives a diachronic analysis in which rhotacism reaches the stem level by the Classical Latin stage, and hence it no longer affects the *prosilire* type (since, under that analysis, prefixes are not part of the stem). And while it could have explained *dirimere* and *diribere* as lexicalised remnants of a previous stage when rhotacism was a word-level rule, it does not say anything about why *dis-* does not combine with vowel-initial stems at a later stage.

[191] Note that instead of a [–son] → [+son] adjustment the C-Place node could also have been deleted, leading to the only [+voice], [+cont], [–son] segment allowed, viz. [h]. This was the path taken in Proto-Greek, followed later by deletion of intervocalic [h] (at least this is a possible analysis, see Sihler 1995: 171 for data).

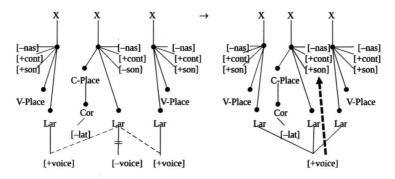

Figure 19. Rhotacism

4.5. Degemination

4.5.1. General degemination

In both simplex and non-simplex forms every geminate, whether under-lying or derived, shortens if it cannot be properly syllabified as a coda–onset sequence or, in the case of [s], as extrasyllabic in a licit environment. This rule is fed by the assimilation of [t] to [s] (4.3) and thus indirectly by contact voice assimilation (4.1). In theory, this regularity allows for simple intervocalic geminates ([Vt.tV]), but also for geminates including a complex onset ([Vt.trV]), a complex coda ([Vnt.tV]) or even both ([Vnt.trV]), since proper syllabification is possible in each of these cases. In fact, only the first two of the four possible types are found, and the second only in prefixed forms (e.g. *attrahere* 'attract' ← *ad+trahere*). This results from the lack of underlying geminates next to a consonant as well as from the lack of prefixes ending in a complex coda.[192] Complex codas immediately followed by complex onsets, as in *mulctra* 'milking bucket', are exceedingly rare (see 3.2, subsection 3.3 within Table 6), so geminates of the [Vnt.trV] type are probably barred on a more systematic basis.

Examples of degemination are given in (28) and (29).

(28) Degemination in simplexes

    verr- → *versus* 'sweep' PassPart (cf. *verro* Pres1Sing, *verri* Perf1Sing)

    fall- → *falsus* 'deceive' PassPart (cf. *fallo* Pres1Sing, *fefelli* Perf1Sing)

    mell- → *mel* 'honey' NomSing (cf. *mellis* GenSing)

---

[192] The prefix *trans-* ends in a complex coda underlyingly (placeless nasal + [s]), and its [s] is not affected by the general degemination. It is, however, optionally affected by the specific degemination of [s], see 4.5.2.

oss- → *os* 'bone' NomSing (cf. *ossis* GenSing)
milet+s → *miless* → *miles* 'soldier' NomSing, see 4.3 above[193]
obsed+s → *obsets* → *obsess* → *obses* 'hostage' NomSing
sumps+sti → *sumpsti* 'take' Perf2Sing[194]

(29) Degemination in prefixed forms
      ex+salire → *exilire* 'jump out' ([kss] → [ks])
      sus+spirare → *suspirare* 'sigh'[195]

For comparison, there is no degemination in these and similar prefixed forms:

(30) Lack of degemination in prefixed forms
      ad+suescere → *assuescere* 'get used to' ([ssw])
      ad+probare → *approbare* 'approve'
      ad+quaerere → *acquirere* 'acquire' ([kkw])

Interestingly, the data show that the only consonants affected by the degemination in simplex forms are the coronal continuants [r l s]. The other consonants are not exempt from it but simply never occur in the triggering environment. The consonant [s] is the only segment that undergoes degemination at prefix–stem boundary. This follows by necessity if both prefixes and stems have proper syllabification independently and then resyllabification takes place at the boundary only if without it there would be no onset to the stem-initial syllable (as explained in 3.5). In such a scenario a syllabification problem can be caused only by a prefix-final or a stem-initial extrasyllabic [s], as in *exilire* and *suspirare* in (29), respectively.[196]

---

[193] Words like *miles* scan with a heavy last syllable in preclassical comedy (Plautus), which shows that degemination was not yet fully active at that time. The pronouns *hic* and *hoc* 'this' exceptionally end in an unshortened geminate [kk] even in Classical Latin, as is evidenced by versification and as is explicitly mentioned by the grammarian Velius Longus (*De orthographia*, Keil 1855–78, vol. 7: 54: 'scribendum per duo *c hocc erat alma parens* aut confitendum quaedam aliter scribi aliter enuntiari' 'the word *hoc* in *hocc erat alma parens* should be written with double *c* or else one should admit that some things are written one way and pronounced another way', translation mine); cf. also Allen (1978: 75–77).

[194] For the analysis of these perfect forms see 6.2.3.3.

[195] Note that the degemination in *suspirare* is because [sp] is not an onset cluster in Latin, as opposed to stop + liquid clusters or [sw]. Similarly, the degemination in *exilire* shows that [ks] is not a coda cluster as opposed to e.g. [rs]. Pillinger (1983) as well as Niedermann (1953) suggest that degemination may have taken place in clusters of the type [kkl], [ttr] as well (i.e. where C.CC was a possible syllabification), as in *attrahere* 'pull', though they admit that the evidence for this is meagre.

[196] The verb *surgere* 'rise' shows degemination of [r] if it is analysed on an etymological basis as *sub+regere*, cf. perfect *surrexi*, third stem (supine) *surrectum*. The same stands for *porgere*, a rare by-form of *porrigere* 'extend', etymologically from *por+regere*. In both of these cases, a short vowel was crucially lost historically after the geminate, thus creating the triggering environment for the degemination.

4.5.2. *Degemination of [s]*

As an extension of the degemination rule, [ss] is shortened in simplexes after any consonant or long vowel even if its syllabification would be possible. These instances of [ss] are all derived via the [t]-assimilation rule (4.3); the lexical frequency of such [ss]s is increased by the fact that the affix of the third stem of verbs after [d] and [t] is regularly -*s*- rather than -*t*-. Examples:

(31) [ss]-shortening

cad+sus → *cātsus* → *cāssus* → *cāsus* 'fall' PassPart[197]

mīt+si → *mīssi* → *mīsi* 'send' Perf1Sing

vert+sus → *verssus* → *versus* 'turn' PassPart[198]

spond+sus → *sponssus* → *sponsus* 'promise' PassPart[199]

Degemination follows rhotacism and so these intervocalic instances of [s] do not undergo it (no *cāssus* → *cāsus* → ****cārus*). At prefix–stem boundary, the shortening is optional, e.g. *transsilire* ~ *transilire* 'jump over' (← *trans+salire*).

At first sight, general degemination appears to be driven by the syllable template, but the specific degemination of [s] does not, since the former reduces unsyllabifiable sequences, while the latter reduces legitimate coda–onset sequences. But on closer inspection the contrast between the two degeminations is not so straightforward. Those codas which consist of a consonant + [s] are, in fact, few and far between. Word-internally a coda [s] can only be preceded by vowels (as in *hostis* 'enemy') and the glides, which have a vocalic structure.[200] Word-finally a coda [s] can be preceded by vowels (as in *mus* 'mouse'), by the glides in four words altogether,[201] by [l] in two rarely used words,[202] variably by [m] in *hiems/hiemps* 'winter' and by [r] in a number of *t*- and *d*-stem nouns and adjectives. Of these, only the last group is robustly attested in the lexicon, and in all of these [rs]-final words the postconsonantal coda [s] emerges as a result of nominative singular suffixation with -*s* followed by (voicing assimilation, then) assimilation of [t] to [s], then by degemination of the general kind:

---

[197] For the lengthening of the vowel see 5.4.2.

[198] *Versus* from *vert+sus* 'turn' PassPart is homophonous with *versus* from *verr+sus* 'sweep' PassPart (28) due to the two different degemination rules.

[199] Note that it is irrelevant whether this rule precedes or follows nasal place loss before fricatives (4.6) and coalescence (5.4.4); a form like *sponsus* will undergo [ss]-shortening either because of the nasal consonant (like *versus*) or because of the long (nasal) vowel (like *mīsi* or *cāsus*).

[200] The exhaustive list of examples for the latter, also given in 3.2, is this: *maestus* 'grieving', *quaestus* 'asked', *aestus* 'summer', *caestus* 'boxing gloves', *caespes* 'lawn' for [js].C, and *faustus* 'favourable', *haustus* 'swallowed', *Auster* 'southerly wind', *auscultare* 'listen' for [ws].C.

[201] *Aes* 'bronze', *praes* 'guarantor', *laus* 'praise' and *fraus* 'deceit'.

[202] *Puls* 'porridge', *uls* 'beyond'.

(32) [r]+stop final stems

misericord+s → *misericor*[t]*s* → *misericor*[ss] → *misericor*[s] 'merciful'

The marginal nature of postconsonantal coda [s] may well have contributed to the perception of geminate [ss] after consonants as ill-formed and thus to its reduction to bring the word forms into line with 'core' syllabification (not in the technical sense of the term). On the other hand, coda [s] after long vowels was not at all rare: *bēstia* 'beast', *iūstus* 'just', *prīscus* 'ancient', *rōstrum* 'beak of bird' and many others, including most verbs whose infectum stem ends in [sk], e.g. *crēscere* 'grow', *nōscere* 'know', *hiāscere* 'gape'. Thus syllable structure motivates specific [s]-degemination only in part.

4.6. NASAL PLACE LOSS BEFORE FRICATIVES

The nasal [n] loses its C-Place node before the fricatives [s] and [f], and a placeless nasal results. The placeless nasal never surfaces, before fricatives it always undergoes a further change, viz. coalescence with the preceding vowel (see 5.4.4). This happens in simplexes and non-simplexes alike, and is not indicated in the writing. The two most typical cases are nasal-final prefixes combining with a fricative-initial stem, and the suffixation of [nt] and [nd]-final stems with [s], since the rule is fed by the assimilation of [t] to [s] (4.3 above). It is possible that in higher styles of speech this rule was suppressed and the nasal was restored to a certain extent as a hypercorrection; this aspect of variation is disregarded here.

Of the nasal-final prefixes *in-* shows the relevant alternation in several forms, e.g. *inscius* 'unaware' [ī:skius] vs. *inultus* 'unavenged' [inultus]. The alternation is present also in *manere* [mane:re] ~ *mansi* [mã:si:] 'stay' INF ~ PERF1 SING, where the *-s-* is the perfectum suffix. For [m] followed by [s] see 4.7. Forms where the nasal vowel never alternates with an oral vowel + [n] sequence are discussed in 5.4.4.

4.7. EPENTHESIS AFTER [m]

When [m] is followed by [s] or [t], no place loss results. In fact, the labial place of the nasal is reinforced by the insertion of an epenthetic [p]. This is a highly systematic process in spite of the fact that there are very few [m]-final stems and consequently very few potential inputs (and the written evidence is also somewhat variable).[203] The set of affected forms comprises the noun *hiem(p)s* 'winter' and the following verbs:

(33) Verbs showing [p]-epenthesis after [m]; all forms INF, PERF1SING with -*s*-suffixation (apart from the last six) and PASSPART with -*t*-suffixation[204]
      comere ~ compsi ~ comptus 'comb'
      sumere ~ sumpsi ~ sumptus 'take'
      praesumere ~ praesumpsi ~ praesumptus 'take first'
      resumere ~ resumpsi ~ resumptus 'take back'
      consumere ~ consumpsi ~ consumptus 'use up'
      absumere ~ absumpsi ~ absumptus 'take away'
      adsumere ~ adsumpsi ~ adsumptus 'take to onself'
      promere ~ prompsi ~ promptus 'take out'
      demere ~ dempsi ~ demptus 'take away'
      emere (~ emi) ~ emptus 'buy'
      coemere (~ coemi) ~ coemptus 'buy up'
      adimere (~ ademi) ~ ademptus 'buy'
      eximere (~ exemi) ~ exemptus 'take out'
      perimere (~ peremi) ~ peremptus 'annihilate'
      redimere (~ redemi) ~ redemptus 'buy back'

In a feature geometric representation the entire structure of the epenthetic [p] apart from the Root node and the skeletal node is explicable from the neighbouring segments (see Figure 20).

Comparative evidence shows that a similar insertion happened historically in the original context [m]_[l] as well (e.g. *exemplum* 'example', *amplus* 'large', cf. de Vaan 2008 s.vv. *emo, amplus*); the context [m]_[r] is not entirely clear from this point of view (cf. Weiss 2009: 164).

[203] Álvarez Huerta (2005: 153) claims that ancient grammarians' evidence points to this being a purely orthographic convention rather than a phonological rule, quoting Marius Victorinus 1.4 (Keil 1855–78, vol. 6: 21). In view of the full context, however, that locus cannot be cited in support of such a position. Before mentioning *hiemps* 'winter', *sumpsit* 'he took', *consumptum* 'used up' Marius Victorinus discusses the neutralisation of voice before [s] in words like *ple*[p]*s ~ plebis* 'people', and proffers advice on the spelling of such words. The point he appears to be making with respect to the *sum(p)sit*-type forms is that these are different from the *plebs*-type; since the ⟨p⟩ in these does not alternate with anything, and since leaving it out cannot result in confusion, it should simply not be written. Although he does say that spelling such words with ⟨p⟩ is a mistake (*vitiose scribetis*), he does not imply that the ⟨p⟩ is silent, only that it is not supported by analogy.

[204] Historically all these verbs are prefixed formations based on *emere* 'buy'. Other [m]-final stems take the *t*-suffix with an intervening vowel (*vomere → vomitus* 'vomit'), and either do not take the *s*-suffix at all or are irrelevant on account of some idiosyncrasy (e.g. *premere → pressi, pressus* 'press').

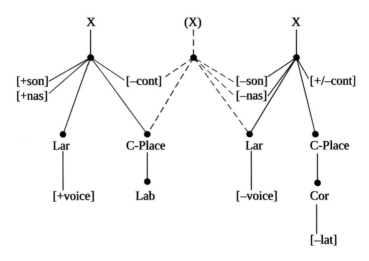

Figure 20. [p]-epenthesis in the environment [m]_[t] and [m]_[s] (collapsed)

4.8. PLACE ASSIMILATION

In Classical Latin there are two place assimilation processes. Typically they result in alternations only at prefix–stem boundaries but they are vacuously true of simplex forms as well.[205] The differences between the two processes are as follows:

(34) Place Assimilation 1:

- affects sequences of a non-peripheral (i.e. coronal or placeless) nasal and any stop;
- C-Place node of stop links to Root node of nasal; and
- probably exceptionless (postlexical?)

Place Assimilation 2:

- affects all consonant sequences where [cont] and [son] specifications do not conflict and where C_2 is non-coronal (i.e. stops assimilate to stops, nasals to nasals, and [s] to [f]; cf. the Generalised Place Condition in 7.3.1.3);
- C-Place node of non-coronal C_2 links to Root node of C_1;
- results in geminates (coupled with voice assimilation for stops); and
- exceptions possible at prefix–stem boundaries.

---

[205] In etymologically related words their diachronic reflexes can be recognised in e.g. *singuli* 'one at a time' with [ŋg] but *simplex* 'simple', both from the root **sem-* 'one' (an earlier form of Place Assimilation 1, affecting [m] too), or *sitis* 'thirst' vs. *siccus* 'dry' (< **sit-kos*, Place Assimilation 2).

Examples for both types of assimilation can be given from the domain of prefixed words.

(35) Examples of place assimilations
    PA 1, [n]: *imbibere* 'drink in', *inquirere* 'inquire' [ŋk] vs. *inest* 'is in'
    PA 1, placeless nasal: *componere* 'compose', *conquirere* 'collect' [ŋk],
        condonare 'give' vs. *coire* 'meet', *cō-nubium* 'marriage'
    PA 2, [d]: *appetere* 'try to reach', *accipere* 'receive' vs. *adesse* 'be present'
    PA 2, [b]: *occludere* 'close' vs. *obaeratus* 'involved in debt'
    PA 2, [n]: *immittere* 'send in'
    PA 2, placeless nasal: *committere* 'bring together'

The rules are formalised in Figures 21 and 22. Both formalisations conflate two configurations each. That of place assimilation 1 (Figure 21) conflates [n] + stop and placeless nasal + stop sequences. That of place assimilation 2 (Figure 22) conflates two configurations as regards the second consonant. C_2 either has a Labial or a Dorsal node, not both; the condition on the assimilation is that C_2 must be peripheral. Also note that the formulation above for place assimilation 2 ('sequences where [cont] and [son] specifications do not conflict') does not say

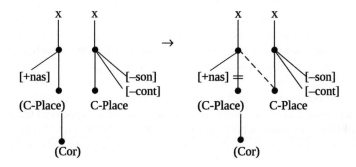

Figure 21. Place assimilation 1 (irrelevant details omitted)

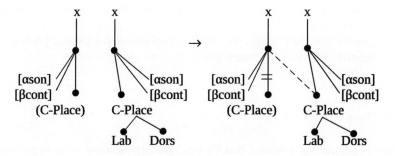

Figure 22. Place assimilation 2 (irrelevant details omitted)

exactly the same as [αson, βcont] for both segments, as in Figure 22. The latter means identical specification for these features and thus identical sonority. But non-conflicting specifications are also possible when a segment does not have a [cont] and/or [son] feature at all (a possibility not included in Figure 22). This is relevant to the pre-classical configuration involving the reconstructed floating C-Place node discussed in 3.6.

The first consonant in both types of place assimilation may or may not have a C-Place node. If it does have one (i.e. it is not the placeless nasal of *con-*), that C-Place node is delinked. The case of the placeless nasal is particularly interesting. The main point is that the placeless nasal of *con-* is able to undergo both place assimilation 1 and place assimilation 2 (and also undergoes total assimilation to liquids, see 7.2.3.2) but when it is followed by [n], neither place assimilation 1 nor place assimilation 2 can take place, since [n] does not satisfy the structural description of C_2 for either. It is not a [−son] segment, so it does not trigger place assimilation 1, and it is coronal, so it does not trigger place assimilation 2. In this case the placeless nasal is lost, probably via coalescence with the preceding vowel (see 5.4.4) — or just possibly lost entirely with compensatory lengthening — (see *cō-nubium* above). When it is followed by a vowel, again the nasal cannot acquire its V-Place node, since V-Place nodes do not link to consonants (unless as secondary place); so the placeless nasal is lost again, and in the resulting hiatus no compensatory lengthening is possible (see *coire* above).

The suffix of the animate accusative singular is a placeless nasal with all vowel-final stems (for a detailed analysis see Chapter 6). In the default case this merges with the stem-final vowel, a process resulting in a long nasal vowel (see 5.4.4). However, if the clitic *-dem* 'same' or *-dam* 'some' is added to the accusative pronouns, the placeless nasal undergoes place assimilation 1 and acquires a coronal place node from the stop [d]. The same happens to the plural genitive of these pronouns, where the suffix ends in a placeless nasal. Thus from the same pronominal stem we get the following AccSing and GenPlur forms:

(36) Alternations involving the placeless nasal (cf. 6 in 2.2.3)
      eam [eã:] 'she' AccSing ~ *eandem* [eandẽ:] 'she, the same' AccSing
      earum [ea:rũ:] GenPlur ~ *earundem* [ea:rundẽ:] GenPlur, stem: *ea-*
      quam [kwã:] 'which' FemAccSing ~ *quandam* [kwandã:] 'some, a certain'
      FemAccSing
      quarum [kwa:rũ:] 'which' GenPlur ~ *quarundam* [kwa:rundã:] 'some, a
      certain' FemGenPlur, stem: *qua-*

4.9. DARK AND CLEAR [l]

There is compelling evidence that [l] was strongly velarised in coda position, and it is highly probable that it was somewhat palatalised in gemination and before [i]. In intervocalic position it was, in all likelihood, velarised before all vowels except [i].[206] Since [l] does not figure in highly productive morpho- logical processes, there are very few alternations in the strict sense of the word that are based on the secondary articulations of [l]; nearly the only such cases are [l]-final stems affixed with vowel-initial vs. consonant-initial suffixes. But these, along with other patterns visible in the lexicon, make it quite clear that, when in the appropriate environment, [l] had a strong velarising effect on preceding short vowels. This is actually the only verifiable case of secondary articulation in the Latin consonant system. The following examples illustrate this:

(37) The darkening effect of single [l] in coda and before vowels other than [i]
  sepelire 'bury' INF ~ *sepultus* PASSPART ~ *sepulcrum* 'grave'
  pellere 'beat' INF ~ *pulsus* PASSPART
  velle 'want' INF ~ *velim* SUBJ1SING ~ *vult* 3SING ~ *volumus* 1PLUR
  familia 'household' ~ *famulus* 'servant'
  ocellus 'eye', *agellus* 'field' ~ *filiolus* 'son', *amiculus* 'friend', all
    diminutives

The conditions of the darkening effect of [l] cannot be defined with precision synchronically because they were obscured by the stress shift mentioned in 5.2.1, by analogical levelling and by recent borrowings. The details of the diachronic process can be found in the major handbooks, e.g. Leumann (1977: 85–7), and most recently in Sen (2015: 15–41). The most important factors are the following:

- the darkening effect is stronger in non-initial than in initial syllables;
- the darkening effect is stronger in coda position than in onset position (coda probably including word-final position, though the evidence here is less unambiguous); and
- the darkening effect is also dependent on the segment preceding the vowel before the [l] (cf. *filiolus* vs. *amiculus* above).

There are thus two interrelated sets of facts. One is the distribution of the variants of [l]; the other is the spreading of the secondary (i.e. vocalic) place features of [l] onto the preceding short vowel. As for the positional variants, it is clear that at least two must be assumed, one with a V-Place node dominating a Dorsal node with [+high] and [+back], the other without. The 'plain' [l] is to be assumed

---

[206] The evidence has been thoroughly assessed in the diachronic literature, see Sen (2012: 472–3; 2015: 15 sqq.), Meiser (1998: 68–9), Leumann (1977: 85–7). The primary direct evidence is a statement by Pliny the Elder reported to posterity by Priscian (book 2 of *Institutiones*, Keil 1855–78, vol. 2: 29), the indirect evidence comes from the prehistory of Latin (vowel weakening and the effect of [l] on preceding vowels) as well as the Romance languages (coda [l] > [w] in French, for instance *alba* 'white' > *aube* 'dawn' or *alter* > *autre* 'other'). Sen (2012: 472) argues that onset single [l] was gradiently velarised depending on the following vowel.

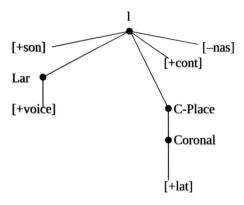

Figure 23. Full structure of plain [l]

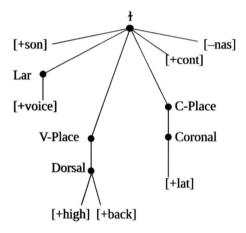

Figure 24. Full structure of velarised [ł] (repeated from Figure 5)

word-initially and after consonants. The representations are shown in Figures 23 and 24.

Historical evidence points to a palatalised quality in geminated [ll] and in [l] before [i]. Representationally this would mean an [l] with a V-Place node dominating [–back] and possibly also [+high]. Since, however, it is impossible to find clear cases of the synchronic spreading of palatality from [l], I will not assume such a representation here (but I do not thereby claim that palatalised surface variants did not exist).

As for the spreading, it is clear that there are two distinct outcomes, [o] and [u]. This implies that, depending on the environment in somewhat opaque ways, either only [+back] spread, leading to [o], or both [+back] and [+high], leading to [u], as in *vel-* → *volumus*, and in *vel-* → *vult* or *sepel-* → *sepultus*, respectively.

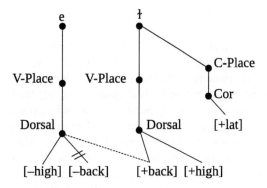

Figure 25. [el] → [ol] (irrelevant details omitted)

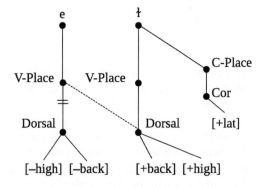

Figure 26. [el] → [ul] (irrelevant details omitted)

In the latter case the entire Dorsal node spreads to the preceding vowel (Figure 26); in the former, only a single feature (Figure 25).

4.10. FINAL STOP DELETION

A process that deletes a final unsyllabifiable stop affects the neuter stems *cord-* 'heart' and *lact-* 'milk' when zero-suffixed, turning them into *cor* and *lac*, respectively (both NomAccSing). In terms of syllable structure this rule is related to the degemination seen in 4.5.1; the motivation in both cases seems to be a segment that cannot be assigned a syllabic position. The cluster [kt] clearly violates the Sonority Sequencing Principle; and while [rd] does not, it was seen in Chapter 3 that voiced stops are not allowed in complex codas and are highly restricted in simple codas. Not all unsyllabifiable consonants are deleted, however; as will be seen in 5.3.1, a final [r] following a stop is saved by vowel insertion.

4.11. LIQUID DISSIMILATION

Latin possessed two liquids, [l] and [r].[207] In terms of phonological structure the distribution of these two segments is very similar: they are both allowed only next to a vowel and constitute clusters with much the same consonants. Both segments also occur in gemination fairly frequently (e.g. *ille* 'that', *error* 'error'), but only between two vowels, as is generally the case with geminates in Latin. At the same time, [l] is found in fewer clusters than [r], and shows a weaker tendency for syllabification as part of a complex onset (see chapter 3). In terms of lexical and morphological incidence too, [l] shows a much narrower range than [r]. The latter occurs in several prefixes (*per-*, *prae-*, *pro-*, *re-*), and numerous inflectional as well as derivational endings both in verbal and nominal morphology (*puellarum* 'girl' GENPLUR, *citior* 'faster', *fecerunt* 'they have done', *amator* 'lover'). By contrast, [l] occurs in no prefix, no inflectional ending, but it does occur in a handful of derivational endings of varying productivity (*regalis* 'royal', *pugil* 'boxer', *querela* 'complaint').

Perhaps the most conspicuous property that has made Latin liquids famous in the phonological literature (Steriade 1987; 1995: 153 sqq.; Kenstowicz 1994: 509; Roca 1994: 54–7; Boersma 1998: 437–40; Odden 2005: 241; Alderete & Frisch 2006: 385; Müller 2013; Bennett 2015: 261 sqq.; Jardine 2016; Payne 2017; Stanton 2017), as well as in the literature on the history of the language (Paucker 1885; Leumann 1917; Kent 1936; Watkins 1970; Dressler 1971; Leumann 1977: 231; Hurch 1991; Sen 2015: 88 sqq.) is the tendency of [l] to dissimilate into [r] where multiple occurrences would have emerged for morphological reasons. In Classical Latin, this is most clearly observable with two suffixes, adjectival *-alis/-aris* and the etymologically related nominal suffix *-al/-ar*. For both suffixes the general rule is that the base form is the one containing [l] (38, 39), but if the stem also has [l] in it, the [r]-variant of the suffix appears (40, 41).

(38) *navalis* 'naval'
      regalis 'royal'
      hiemalis 'winter' ADJ
      autumnalis 'autumn' ADJ
      Augustalis 'related to Augustus'...

(39) *animal* 'animal'
      vectigal 'toll'
      tribunal 'judgment-seat'
      capital 'head-dress'
      cubital 'cushion'

---

[207] Portions of this section first appeared, in somewhat different form, in Cser (2010).

feminal 'female genitalia'
quadrantal 'a liquid measure'

(40) *consularis* 'consular'
popularis 'popular'
militaris 'military'
lunaris 'lunar'
stellaris 'stellar'
Saliaris 'related to Salius-priests'

(41) *pulvinar* 'cushion'
calcar 'spur'
exemplar 'copy'
torcular 'wine or oil press'
lacunar 'panelled ceiling'
laquear 'panelled ceiling'
lupanar 'brothel'
nubilar 'barn'

In the case of both suffixes, if an [r] intervenes between the stem [l] and the suffix itself, the dissimilation is blocked and the [l]-variant of the suffix is selected (42, 43).

(42) *litoralis* 'belonging to sea-shore'
lateralis 'side-, lateral'
floralis 'floral'
pluralis 'plural'

(43) *Lupercal* proper name (only example)

For the adjectival suffix, however, intervening non-coronal consonants also systematically block the dissimilation (44).[208]

(44) *legalis* 'legal'
fluvialis 'belonging to river'
pluvialis 'rainy'
glacialis 'icy'
umbilicalis 'umbilical'
intellectualis 'sensible'
Vulcanalis 'related to Vulcanus'
Flavialis 'related to Flavius'

---

[208] Cser (2010); cf. also the modern formations *labial, global, subliminal*.

> *glebalis* 'consisting of clods'
> *localis* 'local'
> *fulminalis* 'projectile'

Some forms present problems: *letalis* 'deadly' is quite inexplicable, while *palmaris* 'of palm' and *vulgaris* 'vulgar' suggest that if the distance between the two liquids is below a certain threshold the blocking may not always be effective. A few cases of variation are also found, e.g. irregular *Latialis* 'of Latium' next to the regular (and more frequent) *Latiaris*.

Other suffixes including [l] no longer show such an obvious effect, but there is good reason to believe that diachronically liquid dissimilation had been more general (Sen 2015: 88 sqq.). It is assumed, for instance, that the noun- or adjective-forming suffixes in words like *ludicrum* 'sport' and *cubiculum* 'bedroom' are etymologically related and go back to an earlier *-klom*, with the [l] dissimilating in *ludicrum* and similar words because of the [l] in the stem. This, however, is no longer part of the synchronic grammatical system of the language.

On the other hand, diminutive formations show an abundance of [l] sounds in each other's vicinity. Witness the words in (45):

(45) Diminutives in -V[l]-
> *labellum* 'lips'
> *flagellum* 'whip'
> *columella* 'column'
> *Claudilla* proper name
> *hilarulus* 'mirthful'
> *litterulae* 'letters'
> *pallidulus* 'pale'
> *glandula* 'tonsil'
> *cultellus* 'knife'
> *clitellae* 'saddle'
> *gladiolus* 'dagger'
> *luteolus* 'yellow'
> *filiolus* 'son'
> *palliolum* 'mantle'
> *ollula* 'jug'
> *paullulum* 'a little'
> *puellula* 'girl'
> *villula* 'mansion'
> *pullulus* 'young animal'
> *bellulus* 'pretty'

It seems that the conspicuous presence of several [l]s was a salient feature of diminutives (cf. Cser 2010: 42). One may cite authors like Plautus (*Edepol*

papillam bellulam 'By Pollux, nice little breasts' *Casina* 848), Juvenal (*Nullum,
quod tibi filiolus vel filia nascitur ex me* 'is it not [a merit] that you have a boy or
a girl from me?' *Sat*. 9.82–3) or Catullus (*collocate puellulam* 'marry off the girl'
Carm. 61.184). Grammarians were also aware of this special quality of [l].
Martianus Cappella, for instance, describes the articulation of [l] with the words
lingua palatoque dulcescit ('sweetens on the tongue and the palate' *De nuptiis*
3.261), but describes all other consonants in neutral terms, e.g. *K lingua
palatoque formatur* ('*k* is formed on [or by] the tongue and the palate'). It may
be surmised that these '*l*-heavy' words constituted a pattern in themselves, and
their salience was due to the slightly irregular or at least unusual sequence of
laterals they contained.

Similar co-occurrence constraints or tendencies to dissimilate cannot be found
for [r] with the exception of one particular point, which concerns the behaviour
of *re-* (cf. 7.2.1.5). This prefix, while highly productive, never combines with
stems that begin with [r]. This constraint appears to be so persistent that even in
the daughter languages such forms are virtually impossible to find. It is also true
that regardless of prefixation, no Latin word begins with **#(C)(C)[r]V[r], that
is, in initial syllables two [r]s must be separated by at least a long vowel.[209]

In non-initial position, however, sequences including more than one (non-
geminate) [r] are not difficult to find, and not only because many inflectional
suffixes include this sound: *perurbanus* 'highly polite', *perargutus* 'well
argued', *pererro* 'wander over', etc. (with the prefix *per-*); *morerer* 'die'
PassImpfSubj1Sing, *ureris* 'burn' PassSubj2Sing, *quereretur* 'complain' Pass-
ImpfSubj3Sing, *currere* 'run' Inf, *cucurrerim* 'run' PerfSubj1Sing, etc. (inflected
verb forms), *error* 'error', *furor* 'rage', etc. (derived nouns).

4.12. Conclusion

This chapter has discussed segmental processes that affect consonants. The set of
these processes is quite heterogenous; several of them involve assimilation
(spreading; 4.2, 4.3, 4.4, 4.8), some are prosodically motivated (4.5, 4.10). What
is common to them is that they all have consequences for the morphology;
arguably some of them could be analysed as expressing phonologically
conditioned allomorphic patterns rather than purely phonological rules (especially 4.11, given the morpheme-specific nature of the alternation). The
following chapter discusses the phonological processes involving vowels.

---

[209] It is also true that no [r]-initial Latin verb has a reduplicated perfect (which would again be
**rer-*), but since there are only 25 reduplicating verbs or so, this fact may have little significance.

5

PROCESSES AFFECTING VOWELS

5.1. INTRODUCTION

This chapter discusses the alternations that vowels enter into in Classical Latin. The alternations show various properties in terms of generality and dependence on lexical identity or morphological structure. The three sections of the chapter present qualitative alternations, vowel–zero alternations, and length alternations, respectively. The section on qualitative alternations begins with the description of a diachronic change that does not strictly belong to the synchronic phonology of Classical Latin but is nevertheless responsible for a conspicuous pattern of fossilised alternations in a significant part of the lexicon, hence the decision to include it here.

5.2. ALTERNATIONS IN VOWEL QUALITY

5.2.1. *The Old Latin weakening*

In about the sixth–fifth centuries BC a pervasive neutralisation affecting short vowels in non-initial syllables took place. The generally accepted explanation is that in this period word stress was on the first syllable and the neutralisations (mergers) in non-initial syllables were weakenings that are cross-linguistically typical of unstressed vowels. Also, along with syncope (the diachronic loss of short vowels in certain internal syllables), this weakening is practically the sole evidence for word-initial stress in this early period.

The synchronic reflexes of the Old Latin weakening are visible but rather unsystematic in Classical Latin. The change that resulted in the Classical stress pattern (penult if it is heavy and antepenult if the penult is light) had completely obscured the original motivation, and other factors had interfered heavily, including analogical levelling, borrowing and later segmental changes — not always clearly distinguishable from each other. For this reason it is impossible, in my view, to include the weakening in the synchronic phonology of the language. Where differences in form are historically due to the weakening, they must be regarded as lexicalised. Since, however, the patterns introduced by this change are found in a large part of the vocabulary, the basic points of its reconstruction will be presented here.[210]

Some of the most obvious examples come from the set of prefixed verbs, since those can easily be compared to unprefixed base forms (although such examples cannot be found for all phonological configurations). The fundamental regularity for medial open syllables is that all short vowels were raised to [i]:

(46) Open syllable weakening
   eligere 'choose' (cf. *legere* 'gather')
   conficere 'accomplish' (cf. *facere* 'do')
   cupiditas 'desire' (cf. *cupidus* 'desiring' < **kupido-*)
   capitis 'head' GenSing (cf. *caput* NomSing)

The presence of onset [r] after the affected vowel had a lowering effect and allowed the raising to go only as far as [e]:

(47) Weakening before [r]
   peperi 'I brought forth' (cf. *parere* Inf)
   temperare 'regulate' (cf. *tempus* < **tempos*)

In closed syllables the mergers were less pervasive; rounded vowels collapse in [u], and [a] raises to [e]:

(48) Closed syllable weakening
   confectus 'accomplished' (cf. *factus* 'done')
   obsessus 'besieged' (cf. *sessus* 'seated')
   euntis 'going' GenSing (< **ejontes*)
   adductus 'led on' (cf. *ductus* 'led')

The labial consonants [p b f m w] affected preceding vowels in open syllables as is indicated by orthographic variation:

(49) Weakening before labials
   obstipescere/obstupescere 'be stupefied' (cf. *stupere* 'be stunned')
   surripere/surrupere 'steal' (cf. *rapere* 'take away')

---

[210] This brief summary mainly follows Sen (2015: 80–8), but the fundamentals with large sets of data can generally be found in the comprehensive discussions of the history of Latin (e.g. Leumann 1977: 79–91, Sihler 1995: 59–64, Meiser 1998: 67–73, Baldi 2002: 253–6 or Weiss 2009: 116–21). Touratier (2005: 217–21) includes some instances of this weakening in his description of Classical Latin synchronic phonology under a morphological regularity he calls *apophonie synchronique*, covering lexical items he analyses as compositional (e.g. *conficere* 'accomplish') as opposed to lexical items he analyses as simplexes (e.g. *interficere* 'kill', both verbs compounds of *facere* 'do'). I completely disregard the forms of diachronic weakening that affected vowels in final syllables, since those left no alternations behind, or at least hardly any compared to medial weakening.

Whether this variation in the writing points to phonological variation between [i] and [u], or to a high front or central rounded vowel ([y], [ʏ] or [ʉ], cf. Allen 1978: 59 or Sen 2015: 83) is a question I leave open.

Dark [l] (cf. 4.9) also influenced the course that weakened vowels took and led to [u] or [o] where otherwise [i] or [e] would be expected:

(50) Weakening before dark [l]
      insulsus 'dull', orig. 'unsalted' (cf. *salsus* 'salted')
      adolescere 'grow up' (cf. *alere* 'nourish')

Forms involving syllables closed by glides were mentioned in 2.3.2. In these, regular diachronic processes (*[ew] > [uː] and *[ej] > [iː]) produced the long vowels after regular weakening:

(51) Closed syllable weakening before glides
      *[rekajd-] > *[rekejd-] > [rekiːd-] *recīdere* 'cut back/up' (cf. *caedere* 'cut')
      *[reklawd-] > *[reklewd-] > [rekluːd-] *reclūdere* 'close' (cf. *claudere* 'close')

At the same time, a large number of words do not show the effect of Old Latin weakening (*sepelire* 'bury', *alacer* 'swift', *perpeti* 'tolerate', etc.). Different explanations are found in the relevant literature, including analogical levelling, recomposition and vowel harmony-type retention, but with these I will not be concerned here.

5.2.2. *Synchronic alternations between the short vowels*

The most frequent quality alternations affects the two short palatal vowels [i] and [e]. There are four specific environments that trigger an alternation between these two vowels. All the four are effective only in non-initial syllables, but this is caused by three different factors. The alternation in 5.2.2.1 results diachronically from the Old Latin weakening discussed in the previous section, which only affected non-initial syllables. Those in 5.2.2.2 and 5.2.2.3 are confined to non-initial syllables simply because synchronically there are no monosyllabic [i]-final or [is]-final stems. That in 5.2.2.4 is found in suffixes only, which evidently cannot be the first syllable of any word form.

5.2.2.1. *Alternation in closed vs. open syllables*

In non-initial syllables, [i] is very often found in open syllables while [e] in closed syllables, depending on how suffixation affects the syllabification of the post-vocalic consonant. Examples of nouns and adjectives exhibiting this alternation are most easily found in the third declension (consonant- and *i-*

stems), where the NomSing suffix is either zero or -s, but all other suffixes begin with a vowel (such as the GenSing suffix -is) and thus the stem-final syllable is closed in the NomSing but open in all other cases:

(52) [e] ~ [i] alternation

NomSing	GenSing	gloss
pecten	pectinis	'comb'
nomen	nominis	'name'
pontifex	pontificis	'priest'

A stem-final coronal stop is regularly lost before the -s suffix (see 4.3 and 4.5.1):

(53) [e] ~ [i] alternation with coronal stop loss

NomSing	GenSing	gloss
miles (← -et+s)	militis	'soldier'
comes (← -et+s)	comitis	'companion'
deses (← -ed+s)	desidis	'idle'
obses (← -ed+s)	obsidis	'hostage'

Many verbs in their various forms and other derived words show the same phonological relation:

(54) [e] ~ [i] alternation in verbs

perficere 'achieve' Inf perfectus PassPart
praecinere 'sing' Inf praecentor 'lead singer'
accipere 'get' Inf acceptum PassPart

While the number of forms displaying this alternation is high, there are also many exceptions to it, viz. non-alternating short palatal vowels in analogous environments. For instance, non-alternating [e] is found in several verbs:

(55) Lack of [e] ~ [i] alternation in verbs

perpeti 'tolerate' Inf perpessus PassPart
aggredi 'attack' Inf aggressus PassPart

Non-alternating [i] is found in many nouns:

(56) Non-alternating [i]

NomSing	GenSing	gloss
calix	calicis	'chalice'
sanguis (← -in+s)	sanguinis	'blood'
lapis (← -id+s)	lapidis	'stone'

Outside the class of verbs, however, non-alternating [e] is only found in two nouns and two adjectives. They clearly constitute a minor phonological pattern with stem shapes of the form C[e]C(C)[et]-, including a single consonant in the middle in three out of the four cases and two consonants only in *perpes*, an etymologically prefixed word (57).[211]

(57) Non-alternating [e]

NomSing	GenSing	gloss
seges (← -*et*+*s*)	*segetis*	'cornfield'
teges (← -*et*+*s*)	*tegetis*	'covering'
hebes (← -*et*+*s*)	*hebetis*	'blunt'
perpes (← -*et*+*s*)	*perpetis*	'continuous'

5.2.2.2. *Lowering before [r]*

The high vowels [i] and [u] are lowered to [e] and [o], respectively, before [r] in a derived environment. Practically all cases involve [r] resulting from rhotacism[212] (59, 60) as opposed to an underlying [r] (on rhotacism see 4.4). The only convincing example of lowering at morpheme boundary is seen in (58).

(58) Pre-r lowering of [u] before morpheme boundary[213]
fu- 'be' → *fore* Inf, *foret* ImpfSubj3Sing

(59) Pre-r lowering of [u] fed by rhotacism

NomSing	GenSing	gloss
tempus	*temporis*	'time'
corpus	*corporis*	'body'
pignus	*pignoris*	'pledge'

(60) Pre-r lowering of [i] fed by rhotacism

NomSing	GenSing	gloss
cinis	*cineris*	'ash'

---

[211] In Latin historical linguistics the *seges*-class falls under the generalisation called *alacer*-rule, which describes the lack of vowel weakening in the environment (C)V$_i$CV$_i$, see e.g. Weiss (2009: 118).

[212] This feeding relationship is mentioned in passing by Uffmann (2007: 158), but not elaborated in detail. In Latin historical linguistics it has long been claimed that rhotacism *qua* sound change preceded lowering *qua* sound change (e.g. Leumann 1977: 51); in that context it is the *vir* 'man', *hircus* 'goat' type words (see below) that pose a problem and require other explanations.

[213] This is the only example, a highly defective verb overlapping in its paradigms with *esse*. The other so-called *u*-stem verbs (e.g. *metuere* 'be afraid') only take vowel-initial allomorphs (and are probably best analysed as consonant-stems). Historically, there were many verbs whose infectum stem ended in [i], and they showed the same lowering (*capi-o ~ cape-re* 'catch' 1Sing ~ Inf). As I will argue later, there appear to be compelling reasons to believe that such verbs were possibly reanalysed as consonant stems in some of their forms, and so the new morphological analysis was *cap-ere*, etc. with a different suffix allomorph, and there was no synchronic lowering before [r]. The lowering of [u] in *fore* and the lowering of both short high vowels before [r] resulting from rhotacism is not affected by this reanalysis. For more details see Chapter 6.

cucumis   cucumeris   'cucumber'
pulvis   pulveris   'dust'

It appears that neither the [i] → [e] / _[r] nor the [u] → [o] / _[r] rule operates in nonderived environments:

(61) [ir] and [ur] in nonderived environments
      vir 'man', *firmus* 'firm', *hircus* 'goat'
      ursus 'bear', *furor* 'rage', *fulgur* 'lightning', *cicur* 'tame', also in suffixed
      forms *fulguris, cicuris* GenSing

It is interesting to note that insances of [ir] (as opposed to those of [ur]) are practically confined to initial syllables in Classical Latin. Non-initial [ir] is found only in the second half of compounds, mainly of *vir* 'man' (*triumvir* 'one of three associates', *levir* 'brother-in-law'[214]). Initial syllable derived environments are created only via the total assimilation of the nasal in the prefix *in-*, but no lowering is seen in such forms (*in+rigare* → *irrigare*, not **errigare* 'make wet', see 7.2.3.1). Similarly there is no lowering in the historically *dis*-prefixed words *diribere* 'sort (votes)' and *dirimere* 'take away' (see 7.2.4.3).

The lowering rule also does not work at compound boundaries:

(62) No lowering in compounds
      semi-rasus 'half-shaven', *semi-rotundus* 'semicircular', *pinni-rapus* 'crest-
      snatcher'

What this means is that compounds do not constitute derived environment in the required sense. Since many of them are highly transparent and on occasion appear to be of the 'Augenblicksbildung' (hapax legomenon) kind, it is unlikely that they would all be lexicalised. Thus the only plausible explanation that remains is that compounding as a morphological operation is assigned to a different level and either follows the lowering rule (and thus counterfeeds it) or precedes it and so does not constitute a derived environment.

Interestingly, however, there are three examples of lowering at compound boundary: *legerupa* 'law-breaker' (← *leg-* 'law' + *rup-* 'break'), *viveradix* '(plant) having root' (← *vivus* 'live' + *radix* 'root') and *funerepus* 'rope-dancer' (← *funis* 'rope' + *repere* 'creep'). While the forms exhibit variation in the surviving manuscripts of the relevant texts and are somewhat contested by textual critics, there is at least a likelihood that they have historical

---

[214] While *levir* is etymologically not related to *vir*, there is some indication that it was regarded in Antiquity as one of its compounds, and analogical transfer from *vir* to *levir* is not disputed (see e.g. de Vaan 2008 s.v., Lindsay 1894: 200, Leumann 1977: 68). *Satira* 'satire' is a postclassical variant of *satura*.

reality.[215] If we take these forms at face value, the implication is that at some not so distant point in the history of the language compounds did constitute derived environment for lowering before [r], and the latter phonological rule shifted levels later. Since, however, there is no evidence whatsoever that the suffixed and the rhotacised forms failed to also constitute derived environment for the same rule at that time, it is more likely that rule scattering had taken place (for the notion see Bermúdez-Otero & Trousdale 2012, Bermúdez-Otero 2006: 506), i.e. pre-[r] lowering operated for a while both at the level of compounding and at the level of case and verb suffixation, but was later confined to the latter. A third possibility, which I revisit in 6.2.2, is that the lowering of [i] was reanalysed as operating in non-initial syllables generally.

5.2.2.3. Word-final lowering

Word-final short [i] is banned in Classical Latin.[216] When a stem that ends in [i] is zero-suffixed, short [i] is lowered to [e]. This is apparent in nominative-accusative singular *i*-stem neuter nouns and adjectives (63).[217]

(63) Word-final lowering
      mari- 'sea' → *mare* NomAccSing (cf. *mari-a* NomAccPlur)
      celeri- 'swift' → *celere* NeutNomAccSing (cf. *celeri-a* NeutNomAccPlur)

5.2.2.4. Alternation in suffixes

In some derivational suffixes one finds the two vowels alternating, and in verbal as well as nominal inflectional morphology (discussed in Chapter 6) they both alternate with zero (though not with each other in the same suffix). One clear example is the nominal suffix *-itas/-etas/-tas*; there is also a pair of adjectival suffixes *-ius/-eus* (e.g. *eximius* 'exceptional' vs. *aureus* 'golden'), but for their distribution no phonological conditions can be identified. As regards the former, the regularity very clearly is that if the stem ends in [i], the variant can only be

---

[215] The first two forms are mentioned in Lindsay (1894: 192, 373) and Leumann (1977: 81, 280, 390), and *legerupa* is mentioned in Weiss (2009: 264). *Legerupa/legirupa* is found in Plautus' comedies (considerably earlier than the classical period) four times, and once in Prudentius. Editors of Plautine comedies usually settle for *legirupa*, considered by Lindsay the inferior reading. *Viveradix* is also attested as *viviradix* and is mostly found in Pliny and Columella, both first c. AD. *Funerepus* is only attested in Apuleius' *Florida*.

[216] Three function words are exceptions: *nisi* 'unless', *tibi* 'to you' and *mihi* 'to me'; the latter two variably showing short or long [i] in the second syllable, and *nisi* historically also containing a long final vowel.

[217] Historically the same change affected the imperatives of verbs whose infectum stem ends in [i]: *capi-* 'catch' → *cape* Imp (cf. *capi-o* 1Sing, *capi-unt* 3Plur); but, as mentioned earlier and as will be seen in more detail in Chapter 6, an alternative analysis is possible for this category. Under that analysis, the imperative is analysed as a consonant-stem form suffixed with the usual consonant-stem ending *-e* and is then not an example of word-final lowering.

-etas, in all other cases mostly *-itas*, though after continuants a vowel-less allomorph *-tas* is found in a handful of words:

(64) Alternations in suffixes
 novus 'new' → *novitas* 'novelty'
 celeber 'frequented' → *celebritas* 'multitude'
 vastus 'empty' → *vastitas* 'waste land'...

 socius 'companion' → *societas* 'fellowship'
 ebrius 'drunken' → *ebrietas* 'drunkenness'
 varius 'variegated' → *varietas* 'variety'
 contrarius 'opposed' → *contrarietas* 'opposition'

 pauper 'poor' → *paupertas* 'poverty'
 difficilis 'difficult' → *difficultas* 'difficulty'

The alternation between the two vowelled variants is driven by the constraint that bans a sequence of two short [i]s (thus ****sociitas*, ****ebriitas*, etc. are impossible).[218] This is all the more interesting given the existence of the vowel-less variant, since at a purely descriptive level *socitas*, *ebritas*, etc. would be possible both morphologically and phonologically.

5.3. VOWEL–ZERO ALTERNATIONS

5.3.1. *Before stem-final [r]*

There is a widespread [e] ~ Ø alternation found in the final syllable of nominal stems between a stop and a stem-final [r]. The vowel appears if the [r] is not followed by a vowel; if it is, the vowel is absent:

(65) [e] ~ Ø alternation before stem-final [r]
NomSing	GenSing	gloss
pater	*patris*	'father'
mater	*matris*	'mother'
celeber	*celebris*	'frequented'
ager	*agri*	'field'
acer	*acris*	'sharp'
liber	*libri*	'book'

The [e] is present not only when the syllable is final, witness *celeberrimus* 'most frequented', *paternus* 'fatherly/paternal'. It appears that the alternation is best

---

[218] Note, however, that a sequence of a short and a long [i] is allowed, as attested in the GenSing and NomPlur forms of words ending in *-ius*, e.g *socii* 'companion's' or 'companions'. Sequences of two short [i]'s appear marginally and optionally in perfectum-based verb forms, where the second of the two vowels is practically always stressed, see 6.2.3.4.

described as vowel epenthesis rather than deletion, since for the latter there would be many counterexamples:

(66) non-alternating [e] in the same environment
   NOMSING   GENSING   gloss
   socer   *soceri*   'father-in-law'
   cicer   *ciceris*   'pea'
   uber   *uberis*   'fertile'
   līber   *līberi*   'free'
   later   *lateris*   'brick'

By contrast, if the alternating stems are represented as vowel-less underlyingly, the insertion rule, which explains the contrast between the above two types of words (*pater* vs. *socer*, etc.), is not only exceptionless; it is also plausibly motivated by the phonotactics, since a word-final or preconsonantal stop+[r] sequence is ill-formed for sonority reasons. It is interesting to note that this is the only configuration in which an unsyllabifiable consonant is saved via vowel insertion, as opposed to degemination and stop-deletion in *cor* and *lac* (see 4.5 and 4.10, respectively). On the assumption that the latter two rules are motivated by a general tendency to delete unsyllabifiable consonants, it is arguable that [e]-insertion precedes them, even though formally it does not bleed them (the triggering [r] being neither a geminate nor a stop). The rule can be formalised in the following (non-geometrical) fashion:

(67) The [e]-insertion rule
   $\emptyset \rightarrow$ [e] / [–son, –cont] _ [r] {C, #}

In some cases the alternation does not strictly align with the environments dictated by the requirements of syllabification. For instance, the adjective *superus* 'that is above', based on *super* 'above' shows vowelled forms, and so does the verb *superare* 'rise above'. The derived adjective *supremus* 'topmost, last', however, shows the vowel-less stem variant, and so does the adverb *supra* 'on the top'. Such examples are found because these alternations do not have a single historical source.[219]

5.3.2. Prevocalic deletion of back vowels

In derived environments, the back vowels [a] and [o] are deleted when another vowel follows. Examples abound in the relevant types of nominal declensions

[219] The instances of this alternation go back diachronically to two (sets of) completely unrelated sound changes. The alternation in the family relation terms including *pater*, *mater* goes back to Proto-Indo-European ablaut and is widely attested in the related languages. Most of the other instances result from a combination of sound changes specific to Latin and hence much more recent (Weiss 2009: 123).

and in the present forms of verbs. A systematic discussion of these is found in chapter 6, but a handful of examples are given here:

(68) Back vowel deletion
 ara+īs → *arīs* 'altar' DatAblPlur
 amā+ō → *amō* 'love' 1Sing
 amā+ē+t → *amet*[220] 'love' Subj3Sing
 domino+īs → *dominīs* 'lord' DatAblPlur
 domino+ī → *dominī* 'lord' NomPlur

The deletion requires a following filled syllable nucleus rather than a segment vocalic in its internal structure (i.e. a segment possessing a V-Place node). That a structurally vocalic segment is not enough is made clear by the combinations in similar environments of the back vowel [a] and the glide [j], where there is no change apart from concatenation (other derived combinations of a back vowel and a glide do not occur):

(69) No deletion before [j]
 ara+[j] → [aːraj] 'altar' (written ⟨arae⟩) GenDatSing, NomPlur

The question whether the process is relevant to the vowel [u] is essentially a morphological one and its aspects pertaining to inflection are also discussed in detail in Chapter 6. The vowel [u] occurs in derived prevocalic environments in [u]-final noun stems suffixed with the GenPlur ending [ũː] (e.g. *tribuum* [tribuũː] 'tribe' GenPlur), and in adjectives where the gender markers follow the vowel [u] (e.g. *exiguus ~ exigua ~ exiguum* 'small' Masc ~ Fem ~ Neut). In the case of verbs there are reasons to believe that what are traditionally called *u*-stems in fact end in a sequence [uw] except for the strongly defective verb *fore* 'be', whose relevant forms are the *a*-suffixed subjunctives (practically only *fuat* Subj3Sing). The [u] is never lost in these cases; the only instance when it is lost is in the DatAblPlur of some *u*-stem nouns (e.g. *portibus* from the stem *portu-* 'port'). Since, however, many nouns in the same category do not show loss of [u] (e.g. *tribubus* 'tribe' DatAblPlur), and since heteroclisy is a pervasive feature of nominal declension, the *portibus*-type data are probably best analysed as heteroclitic consonant-stem forms rather than forms involving [u]-loss. The upshot is that [u] is indeed excluded from the rule of prevocalic back vowel deletion, which is thus formalised (non-geometrically) in the following way:

(70) The vowel deletion rule
 V[+back, –high] → Ø / _V (in derived environments)

It appears that the loss of non-high back vowels is never fed by prefixation, as forms with *pro-* and *con-* amply show, e.g. *proavus* 'great-grandfather',

---

[220] The shortening of the [eː] before word-final [t] is an independent process, see 5.4.1.

coactus 'coerced', the latter with prevocalic loss of its placeless nasal (see 5.4.4).

5.3.3. *Vowel–zero alternation in suffixes*

In the discussion of the suffix *-itas/-etas/-tas* in 5.2.2.4 it was seen that zero was a possibility in the place of the suffix-initial palatal vowel. There, however, the focus was on the regularity governing the distribution of the two vowelled variants rather than on the vowel–zero alternation. Some other derivational suffixes show an [i] ~ Ø alternation, and in verbal inflection [i] ~ Ø and [e] ~ Ø alternations are found too. For example, one may consider the noun-forming suffix *-(i)mentum*:[221]

(71) V ~ Ø alternation in suffixes
     alimentum 'nourishment'
     sedimentum 'settling'

     fragmentum 'fragment'
     armentum 'cattle'
     augmentum 'growth'
     fermentum 'yeast'
     incrementum 'increase'
     pigmentum 'colour'

The choice of the suffix cannot be motivated phonotactically, since the cluster [gm] is only ever found in [k]-final and [g]-final stems affixed with *-mentum* or *-men*, two etymologically and functionally related endings.[222] By contrast, a form such as **almentum without the suffix-initial [i] would be perfectly well-formed, since the cluster [lm] is found in simplex forms (e.g. *ulmus* 'elm-tree', or indeed *almus* 'nourishing' from the same etymological root as *alimentum*).

    Many examples of vowel–zero alternations are discussed in Chapter 6, which presents the verbal and nominal inflection, the extensive and varied allomorphic variation found in it and its phonological conditioning in detail.

5.4. LENGTH ALTERNATIONS

Systematic length alternations in Latin include the shortening of long vowels in several environments, the lengthening that accompanies the devoicing of voiced stops, the lengthening resulting from coalescence with an empty vowel, and the lengthening and concomitant nasalisation resulting from coalescence with a

---

[221] Note that in many cases the stem itself ends in ī and so while the form appears to end in ⟨imentum⟩, the suffix itself is *-mentum*, e.g. *condīmentum* 'spice', *detrīmentum* 'rubbing off'.

[222] Voiced obstruents are never found in coda position in unprefixed and uncliticised forms except for the case above plus the final [d] of neuter pronouns (see Chapter 3). At prefix–stem boundaries different generalisations are valid.

placeless nasal. These will now be discussed in this order. The historical lengthening following loss of [s] is not a systematic synchronic process any longer; it is discussed in 4.2.1 above and in Chapter 7.

5.4.1. *Shortenings*

Long vowels are systematically shortened in the following environments:

- (i)   before [nt], [nd];
- (ii) before another vowel;
- (iii) before word-final [t]; and
- (iv) before word-final liquids in polysyllables.

In (i) and (ii) nothing else matters but the following segmental portion. By contrast, following [t] and the liquids only have a shortening effect word-finally, and the liquids only in words of more than one syllable. Some of these environments are made up of a single affix; final shortening [t] is always the 3Sɪɴɢ affix (but distributionally all final [t]s are preceded by short vowels, e.g. *caput* 'head'), shortening [nd] is the PᴀʀᴛPᴀssFᴜᴛ affix; and the shortening effect of [l] is only visible in nouns derived with the suffix *-āl(i)-*, but these processes are exceptionless all the same. Examples:

(72) Exampes of vowel shortening
- (i)   *vidē-* 'see', *amā-* 'love' → *vidĕnt, amănt* 3Pʟᴜʀ, *vidĕntem, amăntem* PᴀʀᴛAᴄᴄSɪɴɢ, *vidĕndus, amăndus* PᴀʀᴛPᴀssFᴜᴛ
- (ii) *vidē-* 'see' → *vidĕo* 1Sɪɴɢ, *vidĕam* Sᴜʙᴊ1Sɪɴɢ
- (iii) *vidē-* 'see', *amā-* 'love' → *vidĕt, amăt* 3Sɪɴɢ
- (iv) *videā-* 'see' Sᴜʙᴊ → *videăr* PᴀssSᴜʙᴊ1Sɪɴɢ
  oratōr- 'speaker' → *oratŏr* NᴏᴍSɪɴɢ (cf. *oratōris* GᴇɴSɪɴɢ)
  animāl(i)- 'animal' → *animăl* NᴏᴍSɪɴɢ (cf. *animālis* GᴇɴSɪɴɢ)

Monosyllables show shortening only before [t] and [nt] (word-finally [nd] does not occur so it never creates a monosyllabic environment):

(73) Shortening in monosyllables
  năt, nănt 'swim' 3Sɪɴɢ, 3Pʟᴜʀ, *dĕt, dĕnt* 'give' Sᴜʙᴊ3Sɪɴɢ, Sᴜʙᴊ3Pʟᴜʀ; but
  pār 'equal', *fūr* 'thief', *cūr* 'why', *sōl* 'sun' with no shortening

Shortening in hiatus has only the exceptions that were listed in 2.3.3: the *ē*-stem noun DᴀᴛGᴇɴSɪɴɢ forms ending in *-iēī*, the disyllabic forms of the verb *fieri* 'become' (*fīo* 1Sɪɴɢ, *fīunt* 3Pʟᴜʀ, *fīat* Sᴜʙᴊ3Sɪɴɢ) and the pronominal genitives ending in *-īus*.

5.4.2. *Lengthening before voiced stops*

It is a clearly observable regularity that in non-final syllables short vowels undergo lengthening before an underlying voiced stop when that stop is devoiced via contact voice assimilation.[223] There are exceptions, and there is also the occasional problem of determining vowel length in closed syllables, where poetic metre provides no information. Nevertheless, there is a clear majority of eligible forms where this lengthening can be ascertained.

(74) Lengthening concomitant on devoicing
    ag- → *āctus* 'do' PASSPART
    reg- → *rēctus* 'govern' PASSPART
    cad- → *cāsus* 'fall' PASSPART

All the creditable examples have underlying [g] or [d]. The labial stop [b] does not figure either because it is never immediately followed by a voiceless obstruent (e.g. the third stem of *cub-* 'lie down' is *cubit-*, not ***cupt-*), or because the vowel is long anyhow (*lāb-* → *lāpsus* 'totter' PASSPART). When the stop that undergoes the devoicing is [d], the following obstruent is always [s], to which the [t] resulting from [d] assimilates in two steps (see 4.2 and 4.3), and then the [ss] is shortened because of the preceding long vowel, as is explained in 4.5.2 (*cad+sus* → *cātsus* → *cāssus* → *cāsus*). The lengthening does not affect vowels in final syllables (*grĕg-* → *grēx* 'herd', *obsĕd-* → *obsēs* 'hostage' NOMSING, the latter with assimilation of [t] to [s] and with general degemination affecting final [ss], cf. 4.5.1). There is a tendency for [i] to remain unaffected (*scid-* → *scĭssus* 'cleave' PASSPART), though there is *vid-* → *vīsus* 'see' and *divid-* ~ *divīsus* 'divide' PASSPART, two similar but etymologically unrelated stems.

The most productive candidates for creating the required environment are the *-t-* and the *-s-* suffixes of the third stem, and the *-s-* of the perfectum stem of many verbs; for the latter see *intellegere* ~ *intellēxi* 'understand', *dividere* ~ *divīsi* 'divide' INF ~ PERF1 SING. Perfectum-based forms are not often adduced as examples in the literature on Lachmann's Law, since vowel lengthening in the perfectum stem is very frequent independently of the devoicing (*sedere* ~ *sēdi* 'sit' INF ~ PERF1 SING), and so one can never say with absolute certainty that a lengthening such as that seen in *intellēxi* has anything to do with the devoicing of [g]. At the same time there is reason to believe that the vowel is short in several *s*-perfectum forms in which the

---

[223] In Latin historical linguistics the change underlying this phenomenon is called Lachmann's Law, probably one of the most famous and most debated sound changes. The literature on it is enormous, and it was at times in the focus of intense theoretical debates, discussed at length in order to underpin Neogrammarian, analogist or generative rule-based hypotheses about phonological or grammatical change. Collinge (1985) is a good survey of previous research up to that time; Jasanoff (2004) includes a brief but incisive survey and suggests an interesting solution to the diachronic problems surrounding Lachmann's Law; Roberts (2009) includes a very detailed summary of the phenomena, the issues, the evidence, all previous research with assessment, and proposes an analysis in the Stratal OT framework. On the phonetics of similar processes Gussenhoven (2007) is an important work. Note, however, that Lachmann's Law is not exactly coextensive with the phonological process I describe here. For example, *dividere* ~ *divīsi* ~ *divīsus* would not be listed as an example of Lachmann's Law because the etymological root ends in a Proto-Indo-European aspirate (de Vaan 2008 s.v.), and aspirates were not affected by this change.

[s] is preceded by underlying [k] or [t]^224 (*quatere ~ quăssi* 'shake', *illicere ~ illĕxi* 'entice', *conspicere ~ conspĕxi* 'catch sight of'), which is at least suggestive of a relation between the lengthening and the devoicing.

If one assumes that we are here dealing with a special kind of compensatory lengthening triggered by the loss of underlying voice – rather than allomorphy – this can be formalised as a four-step process (see Figure 27): (i) voice assimilation, i.e. the delinking of the Laryngeal node of the first obstruent, which dominates a [+voice] feature, and the linking of the Laryngeal node of the second obstruent, which dominates a [–voice] feature, to the Root node of the first obstruent (see 4.2); (ii) the projection of a Root node and a skeletal slot by the delinked Laryngeal node; (iii) the spreading of the vowel onto the newly projected skeletal slot; and (iv) the deletion of the structure dissociated from the devoiced stop, that is, of the Larnygeal node and the [+voice] feature it dominates, along with the Root node it projected in step (ii). Of the four sub-processes, only (ii) is lexically conditioned: it is only in a subset of the phonologically eligible forms that a Root node and a skeletal slot are projected by the delinked Laryngeal node. Step (iv) is not a separate process in the sense that it instantiates the general rule deleting all incomplete segments at the end of the derivation, such as a placeless nasal that neither acquired a C-Place node nor merged with a preceding vowel.

Since no segment can have two Laryngeal nodes, the delinked Laryngeal node will not link to the Root node of the vowel; and since vowels are redundantly voiced, the vowel before the devoicing site will also not host the delinked voice feature. Thus the Laryngeal node delinking from the stop is deleted in the end – a major difference *vis-à-vis* the lengthening and concomitant nasalisation resulting from coalescence with a placeless nasal (see 5.4.4). The transient Root node is

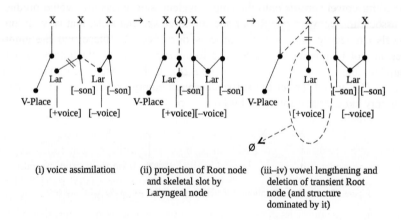

(i) voice assimilation	(ii) projection of Root node and skeletal slot by Laryngeal node	(iii–iv) vowel lengthening and deletion of transient Root node (and structure dominated by it)

Figure 27. Lengthening concomitant on devoicing (irrelevant details omitted)

---

^224 See Allen (1978: 67), Leumann (1977: 591), and the most detailed Meiser (2003: 107–46) on *s*-perfects.

necessary only because a melodic node cannot link immediately to a skeletal slot and, *a fortiori*, cannot project one.

Note that in prefixed forms the quality of the vowel is unpredictable from the infectum because of the historical weakening (see 5.2.1); e.g. both *peragere* 'transfix' and *redigere* 'drive back' have the same long vowel in the third stem (*perāctus, redāctus* PassPart) because they both derive from *agere* 'do'. Also note that vowels in prefixes never undergo the lengthening even when the segmental environment could in principle trigger it (e.g. *adfui* 'I was present', *obtinere* 'maintain'). Clearly there are elements of opacity here both in the unpredictable quality of the alternating vowels and in the morphological and phonological constraints that obtain. Another type of opacity is present in the unusually complex phonological process as described above. These factors may well have contributed to the process being restricted to a narrow domain, partly losing its original phonological motivation. It is not entirely impossible that it was fully morphologised or lexicalised by the Classical period.

5.4.3. *Coalescence with empty vowel*

Some suffixes in the nominal declension begin with an empty vowel, that is, an empty skeletal slot in a syllable nucleus; to wit, particular allomorphs of the ablative and dative singular, and the nominative, accusative and genitive plural endings (for details see Chapter 6). Because of the relevant allomorphic distributional regularities, these allomorphs are associated only with vowel-final stems. The empty vowel does not induce the prevocalic deletion of back vowels (5.3.2), but is instead filled by the vowel before it via linking to its Root node (irrespective of its quality). In these configurations, the Root node of the preceding vowel spreads onto the empty skeletal slot unless this would produce an association between one Root node and three skeletal slots; that is, with long vowels (in reality only [eː]) the process does not take place and the empty skeletal slot is ultimately deleted. The following examples illustrate an *a*-stem noun in the ablative singular (Figure 28) and in the accusative plural (Figure 29); in the former the suffix is a plain empty skeletal slot, in the latter an empty skeletal slot followed by [s].

Figure 28. AblSing affixation of *a*-stem (e.g. *puella-* → *puellā* 'girl' AblSing)

Figure 29. AccPlur affixation of *a*-stem (*puella-* → *puellās* 'girl' AccPlur)

5.4.4. *Coalescence with placeless nasal*

Whatever its source, a placeless nasal that is preceded by a vowel (but crucially not followed by a vowel in the same word) merges with that vowel to produce a long nasal vowel. As explained elsewhere (cf. 2.2.3, 2.3.1 and 4.6), such a sequence may result from nasal place loss before fricatives or from affixation with an ending consisting of a placeless nasal and nothing else, but it may also be lexical (see below). The placeless nasal is in all cases associated with a skeletal slot; otherwise one could not account for the invariable length of the resulting nasal vowel, and one could not explain the place-assimilated nasal of cliticised forms such as *eandem* 'she, the same' AccSing from the stem *ea-* (cf. 36 in 4.8). For the former, a skeletal slot is needed, for the latter both a skeletal slot and a Root node.

In many words the surface nasal vowel does not alternate with any other segment(s), e.g. *ensis* 'sword', *anser* 'goose', *palam* 'in public'. In theory, the analysis of such forms could go in three directions: (i) the nasal vowel is underlying; (ii) an oral vowel + placeless nasal sequence is underlying; and (iii) an oral vowel + full nasal (i.e. [m] or [n]) sequence is underlying.

Of these, I reject (i) on the basis of economy, for two reasons in particular. One is that most other instances of nasal vowels can arguably be derived from a vowel + nasal consonant sequence, including the *frons* ~ *frondis* 'foliage' type (see 2.3.1) and the accusative singular forms of animate nouns such as *puellam* 'girl' (morphologically with a placeless nasal affix, but phonetically no different from the ending of *palam*). The other is that the non-alternating nasal vowels are invariably long just like their alternating counterparts. Thus I think one would gain practically nothing at the systemic level in exchange for enlarging the underlying vowel inventory with the five nasal vowels.

If one opted for (iii), one would have to decide what the underlying nasal consonant was in each case, or at least in each type. Word-internally, in the *ensis*, *anser* type [n] would be an obvious choice since [n] from other sources actually

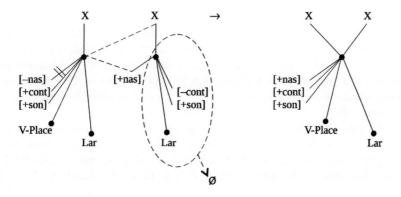

Figure 30. Coalescence with placeless nasal and the representation of a nasal vowel (with place and voice features omitted)

loses its C-Place node before fricatives (4.6). But in this type of words the underlying [n] would absolutely never surface (as opposed to the *frons*-type), which ultimately makes the argument for [n] tenuous and, at a theoretical level, potentially leads to learnability problems.

Word-final nasal vowels are even more problematic with regard to option (iii). They clearly cannot be derived from V[n]#, since such sequences appear on the surface in many words (*pecten* 'comb', *fulmen* 'lightning'). Deriving them from V[m]# – which would replicate their history – is also untenable synchronically in view of the broader category of word-final nasal vowels. These nasal vowels are mostly invariable (the *palam*-type), like those in the *ensis*-type. But final nasal vowels may alternate with a V[n] sequence, mainly in pronouns such as *eandem* (see above), just as the non-final nasal vowels in the *frons ~ frondis* type do. There is, however, no reliable evidence that they ever surfaced as V[m] sequences – perhaps apart from place-assimilated examples before the clitic *-piam*, e.g. *quempiam* 'whoever' AccSing or *quampiam* 'whichever/whatever' FemAccSing.

Since there are thus no grounds for assuming word-final [n] in such words underlyingly, and since assuming a word-final [m] would necessitate processes untypical of [m] elsewhere (i.e. alternation with [n] and with a nasal vowel), the most attractive option is (ii), that is, assuming an oral vowel + placeless nasal sequence underlying word-final nasal vowels. But this also tilts the balance towards assuming the same underlying configuration in the *ensis*-type. In this way no extra machinery is needed in addition to that introduced so far, viz. place assimilation, plus the coalescence process formalised in Figure 30.

It is possible, though not necessary, to hypothesise that all nasals before stops are underlyingly placeless. The phonological rules introduced so far could equally derive the surface forms of all the *frons ~ frondis* type words, regardless of whether the nasal is underlyingly placeless or coronal ([n]). This is because the place of nasals before tautomorphemic stops is always redundant, and place assimilation 1, which operates in a nasal+stop sequence, is independently motivated. The two derivations (both for the NomSing and the GenSing) would look as shown in Figure 31.[225]

If the nasal and the stop are not adjacent underlyingly, that is, there is a morpheme boundary between them, the nasal cannot be underlyingly placeless at the end of lexical stems; as was shown in 4.7, a stem-final [m] triggers the insertion of a labial stop when affixed with [t] or [s] (*comere* → *compsi, comptus* 'comb'), and, of course, pre-vocalic nasals (e.g. *comere*) would be impossible to derive plausibly.

Some aspects of the behaviour of the prefix *con-*, which ends in a placeless nasal, were briefly explained in 4.8; see also 7.2.3.2. The placeless nasal undergoes place assimilation before stops (PA 1) and non-coronal nasals (PA 2); it may also undergo total assimilation to liquids. Before the fricatives [s] and [f]

---

[225] In Figure 31 I use ⟨N⟩ to denote the placeless nasal, a notation I otherwise avoid in order not to evoke the classical notion of archiphoneme (cf. Trubetzkoy 1969: 79 sqq.).

Underlying form:	froNd+s	froNd+is	frond+s	frond+is
voice assimilation (4.2)	froNts	—	fronts	—
t → s / _s (4.3)	froNss	—	fronss	—
degemination (4.5.1)	froNs	—	frons	—
nasal place loss (4.6)	—	—	froNs	—
place assimilation 1 (4.8)	—	frondis	—	—
coalescence	frõ:s	—	frõ:s	—
Surface form:	frõ:s	frondis	frõ:s	frondis

Figure 31. Derivation of nasals before stops: underlyingly placeless vs. full segment; example: *frons ~ frondis* 'foliage' NomSing ~ GenSing

it coalesces with the preceding vowel. Before the glides [j] and [w] it probably coalesces with the vowel just like before fricatives, though the evidence is less clear on this point. The most interesting cases are the combinations of *con-* with vowel-initial stems (e.g. *coire* 'meet'). In these, the placeless nasal cannot acquire a C-Place node from the following segment, since the latter is a vowel; it also cannot coalesce with the preceding vowel, since that would result in a long vowel in the first part of a hiatus, a configuration strictly banned in Classical Latin (on hiatus see 2.3.3). Before [n], contrary to what one would expect, there is no assimilation. Metrical and graphic evidence points to a long vowel and a single [n], as in *cō-nubium* 'marriage'. This is explained in 4.8 as resulting from the properties of the two place assimilation processes; a sequence of a placeless and a coronal nasal simply does not match the structural description of either. What happens is probably coalescence, though the nasality of the vowel was not indicated in the spelling with an extra ⟨n⟩ before the stem-initial ⟨n⟩; in this case the suface representation would be [kõ:nu:biũ:]. The other possibility is that instead of coalescence the placeless nasal (but not its skeletal slot) was simply deleted and the vowel underwent compensatory lengthening, thus resulting in [ko:nu:biũ:]. The latter process would be unparallelled,[226] the former would be in harmony with independently estlablished rules; but I see no way to decide between the two.

5.4.5. The abïēs-pattern

As was seen in 4.5 and in 5.2.2.1, degemination does not lead to compensatory lengthening in Latin (*milets → miless → miles* 'soldier' NomSing). However, three nouns which belong to the same class as *miles* constitute a minor sub-

---

[226] Deletion with compensatory lengthening but without coalescence, that is, without nasalisation of the vowel would be unparallelled within Latin but it would be in harmony with certain cross-linguistically observable patterns. Nasal vowels are not permitted before nasal consonants in French, for instance; if a similar constraint was stipulated for Classical Latin, it would automatically result in non-nasalising compensatory lengthening.

pattern with an interesting phonological quirk, the lengthening of the vowel in the NomSing. These are the following:

(75) The *abies*-words

NomSing	GenSing	gloss
abiēs	*abiĕtis*	'fir-tree'
ariēs	*ariĕtis*	'ram'
pariēs	*pariĕtis*	'wall'

In Latin there are no more -*ieC*-final nominal stems apart from these three plus *hiem(p)s* 'winter' (GenSing *hiemis*), which shows no lengthening and also no loss of the stem-final consonant. The phonological similarity of the three stems is conspicuous, all of them being of the shape (C)*aCiet-*. There does not appear to be any convincing attempt at an explanation of the vowel lengthening (see De Vaan 2008 s.vv. and the references there). One notes, however, that in these three words (and in *hiems*) the appearance of an [i] in the oblique cases, where the stem-final syllable would be open, is precluded on phonological grounds. As was pointed out in 5.2.2.4, an [ii] sequence is ill-formed in Latin: **abiitis as the hypothetical genitive of *abiēs* is impossible in the same way as **sociitas instead of *societas* 'society'. It is at least hypothetically possible that the unexplained lengthening in the NomSing serves as a phonological device to increase the distance between that form and the other forms, since the [e] ~ [i] alternation, which could otherwise contribute to increasing this distance, is excluded.

One might argue that the distance between the NomSing and the other forms is minimal in the case of both noun types that are exceptions to the closed syllable ~ open syllable [e] ~ [i] alternation, namely the *seges*-type and the *lapis*-type (see 5.2.2.1 above), where there is neither qualitative alternation nor quantitative alternation. This is true but it is to be noted that the *seges*-type and the *lapis*-type exceptions are fully arbitrary in the sense that there would be nothing phonologically ill-formed about a hypothetical **lapes NomSing (instead of *lapis*) or a hypothetical **segitis GenSing (instead of *segetis*). These forms simply do not exist — although they could. By contrast, as was explained above, forms like **abiitis, etc. are not only non-existent, they are also impossible, so the lack of a qualitative alternation is not arbitrary in their case. I will make no attempt here to formalise this insight, and given the small number of items involved I cannot say that I have discovered a robust generalisation. Nevertheless there seems to be a pattern here, even if only a minor one.

Another possibility is analogical attraction from ē-stem nouns.[227] In Latin, no word ends in [ies] in any form but many nouns end in [ie:s] in the NomSing. The latter kinds of nouns, however, mostly belong to a different inflectional class called ē-stem or fifth declension (*faciēs* 'face', *aciēs* 'edge', *caesariēs* 'long hair', etc., see Chapter 6) — the only exceptions being *abiēs*, *ariēs* and *pariēs*, in

[227] Thanks to László Kálmán (p.c.), who drew my attention to this possibility.

which the length of the vowel in the NomSing can then potentially be explained with reference to the analogy of ē-stem nouns.

5.5. Conclusion

This chapter has surveyed those phonological processes that affect vowels in Latin. Three major types were distinguished, qualitative alternations, vowel–zero alternations and length alternations. As in the case of consonantal rules, it is the case with vowel processes too that they show varying degrees of morphologi-sation (or lexicalisation): some are practically automatic and nearly exception-less, but some have a narrower range with more exceptions and are more sensitive to morphological structure. The latter type of rules arguably verge on allomorphy (e.g. the lengthening described in 5.4.2) and could be analysed as not part of phonology on a narrower interpretation.

Many of the rules introduced in this as well as the previous chapter will play an important role in the following chapter, which surveys the morphophonology of regular inflection.

6

THE INFLECTIONAL MORPHOLOGY OF CLASSICAL LATIN

6.1. INTRODUCTION

In Classical Latin both the nominal and the verbal inflectional system involves intricate patterns of allomorphy, which are the basis of the traditional classification of verbs into four conjugations, and of nouns/adjectives into five declensions (i.e. paradigm classes).[228] This chapter attempts to give a comprehensive and systematic description which is theoretically informed and which articulates an important insight regarding the relation between phonology and morphology. It is demonstrated that the apparent variety found in the inflectional system can be reduced to patterns of mostly binary allomorphy which are phonologically conditioned by the stem-final segment. The conditioning appears to be a function of a scale of vocalicness, which is here argued to be nothing else but the sonority scale of vowels.[229]

A crucial observation with respect to the vocalic scale – in relation to the allomorphy conditioned by it – is contiguity: if two environments that are not adjacent on the scale select the same allomorph, then all the environments between the two select the same allomorph. Without contiguity, the scale would be of no descriptive or theoretical significance whatever. The vocalic scale is the same for verbal and nominal morphology, and it is non-arbitrary in the sense that it corresponds to vowel height. The relation between this vocalic scale and the sonority scale is taken up in section 6.5. To anticipate a point to be made there, it is reasonable to identify the vocalic scale with the sonority scale of vowels, but for sonority to play such a pervasive role in inflectional morphology is an unusual feature not previously highlighted in the literature (though the traditional classifications of Latin inflectional patterns show that the intuition was certainly present).

---

[228] Portions of this chapter first appeared, in somewhat different form, in Cser (2015).

[229] The application of this idea to nominal inflection is explored in Spaelti (2004) and, with very minor modifications, in Emonds & Spaelti (2005), an upgraded extension of the former, and then revisited in Emonds (2014). My work, including Cser (2015) and the present chapter takes broader scope than either of these in giving a unified account of nominal and verbal inflection, and also treats significant aspects of nominal morphology (e.g. *i*-stems) differently. Details of the analysis that are identical to Spaelti's (e.g. the phonological formalisation of certain endings) are pointed out in due course.

In this work, stem is generally defined as the infectum and the perfectum stem for verbs and the portion preceding the case endings for nouns or adjectives. This is in harmony with the traditional use of these terms in Latin linguistics. Most verbs also have a third stem, on which no finite forms are based, but which has an important function in the formation of other participles, a defective nominal form (called supine) and several derived nouns, adjectives and verbs. In this chapter I will not be concerned with any forms based on the third stem.

It will be seen that the traditional classification into stem types, which is based on etymological and comparative considerations, is insufficient for a theoretically informed description. My phonological specification of nominal as well as verbal infectum stems, more precisely of the stem-final segments, will depart slightly from what is found in the descriptive literature. The phonological specification of the endings will be, at certain points, radically different from it. This is mainly because my characterisations are not etymologically based but are meant to capture synchronic patterns and alternations. Relevant differences will be highlighted and explained at the appropriate points.

Importantly, the putative morphological status of the stem-final segment proves to be irrelevant (cf. the discussion in 1.4). In some cases systemic considerations clearly indicate a morphological formative (e.g. when the $\bar{e}$ or $\bar{a}$ regularly appears in the infectum-based forms of the verb but nowhere else, or when the perfectum stem ends in a v or s not found in any non-perfectum-based verb forms; or when nominal/adjectival stem-final a and o/u alternate as a function of gender). In many cases there is no compelling reason to assume any morphological function. The point is that morphophonologically there is no difference whatsoever between identical stem-final segments, the only exceptions being the deletability of stem-final v and s in perfectum-based verb forms, but these may simply be cases of optional affixation (see 6.2.3).

As a consequence, I believe that denoting stem-final segments as e.g. thematic vowels (as in Aronoff 1994) or any other morphological or quasi-morphological entity is of little use. As another consequence I will generally not be concerned with the formal relations between the three stems of a verb. This relation shows extensive variation from lexeme to lexeme, and generalisations can be made only in certain types of cases, and even then of restricted validity. Because of this, I take it without further argumentation that this relation is lexically specified for each verb. A third consequence is that even where all three verb stems show concatenative affixation, and thus a common morphological 'core' could be formally isolated, I will refrain from identifying such entities as morphological units of any kind.

A case in point is the verb *monere* 'warn': infectum stem *monē-*, perfectum stem *monu-*, third stem *monit-* with the productive or at least frequent affixes -$\bar{e}$-, -*u*-, -*(i)t*-, respectively. The common unit *mon*- can be easily isolated as a root, and this is indeed the well justified etymological practice in Indo-European linguistics (e.g. Baldi 2002: 381, passim, de Vaan 2008 s.vv. *memini*, *mens* and *moneo*). But in a synchronic analysis of Latin there is no such straightforward segmentation for most verbs, so an analysis of this kind is simply impracticable in general; furthermore, it would lead to irrelevant information at best, since the morphology of *monere* does not differ from that of e.g. *delere* 'delete' in the infectum (where the stem-final [e:] is definitely not an affix), or from *fui* 'be' in the perfectum, where the [u] is again not an affix. What is presented here does not depend on assumptions about the morphological structure of stems, or about the relations between the stems. References will be made to morphological exponence but only where a fairly obvious agglutinating structure can be discerned.[230]

The structure of this chapter is the following. In section 6.2 the patterns of allomorphy found in verbal inflection are presented under three main headings after a general discussion of the structure of verbal inflection (affixes immediately following the infectum stem in 6.2.2, affixes immediately following the perfectum stem in 6.2.3, affixes following extended stems in 6.2.4). In section 6.3 nominal inflection follows, with a lengthier discussion of the nominative and accusative singular (6.3.2), then all the other cases (6.3.3). The morphophonological analysis in 6.4 summarily presents the relation between the vocalic scale and all allomorphy. In 6.5 the relation of the vocalic scale to sonority is explored.

6.2. ALLOMORPHY IN THE VERBAL INFLECTION

6.2.1. *The general structure of verbal inflection*

In Latin, all finite verb forms are based on either the infectum stem or the perfectum stem. In addition, two infinitives and two participles are also based on the infectum stem, and another infinitive on the perfectum stem. These two stems can be followed by a variety of elements in a concatenative fashion. Figure 32 gives a conspectus of all the forms based on these two stems. The morphemes can combine left-to-right as the lines indicate; morphemes in the same column do not combine with each other. Figure 32 also lists all the allomorphs that the post-stem formatives have.[231]

---

[230] That said, there is a wealth of literature on the formation of the three verb stems and the relations between them. Of the diachronic literature Meiser (1998; 2003) stand out; of synchronic analyses Matthews (1974), Aronoff (1994), though I disagree with the latter's analysis of the infectum, and Steriade (2012), which is specifically concerned with the relation between the perfectum and the third stems and presents an OT analysis of that relation.

[231] The passive perfect and pluperfect in Latin consists entirely of participle + *esse* 'be' combinations. Not being morphological constructions these will not be discussed here. I will also not cover the handful of verbs that show irregular allomorphic patterns (e.g. *ferre* 'take', *esse* 'be', *velle* 'want'). Of the simple imperatives, only the active endings are included, since the passive (singular and plural) endings are identical to the active infinitive ending and the passive 2PLUR personal ending, respectively. There is no discernible difference in the meaning of simple imperatives and what are traditionally called future imperatives. For a descriptive conspectus of all regular forms see Clackson (2011).

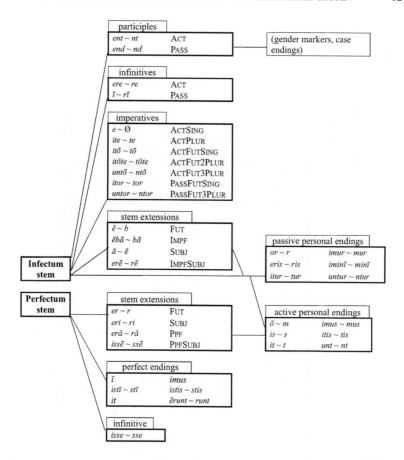

Figure 32. The general structure of Latin verb forms based on the infectum and the perfectum stems

First I look at the distribution of the allomorphs of formatives immediately following the infectum stem. This means mood and tense formatives (which I here call stem extensions), infinitival and participial affixes, and personal endings with no stem extensions intervening, among them the imperative endings. Then I look at those affixes that can immediately follow the perfectum stem. Finally I look at the personal endings following extended stems (both infectum and perfectum).

6.2.2. Affixes immediately following the infectum stem

On the left of Tables 10 and 11, infectum stem types are listed according to their final segment (consonant, high vowels, non-high vowels, with one example for each type). The columns are numbered for reference. The infectum stem

Table 10. Type 1 affix variants immediately following the infectum stem[232]

Type 1	1	2	3	4	5	6	7
	is, it, imus, itis, ite, itō, itōte,	*e*	*itur, imur, iminī, itor*	*eris*	*ere*	*erē-*	*ī*
ag-/cap-							
tribu-							
ferī-							
vidē-							
amā-							
	s, t, mus, tis, te, tō, tōte	Ø	*tur, mur, minī, tor*	*ris*	*re*	*rē-*	*rī*
	act. p. e. 23SING, 12PLUR; IMP2PLUR, IMPFUTSING, IMPFUT2PLUR	IMP2SING	pass. p. e. 3SING, 12PLUR; PASSIMPFUTSING	pass. p. e. 2SING	ACTINF	IMPFSUBJ	PASSINF

extensions *-erē-*, *-ē-*, *-ēbā-*, *-ā-* as well as the personal endings are distributed between the two tables. Stem extensions can be followed by personal endings, and such constructions will be discussed in 6.2.4. The 1SING ending is added for completeness, but it only appears as *-ō*, never as *-m* (actually, a placeless nasal) when immediately following the infectum stem. The gender markers and the case endings which can follow the participial affixes are discussed under nominal morphology in section 6.3. The number (1) in Table 11 refers to the phonological rule of Prevocalic back vowel deletion repeated from 5.3.2 in the note.

It is to be observed that one specific stem type (here represented by *cap-/capī-*) is found in two different forms and in two different cells in the two tables. Verbs belonging to this type are traditionally called *i*-stems; I regard

---

[232]The stems on the left belong to the verbs *agere* 'do', *tribuere* 'distribute', *capere* 'catch', *ferire* 'hit', *videre* 'see', *amare* 'love'.

Table 11. Type 2 and other affix variants immediately following the infectum stem

Type 2 & other	8	9	10	11	12	13	14
	ē-	*ēbā-*	*ā-*	*ent-*	*end-*	*unt, untur, untō, untor*	*ō*
ag-							
tribu-							
ferī-/capī-							
vidē-							
amā-			(1)				(1)
	b-	*bā-*	*ē-*	*nt-*	*nd-*	*nt, ntur, ntō, ntor*	*(m)*
	FUT	IMPF	SUBJ	ACTPART	PASSPART	p. e. 3PLUR; IMPFUT3PLUR	p. e. 1SING

Note (1) to Table 11: Prevocalic deletion of back vowels (5.3.2): [a (o)] → Ø / _V (in derived environments), thus *amā+ē-* → *amē-* and *amā+ō* → *amō*.

them as systematically heteroclitic. This populous group is basically a subset of *ī*-stems which are inflected as C-stems (i.e. without the *ī*) in certain paradigmatic cells. They do not have a single form that is not identical either with the corresponding C-stem form or with the corresponding *ī*-stem form; hence their assigment to the *ag*-type and the *ferī*-type in the two tables, respectively. The distribution of the two stem-variants is very systematic; apart from one or two lexical items, every verb in this class shows C-stem variants in the same set of forms and *ī*-stem forms in the complementary set of forms.

As can be seen, there are two major types of allomorphy in terms of environment and there are two idiosyncratic ones, namely affixes 10 and 14, which show allomorphic distributions different from all other affixes. The two major patterns are represented by 1–7 on the one hand (henceforth I will refer to these as Type 1 allomorphy) and 8, 9, 11–13 on the other (henceforth Type 2 allomorphy). Both Type 1 and Type 2 allomorphy share a common feature in terms of environment: these affixes select one variant after consonants and [u] (*ag-*, *tribu-*),[233] and another variant after non-high vowels (*vidē-*, *amā-*). The difference between Type 1 and Type 2 is which allomorph is selected after (short and long) [i]. In Type 1, the variant after [i(:)] is the one selected after the non-high vowels, in Type 2 the variant is the one selected after consonants and [u]. This is shown schematically in Figure 33.

As will be seen shortly, these two types recur elsewhere in the verbal paradigms, and Type 2 is found in nominal morphology too.

As can be observed in the two tables, there are two recurring phonological features that separate Type 1 affixes from Type 2 affixes. One concerns syllable weight: the vowel-initial variants of the two types, seen at the top of both tables, are light vs. heavy syllables, respectively (in the case of polysyllabic affixes such as *-imus* this refers to the first syllable). The only exception to this generalisation is the passive infinitive ending *-ī*, which constitutes a heavy syllable but is a Type 1 suffix. Why syllable weight should correlate so clearly with the environment, and crucially with *ī*-final stems is not clear; and, as we shall see below, affixes following the perfectum stem show an inverse relation, viz. light syllables are Type 2 and heavy syllables are Type 1.

The other feature that distinguishes the two types is the initial vowel of the vowelled variant. These show [i] and [e] in Type 1, with the two vowels in complementary distribution: [e] only before [r] and word-finally. To this

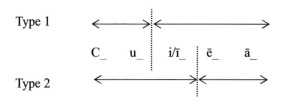

Figure 33. The environments of Type 1 vs. Type 2 allomorphy

---

[233] In fact, it is possible to argue that [u]-final stems are not vowel-final at all but consonant-final (phonologically — and perhaps phonetically — [uw]). One point to consider is that they absolutely never pattern differently from consonant-final stems proper. Another is that no infectum stem ends in [o] or [o:], which looks like an accidental gap since all other vowel qualities are attested. If [u] and [u:] are also added, one is at least able to make a more general statement: infectum stems never end in a round vowel. The third point is the marginal existence of a single 'true' *u*-stem verb, *fore* 'be', with the [u] showing the lowering of the high vowel before [r] (*fu-* → *fore*, see 5.2.2.2). The only attested forms of the verb *fore* are the *-re*, *-rē-* and *-ā-*suffixed ones, and the former two show their vowel-less variants. The idea that what are called *u*-stems (and also *u*-final perfectum stems) are to be analysed as [uw]-final is found in different versions, underpinned by different arguments, in Juret (1913: 200), Moralejo (1991) and Touratier (2005: 68 sqq.), among others. If this analysis is adopted it follows that the difference between '*u*-stem' verbs and 'real' *v*-stems such as *vivere* 'live' is merely orthographic: [w] is not indicated in the writing of verbs like *tribuere* but it is in verbs like *vivere*. For a conspectus of the history of all *u*-stem verbs see Szemerényi (1980).

generalisation there is no exception; the passive infinitive ending -ī falls naturally within the [i]-initial category.

It is therefore at least a hypothetical possibility that underlyingly the vowel-initial variants of all Type 1 affixes begin with [i], which regularly turns into [e] word-finally (in the imperative, cf. 5.2.2.3) and before [r] (in -eris, -ere and -erē-, cf. 5.2.2.2). This would very simply explain why the vowel-initial variants of Type 1 affixes avoid ī-final stems, the sequence [ii] being disallowed (cf. 5.2.2.4), and thus the difference between Type 1 and Type 2 affixes would be reduced to a phonological difference between [i]-initial affixes (including -ī) and everything else.

There are two possible objections to such an analysis. One is that the lowering of [i] into [e] is arguably a rule that operates in derived environments, and no derived environment in the relevant sense is created here because both the target and the environment of the process are inside the affixes -eris, -ere and -erē-. The other problem is the following: if, as was hinted at in 5.2.2.4, the appearance of [e] in an affix can be motivated by the ban on [ii] (e.g. soci_etas 'fellowship' vs. novi_tas 'novelty'), why is the same not possible for forms like ferīre (i.e. why could it not be **feriere)? The putative parallel is then lost and the explanation is not as general as would be desirable.

However, neither of these objections presents unsurmountable difficulties. As for the first, it was pointed out in 5.2.2.2 that surface [ir] sequences are practically confined to initial syllables; it is therefore not inconceivable that the lowering of [i] before [r] was reanalysed as a pattern that generally obtains in non-initial syllables and could thus encompass suffixes. And as for the second objection, it is not infrequently seen even in one and the same language that more than one operation is made use of to avoid a certain phonological configuration (e.g. long vowels in hiatus are either shortened or followed by a consonant that fills the hiatus, cf. 2.3.3). If one accepts this argumentation, the difference between Type 1 and Type 2 affixes simply boils down to the independently motivated avoidance of [ii] sequences.

6.2.3. Affixes immediately following the perfectum stem

6.2.3.1. Classification of affixes

The affixes that can be adjacent to the perfectum stem fall into three categories functionally. Like with the infectum, there are mood and tense formatives (stem extensions), there is an infinitive ending, and there is a set of active personal endings found only in the perfect indicative paradigm. (As will be seen later, stem extensions can be followed by active personal endings identical to those found in infectum-based forms.)

The perfect indicative paradigm requires some explanation. These endings are a heterogeneous and partly idiosyncratic set (also etymologically problematic to a certain extent, see Leumann 1977: 606–8; Clackson 2007: 120–8; Clackson & Horrocks 2007: 98–101; Weiss 2009: 390 sqq.). Two of the endings are not

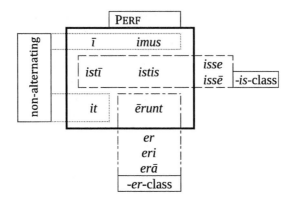

Figure 34. Formal types of affixes immediately following the perfectum stem

found anywhere else in the verbal morphology (1Sing -ī, 2Sing -istī), two are the same as their counterparts elsewhere (3Sing -it, 1Plur -imus), and two look as if they consisted of a stem extension and a personal ending seen elsewhere (2Plur -istis, 3Plur -ērunt[234]). The unusual composition of this paradigm warrants its separate placement in Figure 32.

In terms of form and alternations, these affixes (including the stem extensions, the infinitive ending and the perfect endings) are traditionally classified into two sets with self-explanatory names, the *is*-class and the *er*-class (e.g. Leumann 1977: 608–9). As a third class one may add that of non-alternating suffixes (comprising the perfect endings -ī, -it and -imus, though it will be shown below that even this group is heterogeneous). This tripartite formal division cross-classifies the functional categories, as is shown in Figure 34.

In the following sections I look at the patterns of alternation in affixes adjacent to the perfectum stem.

6.2.3.2. The general pattern of affix alternations

The alternations of the affixes are conditioned by the phonological shape of the stems, in particular by their final segments. As we saw above, in the infectum it is a lexical property of verbs what the final segment of the stem is (both when

---

[234] The suffix *-ērunt* has two further variants: earlier *-ēre* and *-ĕrunt*. Of these three *-ērunt* appears to be continued by the Romance languages, and since *-ĕrunt* and *-ērunt* are not graphically distinguished, it is not entirely clear what their respective incidence was. In classical poetry, however, *-ērunt* was the norm, although there are quite a few occurrences of *-ĕrunt* too. There was variation also in the length of the [i] vowel in the *-eri-* and *-er*-affixed forms, e.g. *fec-eri-mus* PerfSubj 'we should have done' and *fec-er-imus* FutPerf 'we will have done', where both are found with short as well as long penultimate vowels (*fecerimus / fecerīmus*). This has to do with the different prehistory of the two stem extensions, the perfect subjunctive originally including [i:]. For some poetic data see Platnauer (1951: 53–6).

THE INFLECTIONAL MORPHOLOGY OF CLASSICAL LATIN

that segment can be analysed as an affix and when it cannot). This gives ample room for the conditioning of various kinds of allomorphy. In the perfectum the possibilities are much more restricted: perfectum stems in Latin end either in a consonant or in [u].[235] There are no other vowel-final perfectum stems apart from two: *ī-* 'go' (e.g. *iī* 'I went', *ierat* 'he had gone', also in prefixed forms such as *abiī* 'I left' or *periī* 'I perished', etc.), and *desī-* 'desist' (*desiī, desierat,* etc.), the latter with many postclassical instances of *v*-addition (e.g. *desīverat*).

What leads to different environments conditioning the appearance of different affix variants in the set of perfectum-based forms is primarily an optional but very frequently occurring process of *v*-deletion. The final [w] of perfectum stems such as *nōv-* 'know' may delete, creating a vowel-final truncated stem, which then selects the affix variant without the initial vowel:

(76) Perfectum *v*-deletion
  nōv-ērunt ~ nō-runt 'they knew'
  nōv-isse ~ nō-sse 'know' PERFINF

The process of *v*-deletion is variable and subject to a combination of lexical and morphophonological conditions. One important factor is that [w] can only delete if it is an affix, not if it is part of the lexical make-up of the verb (this is clear from the data enumerated in Leumann 1977: 598–601). Though very similar to *nōv-*, the final [w] of *mōv-* 'move' almost never deletes, and *fōv-* 'warm' is absolutely unattested with deletion.[236] Similarly, the [w] of *probāv-* 'approve' has a strong tendency to delete (**probavisti* 2SING is unattested, including all prefixed forms!), whereas that of *fāv-* 'favour' is stable (cf. the infectum stems *probā-* vs. *favē-*). But even where the [w] is an affix, it is lexically specific whether it deletes or not; e.g. in *crēv-* 'separate' it does, in *sprēv-* 'despise' it does not.

Another factor is that *v*-deletion is much more frequent before -*is*-class affixes than before -*er*-class affixes, and it does not normally occur before the three non-alternating affixes.[237] The difference in the capacity of -*is*-class vs. -*er*-class

---

[235] The stem-final segment can often, but not always, be analysed as an affix. The most frequent analysable perfectum stem-forming affixes are -*v*-, -*u*- and -*s*-. Of these, -*v*- and -*u*- are in complementary distribution: -*v*- only occurs after long vowels, -*u*- only after consonants. Interestingly, stem-final [w] is always preceded by a long vowel even if it is not an affix.

[236] For *nōv-* with -*is*-class affixes, the ratio of deleted forms in the corpus I used is 96.3 per cent, for *mōv-* (including prefixed forms) only 3.6 per cent. In *nōv-*, the [w] is an affix that forms the perfectum stem (the infectum stem is *nōsc-*), whereas in *mōv-* and *fōv-* it is lexically part of the verb (cf. the infectum stems *movē-* and *fovē-*). The restriction of *v*-deletion to suffixes can be seen as an effect of the derived environment condition (see 1.4) if the process is phonological; if, alternatively, it is part of the morphology, it can be described as optional affixation.

[237] The deletion of [w] before the two singular non-alternating suffixes is possible only if the truncated perfectum stem ends in [i], e.g. *petii* 'I strove for', *nequiit* '(s)he was unable to' (the full forms being *petivi* and *nequivit,* respectively); more will be said about this later. On putative examples involving *v*-deletion and the concomitant appearance of vowelless variants of the affixes -*it* and -*imus,* see Leumann (1977: 599 sqq.).

affixes to induce *v*-deletion perhaps has to do with the large number of affixes including [r] overall in the Latin verbal paradigms: *v*-deleted forms, which also automatically lack the initial vowel of alternating suffixes, are at great risk of being confused with other verb forms. Add to this that, as my own statistical counts prove (Appendix 1), [r] is the most frequent consonant word-internally. By contrast, the [ss] and the [st] sequences of the *-is*-class affixes are unique to them and mark their categories (PPFSUBJ and INF, and second person, respectively) very saliently.

Table 12 gives a preliminary presentation of the kinds of allomorphy that the alternating affixes following perfectum stems display.[238] It is clear that the two classes of affixes take part in precisely those two types of allomorphy that were identified for the affixes following the infectum stem, with [u] always patterning with the consonants (therefore perhaps [uw] rather than [u]), and [i(:)] patterning either with the consonants and [u(w)] or with the non-high vowels. Thus, Figure 33 can be repeated here virtually unchanged, with only [o:] added to the environments (Figure 35).

As can be seen, the generalisation made about Type 1 vs. Type 2 suffixes above is true in the context of the perfectum stem as well as in that of the infectum stem. Since only Type 1 affixes begin with [i], and the only difference

Table 12. Affix variants immediately following the perfectum stem (preliminary)

	-isse -issē- -istī -istis	-er- -erā- -eri- -ērunt
-C_	nōv-isse amāv-isse tetig-isse	nōv-ērunt amāv-ērunt tetig-ērunt
-u_	monu-isse	monu-ērunt
-i/ī_	abī-sse	abi-ērunt
-V[–high]_	nō-sse complē-sse amā-sse	nō-runt complē-runt amā-runt
	-sse -ssē- -stī -stis	-r- -rā- -ri- -runt

[238] The examples are *no(v)-* 'know', *ama(v)-* 'love', *tetig-* 'touch', *monu-* 'warm', *abi-* 'leave', *comple(v)-* 'complete' (the respective present inifinitives are *noscere, amare, tangere, monēre, abire* and *complēre*). The forms in the shaded bottom part of the chart are usually referred to as contracted in Latin linguistics (e.g. Baldi 2002: 381; Clackson & Horrocks 2007: 280). I do not follow this practice and reserve the term contraction for a different set of phenomena (e.g. for a reduction in the number of syllables in certain prefixed forms, see 7.2.1).

in the behaviour of the two types is which of their variants combines with [i(:)]-final stems, the patterns of allomorphy they display can again be reduced to the avoidance of [ii] sequences (but for a caveat in 6.2.3.4). The only difference *vis-à-vis* the infectum is that in the perfectum-based forms it is not possible to synchronically derive the [e] of the *er*-endings from underlying [i], since that would erroneously imply that the choice of the vowelless variants of these endings after [i]-final stems is at least a possibility; see present infinitive *abi-re* 'to leave' as opposed to perfect *abi-erunt* 'they left' or pluperfect *abi-erat* 'he had left', with **abi-runt, **abi-rat categorically excluded.

6.2.3.3. *Vowel deletion after [s]*

One minor point of complication involves [s]-final perfectum stems (excluding -[ls]-, -[rs]-) combining with *is*-affixes. In more than just a handful of cases the vowelless affix variant appears, and the number of adjacent [s]s is reduced. Thus *derexisti* ~ *derexti* 'arrange' Perf2Sing, *divisisse* ~ *divisse* 'divide' PerfInf, *accessistis* ~ *accestis* 'approach' Perf2Plur, *admisisse* ~ *admisse* 'send to' PerfInf, and many others. On the face of it this looks like the loss of an [is] sequence specifically after [s] in these particular constructions (as is the traditional account, see Leumann 1977: 598). It is, however, more economical to analyse the disappearance of the vowel as being the same allomorphic variation as that seen after vowel-final stems, and the disappearance of [s] as resulting from an independently motivated phonological process of degemination (4.5.1).[239] In this case we do not need any extra processes such as an ad hoc [sis] > [s] reduction – though we need to stipulate the somewhat odd context [s]_ for the otherwise postvocalic morpheme variants.

An interesting consequence of this allomorphic choice is that since the perfectum marker -*s*- itself is deleted, in morphological terms the two transparent, agglutinating perfectum markers -*v*- and -*s*- (but apparently only these) are, in fact, optional. It is not, however, the case that -*s*- is simply optionally deleted before the allomorphic choice is made, since that would result is forms like **derecisti instead of *derexti*. The postvocalic suffix allomorph is chosen in the position after the -*s*-, and after that the -*s*- itself is deleted. With -*v*- it is different, since that ending is always preceded by a vowel, so the choice of the postvocalic suffix allomorph is inevitable after *v*-deletion.

6.2.3.4. *Hiatus and i-final perfectum stems*

Those perfectum stems that are [i]-final (whether truncated or not) present minor issues in connection with hiatus that merit a brief excursus. One fact to note is that – fully in line with the general rule of hiatus, see 5.4.1 – if a stem ending in

---

[239] Note that in *accestis* the rule deletes two [s]s.

-*is*-class (=Type 1)

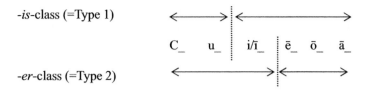

-*er*-class (=Type 2)

Figure 35. The environments of -*is*-class vs. -*er*-class allomorphy

long [iː] is followed by the vowel-initial suffixes, the [iː] shortens: *finīv-erat* but *finĭ-erat* 'he had finished'; cf. *finī-sse* PERFINF.

Another, somewhat more complicated, point to note is that with [i]-final stems, especially if they do not result from the truncation of [iːw]-final stems, the choice of the vowelled variant is marginally possible with the -*is*-class too: *abiisse* next to the majority *abisse,* etc. forms. Morphologically this represents nothing but a minor variation within the pattern described above. Phonologically it is more tantalising, however; forms like *abiisse,* though marginal in terms of numbers, clearly contradict the generalisation that a sequence of two short [i]s is forbidden in Latin (we do not have even marginal ***sociitas,* etc.).

One way to circumvent this irregularity would be to claim that ⟨ii⟩ was simply a way to write [iː] and so ⟨abiisse⟩ and ⟨abisse⟩ are plain spelling variants representing [abiːsse], the expected (morpho)phonological form. While we cannot say with absolute certainty that ⟨ii⟩ never represented [iː] in such (or in other) cases, it would be incongruous with our knowledge of the history of Latin writing, and also plainly contradicted by several attestations in poetic texts where ⟨ii⟩ sequences are disyllabic.[240] Thus we must conclude that in at least some cases ⟨ii⟩ represented [ii].

Another way out would be to claim that the second [i] in these sequences was long; in that case it would not contradict the ban on **[ii]. However, there is no evidence whatsoever for the length of the [i] of the -*is*-suffixes, and etymological considerations clearly point to a short vowel.[241]

A third way of looking at these forms concentrates on word stress. If one considers where stress occurs, the *abiisse*-type is markedly different from the

---

[240] Cf. the hexameter line Stat. *Theb.* 10.237: *(numina) qui fractos superi rediistis ad Argos* 'What gods are ye, who have turned again to Argos in her distress?' (translation from Mozley 1928), where *rediistis* must scan as four syllables (light–light–heavy–light).

[241] Diachronically the [is] part and the [er] part of the suffixes in question is identical, differentiated by rhotacism ([s] > [r] / V_V) and pre-r lowering ([i] > [e] / _[r]). Though both rules are arguably present in the synchronic phonology of Latin (see 4.4 and 5.2.2.2), I would not want to derive these perfectum suffixes from a common underlying form because in order to create a derived environment for rhotacism (a lexical rule in Classical Latin) one would need to further analyse the stem extensions as composites, which in the end would simply replicate the accepted etymological analysis (see e.g. Baldi 2002: 387 sqq.). Such a synchronic analysis would also lead to problems in differentiating between infectum and perfectum affixes, see the argument in the final paragraph of 6.2.3.2.

societas-type. In nouns such as the latter, stress can simply never fall on the alternating short vowel. In the NomSing it falls on the vowel before it (*nóvitas, socíetas*), in all other forms it falls on the vowel following it (AccSing *novitátem, societátem*, DatAblPlur *novitátibus, societátibus*, etc.). By contrast, in the perfectum-based verb forms with -*is*-type suffixes stress falls on the [i] in question in seven out of the nine possible forms (*abiísse, abiíssem, rediísses, abiísset, rediíssent, rediísti, rediístis*).[242] The only forms in which they could possibly fall elsewhere are the PpfSubj1Plur and PpfSubj2Plur *redissémus, abissétis*. But such forms ending in ⟨iissemus⟩ or ⟨iissetis⟩ (i.e. including a sequence of two unstressed short [i]s) are not attested apart from a single instance of *obiissemus* (in Tertullian's *De ieiunio*) in the entire corpus. Whether the absence of such forms is statistically significant I cannot establish, given the relatively small number of the relevant forms overall and given that the 1Plur and 2Plur verb forms are in general rarer than third person or 1Sing forms. But at least tentatively one could say that the ban on **[ii] is categorical only with respect to unstressed vowels; an [ií] sequence is marginally possible – though in the majority of such cases the vowel-less allomorph is selected by the stem and so no sequence of vowels results.

6.2.3.5. *The non-alternating suffixes*

The three remaining suffixes 1Sing -*ī*, 3Sing -*it* and 1Plur -*imus*, which I earlier termed non-alternating, present special problems. The data are somewhat messy, with textual editions reflecting manuscript variation, and their interpretation is not always straightforward, but the main thrust of the evidence seems to be the following.

1Sing -*ī* and 3Sing -*it* are categorically non-alternating, and *v*-deletion before them is possible only if the vowel preceding the [w] is [iː]; thus, *audīvi(t) ~ audii(t)* 'hear',[243] *finīvit ~ finiit* 'finish', but only *novi(t)* 'know', *amavi(t)* 'love', etc. (This may reflect the analogical pull of the only truly vowel-final perfectum stems *ī*- 'go' and *desī*- 'desist', but is perhaps simply the residue of a well-known earlier sound change that deleted [w] between identical vowels.) As is often seen in morphophonological variation in Latin, individual verbs of a similar phonological shape show differing ratios of truncated vs. non-truncated forms, and a variety of lexical factors appears to play a role.[244] Where the perfectum stem ends in [iː] with no original [w] at all (i.e. *ī*- together with prefixed forms, and *desī*-), one finds invariable -*ii(t)*: *abii(t), redii(t), desii(t)*, with very rare, largely postclassical

---

[242] This list includes forms of *ire* 'go' with two different prefixes because no single verb has all the forms in question attested.

[243] As a famous example note Vergil's extensive use of both *audivit* (metrically heavy–heavy–light) and *audiit* (heavy–light–light) in his *Aeneid*.

[244] For instance, *petere* 'strive for' mostly has truncated *petii(t)*, but its prefixed forms prefer the untruncated variants (*repetivi* 'I struck again', etc.).

secondary *v*-additions (*perivit* in Apuleius, *desivit* once in Quintilian, then several times in the Church Fathers). On some occasions the spelling only has one ⟨i⟩ which may scan long in poetry.[245] When these can be taken at face value, they represent genuine cases of vowel contraction, which makes them doubly exceptional (contraction plus vowel length before final [t]). At the same time, uncontracted *abiit*-type 3SING forms are also exceptional in that they contain an [ii] sequence within which neither vowel is stressed; but in verse, the metre usually makes it clear that forms like *abiit* are indeed trisyllabic. Note that for some poets in such constructions a long suffix vowel was a possible option depending on metrical exigencies (i.e. -*īt* instead of -*iīt*, see Castillo Herrera 2009 for a conspectus of the data). 1SING forms such as *abiī* are unproblematic because the second [i] is always long in them.

Before 1PLUR -*imus* *v*-deletion is almost completely unattested, even with -[i:w]-final stems. This means that this suffix can only be preceded by consonants, [u] or the [i:] of *ī*- 'go' and *dēsī*- 'desist'. After consonants and [u] no suffix ever shows a vowel-less variant. After the [i:] of *ī*- and all its compounds, however, -*imus* drops the initial [i] quite categorically (*īmus, abīmus, obīmus, redīmus, exīmus* with rare instances of *adiimus, periimus*) in spite of the resulting homophony with the corresponding present forms. With *dēsī*- there are far fewer forms in the corpus: one single *desīmus*, six occurrences of *desiimus* (and eleven of *desīvimus*, all postclassical). One would expect the usual form to be *desīmus*, all the more so since this would not coincide with the present *desinimus* — but apparently here we have to do with the odd counterexample again, similarly to the two instances of *repetiimus* for the default form *repetīvimus*. So, revising the categorisation given above, one might reclassify -*imus* as a semi-alternating or marginally alternating affix. Another way of capturing its special status is that it is actually an alternating affix (Type 1), just like *is*-class affixes in general, but for an independent reason (viz. the impossibility of *v*-deletion before it) it only occurs in a restricted set of environments and can never follow a non-high vowel.[246]

At this point it is useful to present a small but particularly instructive piece of textual philology, which illustrates the nature of the data we work with. When looking for evidence for the behaviour of -*imus* in the corpus, I came across a contrast between *petĭmus* ('we strive for') and *petīmus* ('we strove for') within a single work, Lucanus's *Pharsalia*.[247] In theory, this could be a contrast between a present and a perfect form, not otherwise visible in writing but highlighted in this case by the metre. The interpretation of the perfect form would then be *v*-deletion of *petīv*- (*contra* the generalisation above) and vowelless -*mus*. However, the critical apparatus of the Teubner edition (Shackleton Bailey 1997:

---

[245] E.g. Verg. *Aen.* 9.418: *it hasta Tago per tempus utrumque* 'the javelin went through both Tagus' temples'.

[246] Note, however, the celebrated pre-classical hapax *nōmus* for *nōvimus* 'we know', found in a fragment attributed to the early poet Ennius.

[247] Also known as *Bellum civile;* the occurrences are *petĭmus* in 4.362, 7.803, 8.441, 9.878, *petīmus* in 9.430.

Table 13. Affix variants immediately following the perfectum stem (revised and extended from Table 12)

	-isse -issē- -istī -istis	-er- -erā- -eri- -ērunt	-imus	-ī -it
-C_	nōv-isse amāv-isse audīv-isse tetig-isse	nōv-ērunt amāv-ērunt audīv-ērunt tetig-ērunt	nōv-imus amāv-imus audīv-imus tetig-imus	nōv-it amāv-it audīv-it tetig-it
-s_	(dīvīs-(s)se) dīvīs-isse	dīvīs-ērunt	dīvīs-imus	dīvīs-it
-u_	monu-isse	monu-ērunt	monu-imus	monu-it
non-truncated -i/ī_	abī-sse (abi-isse)	abi-ērunt	abī-mus	abi-it
truncated -ī_	audī-sse (audi-isse)	audi-ērunt		audi-it
-V[–high]_ (always truncated)	nō-sse complē-sse amā-sse	nō-runt complē-runt amā-runt		
	-sse -ssē- -stī -stis	-r- -rā- -ri- -runt	-mus	

241) makes it clear that the manuscripts have four different readings for the end of the hexameter line in question: besides ⟨petimus ab orbe⟩, the reading that made its way into the main text of this edition and thus also into the Brepols-corpus, there is ⟨petivimus orbe⟩ (non-*v*-deleted perfect), ⟨petemus ab orbe⟩ (future, which can be excluded on contextual grounds) and the metrically impossible ⟨petimus orbe⟩.[248]

The moral of this brief excursus is that the limitations on what one can do with a textual database for Latin become quite severe when trying to disentangle issues such as the (morpho)phonological interpretation of ⟨desiimus⟩, ⟨repetiimus⟩, ⟨abiisse⟩ and similar forms. It would be unrealistic not to admit that combinations of [i]-final stems and [i]-initial affixes will always represent a bit of a grey zone and a full understanding of them may well remain impossible.

That said, the generalisations regarding the distribution of the perfectum affixes will now be revised to encompass what I have termed non-alternating affixes and to encompass the minor variations described above; see Table 13.

6.2.4. *Affixes following the extended stems*

Extended stems, whether perfectum or infectum, can only be followed by the personal endings. These featured already in Tables 10 and 11 since they can

---

[248] The full line (in this edition) is *extremoque epulas mensasque petimus ab orbe*, in a free translation 'we strove to bring tables and food from the limits of the world'; Sir Edward Ridley's translation is available at http: //www.perseus.tufts.edu/hopper/text?doc=Perseus%3atext%3a1999.02.0134.

also follow the infectum stem immediately. After extended stems, however, their distribution is somewhat different. First, while infectum and extended infectum stems can be followed by active as well as passive endings, extended perfectum stems can only be followed by active endings. Second, after extended stems the 1SING ending displays allomorphy too (when immediately after the infectum stem, it is invariably -ō).[249] Third, after extended stems all personal endings, even 3PLUR -unt, display Type 1 allomorphy. This is clear even though the set of actual segments found at the end of extended stems is quite small: [r b i a: e:]. The crucial point is that in this morphological construction all three vowels, including [i], pattern together as environments; see Table 14.[250]

There are two local irregularities to mention, and with these the description of the systemic morphophonology of Latin regular verbal inflection is complete. One irregularity is that in the FutPerf3Plur the forms end in -erint (fuerint, audierint), though they should end in **-erunt, since these forms consist of the perfectum stem, extension -er- plus the 3PLUR suffix -(u)nt.[251] This is not a morhophonological irregularity; the fuerint-type forms have simply spilled over from the accidentally highly similar PerfSubj paradigm, where the stem extension is -eri-. (Consequently, the only difference between the two paradigms is in the 1SING fuero vs. fuerim.)

Not unlike this is the case of the Fut1Sing of consonant- and i-stem verbs. These forms end in -am (agam, capiam, veniam), although the stem extension here is -ē-; again, this is a case of contamination from the corresponding PresSubj paradigm, where the stem extension is -ā-.

Table 14. Affix variants following extended stems

	ō/or, is/eris, it/itur, imus/imur, itis/iminī, unt/untur
-C	
-V	
	m/r, s/ris, t/tur, mus/mur, tis/minī, nt/ntur

---

[249] The 1SING ending written ⟨m⟩ is phonologically a placeless nasal which is realised as nasalisation and lengthening on the preceding vowel (see 5.4.4).

[250] In particular, the contrast can be captured at two points: (i) -i+(u)nt constructions, e.g. veni-unt 'come' PRES3PLUR vs. ven-eri-nt PERFSUBJ3PLUR; (ii) nearly all 1SING forms, e.g. vide-o 'see' PRES1SING vs. am-e-m 'love' PRESSUBJ1SING or vide-or vs. am-e-r, the same forms in passive. The first contrast is due to Type 2 vs. Type 1 allomorphy of -(u)nt after infectum and extended stems, respectively; the second is due to the wholly idiosyncratic behaviour of the 1SING suffix.

[251] Such forms do exist, but only as by-forms of the PERF3PLUR in the indicative (fuērunt ~ fuĕrunt), see note 234.

6.3. ALLOMORPHY IN THE NOMINAL INFLECTION

6.3.1. *Introductory remarks*

As was seen above, the environments of the allomorphic alternations encountered in verbal inflection can be defined over a scale of vocalicness, with consonants at one end, non-high vowels at the other, and the high vowels in between, patterning partly with the consonants, partly with the non-high vowels. Something very similar is found in nominal inflection, an insight expressed already in Spaelti (2004), Emonds and Spaelti (2005) and Emonds (2014).

Nominal inflection is structurally simpler but morphophonologically more complex than verbal inflection. It is structurally simpler because all forms consist of a stem and an ending; unlike with verbs, there are no subsystems of extended stems apart from a certain kind of gender marking (see below); and, of course, various kinds of nominal derivations are found, which are not discussed here. In terms of morphosyntactic properties, nominal inflection includes cumulative case/number marking (henceforth referred to as case marking) for all kinds of nouns and adjectives, as well as gender marking for some nouns and many adjectives. Gender is encoded partly in the differential marking of the nominative and accusative cases, partly in the stem-final vowel. These details will be explained below.

Stems can end in all five vowel qualities and any of the consonants except [f], [j] and [h].[252] In particular, the stem-final segments which define the types by conditioning allomorphy in case marking are the following:[253] -ă -ŏ/ŭ -ē -ū/ŭ -ĭ -C. While this list largely corresponds to the traditionally distinguished declensions, one important difference is to be noted. In the time-honoured classification *i*-stems and consonant stems belong to what is called the third declension and are distinguished from each other on an etymological basis. Since the endings for the two kinds of stems were in several cases identical to begin with, and since subsequent sound changes and analogical levelling obscured some of the existing differences, only five points remained visible, viz. ACCSING -*im* vs. -*em*, ABLSING -*ī* vs. -*e*, NEUTNOMACCPLUR -*ia* vs. -*a*, MASCFEMACCPLUR -*īs* vs. -*ēs*, and GENPLUR -*ium* vs. -*um* (the former typical of the *i*-stem forms, the latter of consonant stems in all the five cases). Third declension nouns and adjectives show immense variation in what endings they show, and the picture is further obscured by the fact that many words are simply not attested in all of their case forms.

---

[252] Note that [f] and [j] are also never found in verb stem-final position.

[253] The type here marked ŏ/ŭ is traditionally called *o*-stem on an etymological basis. By the Classical Latin period the original stem-final *[o] developed into [u] in some forms. Thus these stems as a type may be described as ending in an unspecified back round vowel; this contrasts with the non-round vowelled stems, and it also contrasts with the clearly *u*-final stems. Nevertheless, for practical purposes I will continue to refer to this class as *o*-stems. The stems here marked as ū/ŭ end in an [u] unspecified for length, which appears either as long or as short in the case-marked forms, without any regularity that could be phonologically specified; the quality of the vowel is stable, as opposed that seen in *o*-stems.

The details of this variation have been thoroughly described[254] and will not be rehearsed here. I will not treat the issue of *i*-stems vs. consonant stems as a matter of inflectional variation, i.e. as variation in the endings within a single general paradigm type. I will treat stem-final [i] as inherently unstable: if it is present, the given instantiation of the stem selects the appropriate allomorph typical of an *i*-stem; if it is not present, it selects an allomorph typical of a consonant stem. I regard this phenomenon essentially as heteroclisy. Some nouns in Latin display forms based on two different stems, e.g. *elephant-/ elephanto-* 'elephant', *opulent-/opulento-* 'rich', *barbaria-/barbariē-* 'strange land', *materia-/materiē-* 'stuff', *domo-/domū-* 'house', and several others. What are called *i*-stems all belong to this set. In a few nouns such as *mare* 'sea' the stem-final [i] is present in most forms;[255] in some it is present only in one distinguishable form (e.g. *urbs* 'city' → GENPLUR *urbium*); and there is a huge number of pure consonant stems with no *i*-stem forms at all.

The relation between *i*-stems and consonant stems is thus a kind of pervasive heteroclisy. The presentation of the allomorphic variation that follows does not explicitly show this or any other heteroclisy: stem types are listed as environments conditioning allomorph choice, and it is understood that certain lexical items shift between these stem types. It so happens that *i*-stem nouns and adjectives are a much less stable category, i.e. more prone to shifting between stem types, than most other stem types.[256] Furthermore, it is important to note that etymological considerations will be explicitly disregarded here in assigning either stems or endings to the *i*-stem class and consonant stem class.[257]

We saw above that verbs also show systematic heteroclisy between *ī*-stem and C-stem. The two types of heteroclisy are parallel to a certain extent in involving the presence vs. absence of the same vowel in stem-final position. The important difference between verbal and nominal *i*-stem heteroclisy is not in the length of

---

[254] For a detailed conspectus see Leumann (1977: 342–53, 429–41).

[255] One could actually argue that *mare* is an *i*-stem throughout if one assigns the surface-ambiguous forms to the set of *i*-stem forms, e.g. GENSING *mari-s* rather than *mar-is*, which would be the consonant-stem form. I do not believe this ambiguity can be resolved, but I also do not believe very much hinges on it.

[256] The class of *ē*-stems is, in fact, also unstable in a slightly different and much less problematic way. The number of *ē*-stem nouns is rather small, only a handful show a full attested paradigm, and several are heteroclitic, see *materies* 'stuff' and *barbaries* 'strange land' above. However, the marginal nature of this stem type is unproblematic from a descriptive point of view because, unlike with *i*-stems, if a noun shows *ē*-stem forms, those are easily distinguished from forms based on other stems.

[257] For example, I classify the NOMSING *-ēs* ending as a consonant stem ending because formally this is more straightforward than classifying it as an *i*-stem ending and then deleting the [i] in actual forms like *fames* 'hunger', *nubes* 'cloud', *clades* 'destruction', *vulpes* 'fox'. Another motivation for this choice is that these words do not show other *i*-stem forms apart from GENPLUR *nubium*, *vulpium* and *cladium* (the latter varying with consonant-stem *cladum*; no GENPLUR forms attested for *fames* at all). In Latin historical linguistics *-ēs* is known as a typical feminine *i*-stem ending for the NOMSING originally.

the vowel (which varies on the surface under well-defined conditions anyway) but in the patterning and symmetry of the variation.

Patterning in this case means a uniform behaviour for verbs: all verbs belonging to the class in question show C-stem forms in exactly the same paradigmatic cells and ī-stem forms in the complementary set of those paradigmatic cells.[258] By contrast, the nouns and adjectives that show *i*-stem forms as well as C-stem forms do so in a largely unpredictable paradigmatic distribution. There are hardly any discernible regularities in the stem allomorphy, or interdependencies between *i*-stem forms and consonant stem forms at a paradigmatic level.[259] Nominal heteroclisy is thus not systematic in the same way as verbal heteroclisy is.

Symmetry means that both 'sides' of the heteroclisy exist in unadulterated form in the morphological system. This is unambiguously true only for verbs: there are pure ī-stems and there are pure C-stems, and there is a class of verbs that systematically shift between the two in particular forms. For nouns this is not the case. While there are pure C-stems, there are no unambiguously pure *i*-stems (see note 255); the tantalising variation is not found between two extremes but at a lopsided periphery of a category.

6.3.2. *Case endings and allomorphy: nominative and accusative singular*

The case endings that different nominal stems take will be summarised in the following four tables. The nominative and accusative cases are presented separately from the other three cases in both numbers because they involve gender differentiation, and because they involve greater variability and require more explanation (especially the nominative singular). The nominative and accusative singular endings are shown in Table 15.[260]

The most typical NomSing ending is -*s* (with variant -*ēs*) for the animate genders, and zero for neuters and for *a*-stems (which are overwhelmingly feminine, with very few masculines). Zero is also found with most sonorant-final and all [s]-final stems of any gender. Animate *u*-stems show the short vowel, neuter *u*-stems presumably show the long vowel in the NomSing, though the latter cannot be definitively established (Leumann 1977: 441). The placeless nasal (written ⟨m⟩ in word-final position) is the general AccSing ending for all vowel-final stem types, the only exceptions being the zero-marked neuters of the high vowel stems.

---

[258] With the notable exception of *oriri* 'arise', which shows more ī-stem forms than the other verbs in the same class.

[259] To note one such rare regularity, also mentioned in Spaelti (2004), if a stem ends in a consonant cluster that cannot be a complex onset, it shows an *i*-stem form in the GenPlur: *urbium* 'city', *amnium* 'river' vs. *patrum* 'father', *volucrum* 'bird'. An example of interdependency is that the *i*-stem AccSing form implies the *i*-stem NomSing form for any given lexeme (*puppim* → *puppis* 'ship'), but not the other way round (*hostis* but *hostem* 'enemy').

[260] In Tables 15 and 17 the shaded area marks forms typical of neuter nouns and adjectives. For each table, orthographic forms are added below. The examples are *ara* 'altar', *annus* 'year', *pilum* 'javelin', *dies* 'day', *puppis* 'ship', *mare* 'sea', *tribus* 'tribe', *cornu* 'horn', *fames* 'hunger', *rex* 'king', *pater* 'father', *caput* 'head'.

Table 15. Nominative and accusative singular endings

	NomSing	AccSing
ă-	Ø	
ŏ/ŭ-		
ē-		m
ĭ-	s	
ū/ŭ -		Ø
C-	ēs	em

ara		*aram*
annus	*pilum*	*annum*
diēs		*diem*
puppis	*mare*	*puppim*
tribus	*cornū*	*tribum*
famēs/	*caput*	*famem/regem/patrem*
rex/pater		

Combined with a stem-final vowel this placeless nasal results in a long nasal vowel written ⟨Vm⟩, which inherits the quality of the stem-final vowel (for the phonological process see 5.4.4). After consonant stems the suffix is [ě:] (written ⟨em⟩). As a rule without exception, neuters have the same nominative and accusative forms; this is indicated as the shaded area overlapping the two cases in the table above. For *o*-stem neuters, the nasal-affixed accusative form functions also as the nominative. There are no neuters among *a*-stems and *ē*-stems.[261]

6.3.2.1. *Phonological alternations in the nominative singular*

The NomSing of nouns and adjectives often shows peculiarities which I here only mention briefly. One example that was mentioned at several points earlier is the disappearance of a dental stop before [s] (*mile-s* ~ *milit-em* 'soldier' NomSing ~ AccSing), the result of assimilation followed by degemination, phonological processes attested independently of nominal morphology (see 4.3 and 4.5). Also, the vowel of the last stem syllable often differs in this form from that found in all other cases. Some such alternations are phonologically systematic, such as the [e] ~ [i] alternation in closed vs. open syllables, as in *miles* (quoted above; on the alternation of vowels see 5.2.2.1). In *i*-stem neuters the lowering rule

---

[261] Emonds & Spaelti (2005) establish the generalisation that among vowel-final stems genders show near-complementary distribution, with non-round-vowel stems being typically feminine and round-vowel stems typically masculine and neuter. They claim this can only be overridden by natural gender. This generalisation is highly problematic for two reasons. One is that it disregards the many *i*-stem neuters (such as *mare* 'sea') and the *u*-stem feminines (e.g. *domus* 'house', *manus* 'hand'). The other is that they use the term natural gender beyond reasonable limits. For instance the feminine gender of *fagus* 'beech-tree' is explained with reference to the fact that trees are usually feminine in Latin. While this is a true generalisation, it has nothing to do with natural gender (as opposed to, say, *nurus* 'daughter-in-law').

[i] → [e] / _ # applies (*mari-* → *mare* 'sea', see 5.2.2.3). Some alternations are less systematic, such as the [u] ~ [e] alternation in *genus* ~ *generis* 'kind'. Some are fairly frequent lexically but cannot be described phonologically. The classic example of this is the set of *n*-final animate stems. These are zero-suffixed but the [n] is deleted too, and the NomSing shows final [oː], whether it is present in the stem otherwise or not: *tirōn-* → *tirō* 'new recruit', *origin-* → *origō* 'beginning'.

If a stem ends in C[r], an epenthetic [e] is inserted in the NomSing (*patr-* → *pater* 'father', *agr-* → *ager* 'field', see 5.3.1). Some of these stems are inflected as consonant stems throughout (e.g. *pater*), some are inflected as *o*-stems in all forms except the NomSing (e.g. *ager*); I regard the latter type as formally heteroclitic, even if only marginally. On adjectives of a similar stem shape see below.

6.3.2.2. Gender marking

The following common ways of marking gender in adjectives (and a number of nouns) are found.[262]

(i) Masc, Neut full *o*-stem inflection, Fem full *a*-stem inflection (e.g. *purus* ~ *purum* ~ *pura* 'clean'). In adjectives like these the feminine differs from the other two genders throughout except in the DatAblPlur (see later); the neuter differs from the masculine in the NomSing (Masc *purus*, Neut *purum*), as explained above, and also in the NomAccPlur (see later).

(ii) All three genders heteroclitic *i*-stem/C-stem inflection, but Masc and Fem have NomSing *i*-stem plus -*s* and AccSing C-stem plus -*em*, whereas Neut has *i*-stem plus zero for both (e.g. Masc, Fem NomSing *viridis*, AccSing *viridem*, Neut *viride* 'green').

As a subcategory that cross-classifies both (i) and (ii), there is a populous group of *r*-final adjectives which do not show a stem-final vowel or a suffix in the masculine NomSing (e.g. *tener* ~ *tenerum* ~ *tenera* 'soft', otherwise same type as *purus* above, or *celer* ~ *celere* ~ *celeris* 'swift', otherwise same type as *viridis* above). Unlike *tener* and *celer*, the majority of such stems end in C*ro-*/C*ra-*/C*r*- or C*ri-*/C*r*-. In these the masculine NomSing usually has no stem-final vowel, epenthesises [e] as any C*r*-final noun stem (see above), and is then zero-suffixed as any sonorant-final noun stem.[263] In all other forms these adjectives are regular. Examples:

---

[262] Some adjectives do not mark gender in the singular at all (e.g. *vetus* 'old', *audax* 'bold'). More precisely, they only mark gender by using the NomSing form for the neuter accusative (Masc/Fem *veterem*, *audacem* vs. Neut *vetus*, *audax*). Note that in these neuter nominative-accusative forms the animate NomSing affix -*s* appears on adjectives like *audax* or all the -*ns*-final participles, which is very unusual from a systemic – and also from an Indo-European – point of view.

[263] Formally this means that C*ro-*/C*ra-*/C*r*- adjectives are heteroclitic just like the C*ro-*/C*r*- nouns of the *ager* type. C*ri-*/C*r*- adjectives are also heteroclitic but that is evident since all *i*-stem nouns and all *i*-stem adjectives are.

(77) Adjectives with Cr(V)-final stems in NomSing (*piger* 'reluctant', *acer* 'sharp')

Masc *piger* (stem *pigr-*, zero suffix, *e*-epenthesis)
Neut *pigrum* (stem *pigro-*, placeless nasal suffix)
Fem *pigra* (stem *pigra-*, zero suffix)

Masc *acer* (stem *acr-*, zero suffix, *e*-epenthesis)
Neut *acre* (stem *acri-*, zero suffix, final *e*-lowering)
Fem *acris* (stem *acri-*, suffix -*s*)

6.3.3. *Case endings and allomorphy: the remaining cases*

The genitive, dative and ablative singular endings are shown in Table 16. The genitive forms are quite varied along the vocalic scale, but a fundamental dichotomy between a vocalic (-[j] or -*ī*) and a consonantal (-*s*/-*is*) affix type is easily identifiable. Stems ending in [a] take -[j] (written ⟨ae⟩); *o*-stems take -*ī* and the stem-final vowel deletes due to the back vowel deletion rule seen in 5.3.2; *ē*-stems also take -*ī* and the stem-final vowel shortens in line with the hiatus rule in 5.4.1.[264] *U*-stems and *i*-stems take -*s*, and consonant-stems take -*is*, which on the surface makes these latter forms indistinguishable from *i*-stem genitives — and also makes the analysis equivocal: *reg-is* 'king', because this word has no straightforward *i*-stem forms at all; but *mari-s* (*i*-stem) or *mar-is* (C-stem) 'sea' are, in theory, equally possible analyses.

Table 16. Genitive, dative and ablative singular endings

	GenSing	DatSing	AblSing
ă-		j	
ŏ/ŭ-			V
ē-		ī	
ĭ-	s		
ū/ŭ -			
C-	is		e

arae	*arae*	*arā*
annī	*annō*	*annō*
diēī	*diēī*	*diē*
maris	*marī*	*marī*
tribūs	*tribuī/senatū*	*tribū*
regis	*regī*	*rege*

---

[264] Except when the stem-final [e:] is preceded by [i], the only vowel possible, in which case it remains long, e.g. *rē-* → *rēī* 'thing', but *diē-* → *diēī* 'day', see the discussion of hiatus in 2.3.3.

The dative of *a*-stems is identical to the genitive; the dative of *o*-stems is identical to the ablative, with an empty vowel suffix (see below). For all other stems the affix is *-ī*, resulting in the combinations *eī* and *uī* (with hiatus shortening again), *ī* (stem-final [i] disappears before the suffix)[265] and C*ī*. As a point of variation the dative of *u*-stems can also be identical to the ablative instead of taking the *-ī* suffix.[266]

For vowel-final stems the ablative is uniformly suffixed with an empty vowel,[267] which appears on the surface as the lengthening of the stem-final vowel if it is short, and as vacuous lengthening (sheer stem) if the final vowel is already long. The suffix is *-e* after consonant-final stems.

In the NomAccPlur (Table 17) all neuters are suffixed with *-a*, before which the round stem vowel *ŏ/ŭ* disappears; *ū* and *i* remain but the former shortens in the hiatus. The round stem vowel *ŏ/ŭ* also disappears before *-ī*, as in the GenSing. The *a*-stem NomPlur is formally identical to the GenDatSing (⟨ae⟩).

Table 17. Nominative and accusative plural endings

	NomPlur	AccPlur
ă-	j	
ŏ/ŭ-	ī	a
ē-		Vs
ĭ-	(ēs)	
ū/ŭ -		a
C-	ēs	ēs

arae		*arās*
annī	*pila*	*annōs*
diēs		*diēs*
(puppēs)	*maria*	*puppīs*
tribūs	*cornua*	*tribūs*
regēs	*capita*	*regēs*

---

[265] It is also a possibility to analyse the *marī*-type datives as consonantal stem forms. But in *-io*-stem genitives the [i] remaining after back vowel deletion is also optionally deleted, thus e.g. *offici* or *officii* from *officium* 'office', thus a rule deleting [i] before final [iː] may be posited.

[266] For the *i*-stem dative two other analyses are possible. It can be analysed as suffixed with the same empty vowel as the ablative (much like *o*-stems), in which case no deletion of the stem vowel is required. Or one could claim that there is no *i*-stem dative proper (as there is no NomPlur either, see Table 17), and the lexical items in question all have C-stem datives. Contrary to what Spaelti (2004: 133) claims, the *u*-stem dative without the *-ī* is not more typical of neuters than of masculines and feminines.

[267] Spaelti (2004) describes the AblSing in the same way, as also the other cases that involve empty vowels (AccPlur and GenPlur). Oniga (2014) and Wiese (2013) express the same insight by describing these affixes as including a (non-segmental) length feature.

The AccPlur ending is -V*s*, which manifests itself as [s] preceded by lengthening on short stem vowels and [s] preceded by vacuous lengthening on long stem vowels. The same functions as NomPlur ending on *ē*- and *ū*-stems. With consonant stems, both cases have -*ēs*.

Strictly speaking, there is no *i*-stem animate NomPlur form. All masculine and feminine *i*-stem nouns and adjectives show exclusively C-stem forms in -*ēs*.[268] This is in contrast to the AccPlur, where distinct -*ēs* vs. -*īs* forms are attested.

The GenPlur allomorphy (Table 18) is a very clear case of what I called Type 2 allomorphy in the discussion of verbal inflection. All consonant-final and high-vowel-final stems are affixed with [ŭ:] (written ⟨um⟩), and all other vowel-final stems are affixed with [Vrŭ:] (written ⟨rum⟩), the latter resulting in lengthening on short stem vowels and vacuous lengthening on the long stem vowel [e:]. In the DatAblPlur (which two case forms are never distinguished in Latin) the three endings are -*īs* for back non-high vowels (with loss of the stem-final vowel), -*bus* for front and high vowels and -*ibus* for consonants. Some *u*-stem nouns show -*ibus* instead of -*bus*, which may be analysed as heteroclisy, in this case switching to a consonant stem. Before -*bus* the stem-final [u] is short. The ending -*bus* is also found exceptionally on *a*-stems where an explicit gender distinction is needed between an *a*-stem noun and a corresponding *o*-stem noun, the most typical such forms being *deabus* 'goddess' and *filiabus* 'daughter' (as opposed to *deis/dis* 'god' and *filiis* 'son', all forms DatAblPlur).

Table 18. Genitive, dative and ablative plural endings

	GenPlur	DatAblPlur
ă-		īs
ŏ/ū-	Vrum	
ē-		
ĭ-		bus
ū/ŭ-	um	
C-		ibus

arārum	*arīs*
annōrum	*annīs*
diērum	*diēbus*
puppium	*puppibus*
tribuum	*tribubus/portibus*[269]
regum	*regibus*

---

[268] This is true again *contra etymologiam*, since the nominative plural -*ēs* ending is known to have belonged originally to the *i*-stems as opposed to the C-stem nominative plural, which is reconstructed as *-ĕs*.

[269] *Portus* 'port' is an *u*-stem noun just like *tribus*.

6.4. MORPHOPHONOLOGICAL ANALYSIS: INFLECTIONAL ALLOMORPHY AND THE VOCALIC SCALE

The stem types as environments conditioning allomorphy can be arranged on a scale (see Figure 36) according to vocalicness in both verbal and nominal inflection. At one extreme one finds [a], the most open vowel and therefore the most vocalic of all segments; at the other extreme one finds the set of consonants, undifferentiated from the point of view of the allomorphy in inflectional morphology.[270] The scale has high predictive strength in that there are no discontinuities in it: if two non-adjacent environments share an affix allomorph, then the environments between them also share the same allomorph.

The scale is common to verbal and nominal inflection. Although in verbal inflection the vast majority of allomorphy belongs to either of two types, that is, they only make a two-way distinction over the three categories consonants plus [u] vs. [iː] vs. non-high vowels, the isolated cases of allomorphy articulate the same cline differently without contradicting the generalisation made above: the subjunctive $\bar{e} \sim \bar{a}$ allomorphy (number 10 in Table 11) separates the most vocalic environment from all the others and the 1SING ending is vacuously non-contradictory in Table 11 since it does not alternate; after extended stems (Table 14) it is Type 2 like all affixes.

Affix variation is greater in the nominal inflection than in the verbal inflection, but a similar pattern is observable. The GENPLUR allomorphy is clearly Type 2, but the GENSING allomorphy is also Type 2 with respect to s-ful ([s], [is]) vs. vocalic ([j], [iː]) affixes. In DATABLPLUR forms the -bus/-ibus vs. -īs distinction draws the line between $\bar{e}$-stems and the more vocalic stems, and the same is true of the NOMPLUR (s-ful vs. vocalic affixes). Furthermore, in the animate NOMACCPLUR the full vowelled -ēs is confined to consonant stems as opposed to the empty vowelled variant. The ACCSING forms contrast a full-vowelled and a vowelless affix variant, and the ABLSING forms contrast a full-vowelled and an empty-vowelled affix variant. A very minor exception is seen in animate NOMSING, where the zero suffix is found within a subclass of consonant-stems as one of the three possible endings.

The only notable difference between verbal and nominal allomorphy, which, however, still does not contradict the generalisation, concerns the high vowels.

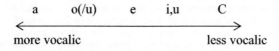

Figure 36. The vocalic scale (length unmarked; high vowels discussed in section 6.5)

---

[270] Though bear in mind that one of the two most vocalic consonants, [j] is not found in stem-final position at all.

As we saw, in the verbal morphology, [u]-final stems always pattern with consonant-final stems (hence it is questionable if they really end in a vowel), whereas in the nominal morphology, [u]-final stems pattern with [i]-final stems, and both types pattern with consonant-final stems in the majority of cases, but in some cases with other vowel-final stems.

Table 19 compares and summarises all cases of allomorphy as functions of the stem-final segment in both nominal and verbal inflection. The list of verb stem-final segments has been reversed to parallel those of nominal stems.[271]

6.5. THE VOCALIC SCALE AND SONORITY

Given the obvious similarity between the vocalic scale that is relevant for the choice of allomorphs in inflection, and the sonority scale, the question must be addressed whether the former is the subsection of the latter as defined on vowels. Does the vocalic scale simply instantiate the sonority ranking of vowels?[272] To

Table 19. Summary of inflectional allomorphy

Noun Adj	Ø	j	īs	j, ī	m	j, ī	Vrum	Vs	m	V	...	...	ē	Verb
ă				—										ă
ŏ/ŭ														ō, (fore)
ē					—									ē
ī				—										ī
ū/ŭ														u
C	Ø													C
	s, ēs	ī	(i)bus	Vs, ēs	Ø	(i)s	um	ēs	em	e	...	...	ā	
	anim. NOM SING	DAT SING	DATABL PLUR	anim. NOM PLUR	NEUT NOM ACC SING	GEN SING	GEN PLUR	anim. ACC PLUR	anim. ACC SING	ABL SING	Type 1	Type 2	SUBJ	

[271] The inclusion of the DATSING in the chart is somewhat tentative since three different analyses are possible for the morphophonological structure of i-stems (see above). It is, however, indicated by the different shading that the DATSING of o-stems takes a suffix not identical to either of the two major types. Cells for non-existent form types are crossed out (neuter forms for a-stems and ē-stems, animate NOMPLUR for i-stems). I have added the marginal verb fu-/fore to the list on the right not because of its systemic importance, which is negligible, but because it is tempting to offer it as a parallel to the nominal stems that end in an unspecified round vowel (o-stems). As was seen above, among nominal stems there is a contrast between those ending in an unspecified round vowel, which function more vocalically, and those that are 'true' u-stems, which function much more like i-stems. As the -re and -rē-suffixed forms of fore show, the stem of this verb is more vocalic than the stem of those traditionally called u-stem verbs, the latter functioning exactly like consonant stems in all respects. This parallel, however, must not be pressed too far, not least because fore lacks Type 2 forms. Verb stem-final [oː] is only found in truncated perfects of the nosse type.

[272] Spaelti (2004) takes it for granted that the arrangement into three groups of the stem-final vowels as environments for allomorphy in the nominal inflection is based on the sonority hierarchy, but does not give arguments pertaining to vowel sonority as such. In Emonds & Spaelti (2005) and in Emonds (2014: 17) the term sonority does not figure at all, though in the former there is reference at one point to the 'more sonorous' (i.e. non-high) vowels.

answer this question we need to consider what the sonority of vowels actually involves.

From discussions of, and analyses invoking, sonority (Kenstowicz 1997; Parker 2002, 2011; Gordon 2006; de Lacy 2006; Gordon et al. 2012; Miller 2012), the following recurring points can be gleaned. Phonological descriptions of sonority pinpoint two dimensions of contrast, high vs. low and central vs. peripheral. It is generally agreed that low vowels have higher sonority than high vowels and peripheral vowels have higher sonority than central vowels. The phonetic correlates of sonority are much more problematic; the parameters that have been proposed are intensity, vocal tract aperture, temporal duration, peak acoustic energy and peak intraoral pressure. It is possible that there is not one single parameter that defines sonority, though intensity takes pride of place (see especially Parker 2002 for arguments in favour of this position and methods of quantifying intensity and thus sonority).

The sonority of vowels manifests itself in certain patterns of phonological behaviour, which are in some cases interrelated. Syllable weight or moraicity, stress avoidance and the tendency to devoice split the set of vowels in several languages along such a scale (vowel height and peripherality in addition to length; see Gordon 2006: 123 sqq.; Parker 2011 section 2.4). In such languages more sonorous vowels contribute to syllable weight while less sonorous vowels do not, and/or more sonorous vowels attract stress more than less sonorous vowels do. In some languages less sonorous (i.e. high or central) vowels are capable of devoicing whereas more sonorous vowels are not (Miller 2012: 285).

The vocalic scale in Latin very clearly shows vowel height as a defining phonological property, with [a] at one end and the high vowels at the other end followed only by consonants. The peripheral vs. central contrast is irrelevant, there being no central vowel in Latin at all. It is not clear if frontness as such plays a role: while [eː] appears to be closer to the consonantal end than [o] in nouns, the latter is actually a vowel alternating between [o] and [u] rather than a plain mid vowel. (In verbs there is no difference between [eː] and [oː].) Furthermore, as was made clear above, there is no difference between [i]-final and [u]-final stems in the nominal inflection, and between [u]-final and consonant-final stems in the verbal inflection. This either means that [u] is more consonantal than [i] (which would be consistent with the verbal but not with the nominal pattern), or that [u]-final infectum as well as perfectum verb stems are, in fact, consonant-final (that is, they end in [uw], see 6.2.2 and 6.2.3.2).

The implication with respect to the relation between the vocalic scale and sonority is that if the analysis of allomorphic patterns expounded here is correct and if the vocalic scale is indeed identical to the sonority scale as defined on vowels then either [u] is less sonorous than [i] or verb stems do not end in [u] and apparently [u]-final stems, whether infectum or perfectum, end in [uw] and are thus consonant-final. Identifying the vocalic scale with the sonority scale is desirable simply on account of simplicity; and since no compelling arguments are found in the literature for the higher sonority of [i] as opposed to [u], we must conclude that there are indeed no [u]-final verb stems.

The phonetic properties that correspond to sonority are mostly not retrievable for Latin, though there is some indication that high vowels may have been somewhat shorter than non-high vowels. More specifically Sen (2014; 2015: 42–78) argues for the relative shortness of [iː]; if similar arguments are not found for the relative shortness of [uː], this may just possibly be a weak indication for another asymmetry between the two high vowels.

In terms of behaviour, vowels of different quality do not show corresponding differences in their contribution to syllable weight or their stressability[273] and there are no vowel devoicing processes at all in Latin. In Classical Latin, then, the only function of the vocalic scale appears to be that found in inflectional morphology. It follows that if we equate this vocalic scale with the sonority scale as defined on vowels (which the central role of vowel height warrants), this is a function or manifestation different from those formerly discussed in the literature. There are known cases of allomorph selection conditioned by high vs. non-high vowel, e.g. an Udihe case mentioned in Nevins (2011), but that involves only a single binary feature; Anttila (1997) discusses the plural genitive suffix in Finnish whose allomorphs are selected in a subset of the lexicon on the basis of the sonority (i.e. height) of the vowel, but there are other factors interfering (word length, stress and syllable weight), and the effect is not systematic even with that proviso since it is demonstrable only for one single suffix. In Classical Latin, however, vowel sonority appears to be the fundamental organising principle of the entire inflectional system.

6.6. Conclusion

This chapter has explored the possibility of analysing the regular inflectional morphology of Latin on a purely phonological basis. It has been demonstrated that nearly all of the inflectional system can be described as a network of binary allomorphic patterns, in which the choice of the allomorphs is governed by the phonological properties of the stem-final segment. The relationship between the conditioning environment and the allomorph can be captured with the help of the sonority scale in a straightforward manner. The property of contiguity, demonstrable for the same scale in both the verbal and the nominal inflection, ensures that this relation is indeed a plausible explanatory factor.

---

[273] In a broader perspective, however, stress and vowel height were related in preclassical Latin. As was briefly explained in 5.2.1, in an early period word stress appears to have been on initial syllables, and short unstressed vowels, i.e. those in non-initial syllables, systematically became higher. However, when stress moved to its Classical Latin position, the quality of vowels proved to be irrelevant and high as well as non-high vowels received stress if in the appropriate position, thus e.g. *pérfacere 'complete' > pérficere > perficere.

7

THE PHONOLOGY OF PREFIXED FORMS

7.1. INTRODUCTION

Prefixed forms display some phonological phenomena that are different from those encountered in simplex forms, and therefore it is necessary to discuss them separately and comprehensively. Some phonological processes that typically occur at prefix–stem boundary were discussed in chapter 4, and some phonotactic aspects in chapter 3. In the present chapter every prefix that can be regarded as a morphological unit in Classical Latin is discussed in detail, specifically with respect to its phonological behaviour.

Morphosyntactically speaking prefixed forms are rigid in the sense that, like prefixed forms in the Slavonic languages, and unlike prefixed forms in German, Old English or Hungarian, they are inseparable. In terms of productivity, transparency and phonological interference they can be arranged on a cline with strongly lexicalised and opaque forms at one end and transparent formations at the other. The difference can be exemplified with *dēgere* 'live' (usu. with an object like 'life' or 'time'), which is composed of *dē* 'from' + *agere* 'do', vs. *perpolitus* 'highly polished', in which the adjective *politus* 'polished' is combined with *per*, which has two meanings, 'through' and 'highly, very'. The transparent nature of *perpolitus* is not only seen in its semantics and in the lack of phonological interference between the two component parts, but also in some instances of its use, where it is used next to other *per*-prefixed adjectives with similar meanings.[274] This cline is related, though certainly not in an isomorphic fashion, to the diachronic emergence of these forms.[275]

The tangled history of prefixed forms will not, in general, be pursued here. I nevertheless note some of its salient points because an understanding of these is indispensable for what follows in the present chapter. Prefixation led in many cases to lexicalisation, which in turn resulted in drastic phonological modifications

---

[274] A case in point is found in the *Rhetorica ad Herennium* 4.32: *ut [continuationes] perfecte et perpolitissime possint esse absolutae* 'so that periods can be finished in a well-rounded and highly polished manner' (translation mine).

[275] The best summary of these issues to date is Prinz (1949–50; 1953), which is based on an extensive study of manuscript and inscriptional evidence as well as grammarians' remarks; one may further consult Leumann (1977: 181–219) on the sound changes that took place in consonant clusters, including those that emerged at prefix–stem boundaries, Buck (1899: 117–18; 156–67) on the assimilation of prefix-final consonants, and García González (1996), a short case-study of the prefix *ad-* and its epigraphic variants based on the Roman inscriptional corpus (*CIL* vol. 6). In the discussion of prefix variability I rely on Prinz (1949–50; 1953) besides my own corpus research.

at the prefix–stem boundary as well as within the stem.[276] The pace and the extent of lexicalisation, however, was highly variable (which explains the cline mentioned in the previous paragraph). Furthermore, prefixation also involved recomposition in all periods of the documented history of Latin. An early case of recomposition is seen in *periūrare* 'forswear', which is the recomposed variant of the older form *peierare* [pejjeːraːre] (same meaning). Later recompositions can be reconstructed on the evidence of Romance languages; reflexes of forms like *rétinet* 'he keeps' (< *re+tenet*) often derive not from the inherited Classical Latin forms but from recomposed variants such as **reténet* (> Fr *retient*, etc.).

The varying pace of lexicalisation and the varying degree of transparency coupled with the phonological processes that took place at prefix–stem boundaries resulted in a not particularly straightforward relation between written forms and probable phonological variants. It is clear that in many cases an assimilation that certainly took place is not indicated in writing (e.g. simple voicing assimilations as in ⟨adtinere⟩ for *attinere* 'hold' or the velarisation of the nasal as in *incipere* 'begin'). It is also clear that beginning with the first century AD etymologically oriented habits of spelling began to gain ground, but did not affect all words of a similar composition to the same extent. Since, however, many of the characteristic traits of the variation that appears in the texts are clearly phonologically based, it can be assumed that the picture is not badly distorted – that is, with all the necessary provisos. In those instances below where there seems to be good reason to believe that the written forms depart from the reconstructible phonological reality, this will be duly pointed out.

The case of *peierare/periūrare* brings us to yet another related issue, that of attestation. The fact is that while the former is evidently the older variant on phonological grounds, its appearance in written documents postdates that of the latter by more than a hundred years (early first century BC for *peierare*, late third century BC for *periūrare*). Furthermore, there appears in some manuscripts of Plautus, Cicero and St Augustine an intermediate form written ⟨peiur-⟩ or ⟨peiiur-⟩, which indicates assimilation of [r] (as in *peier-*) but unweakened stem vowel (as in *periur-*). If one considers word class as well, the picture is further complicated. This particular prefixed stem underlies three words: the verb *peierare/periurare/peiurare*, the noun *periurium/peiurium* and the adjective *periurus/peiurus*. The forms written as *peier-* are all forms of the verb; those written as *periur-* are mostly forms of the noun and the adjective, and only in a few instances are they forms of the verb; those few written as *pei(i)ur-* are all forms of the noun and the adjective until the end of the Republican era, after which one or two verbal formations are attested.

If one assumes that late antique and medieval scribal interference has been factored out by the editors of the texts that found their way into the database (indeed the manuscript evidence for these words is fairly safe), and if one further

---

[276] Within stems, these phonological modifications are virtually confined to short vowels; see the brief discussion of these in 5.2.1.

assumes that the spellings faithfully represent pronunciation variants ([rj] vs. [jj], or [e] vs. [uː] in the stem; note that this assumption is, of course, not self-explanatory), a possible scenario that explains this lexical distribution could be that after an early split into a verb *peierare* and an adjective/noun *perjurus/ perjurium*, a secondary verb was formed on the basis of the nominal forms, which was thus *perjurare*. Yet it remains a problematic point why the attestation of the apparently earlier form is actually later than that of the more recent form.[277]

7.2. THE PREFIXES OF LATIN

Latin prefixes are exhaustively listed in (78).

(78) The prefixes of Latin
  (i)   Vowel-final: *dē-*
                           prō-
                           sē-
                           ne-
                           re-
                           ambi-
                           ante-
                           vē-
  (ii)   Glide-final: *prae-*
  (iii) [r]-final: *per-*
                           super-
                           subter-
                           inter-
                           por-
  (iv)   Nasal-final: *con-*
                           in-
                           circum-
                           an-
  (v)   Obstruent-final: *post-*
                           ex-
                           dis-
                           trans-
                           ad-
                           ab-
                           ob-
                           sub-

---

[277] On the story of these words see Prinz (1953: 52–53) as well as Walde & Hoffmann (1956 s.v.) and de Vaan (2008 s.v.).

7.2.1. *Vowel-final prefixes* + *prae*

7.2.1.1. *dē-*

The lexically frequent prefix *dē* only shows phonological modification when followed by a stem-initial vowel.[278] In such cases the vowel shortens as is normal in word-internal hiatus: *dĕhinc* 'hence', *dĕhiscere* 'swallow', *dĕunx* '11/12'. In some words lexicalised contraction with a short vowel is found:[279] *dēgere* < *dē+agere* 'live',[280] *dēbere* 'owe' < *dē+habere*. Evidence from poetry indicates that those infectum forms of *deesse* 'be missing, absent' where the stem begins with [e] are contracted even if the writing does not normally indicate it, so *deesse* INF, *deerat* IMPF3SING, etc. are disyllabic ([deːsse], [deːrat]), *deest* PRES3SING is monosyllabic ([deːst]).

7.2.1.2. *prō-*

This prefix is also frequent lexically. It has three variants: *prō-*, *prōd-* and *prŏ-*. The first is normally found before consonants. The other two are prevocalic variants: the hiatus is filled with [d] in *prōdire* 'go forward', *prōdesse* 'be of use' and *prōdigere* 'drive'; by contrast, the hiatus remains unfilled and the long vowel shortens in *prŏavus* 'great-grandfather', *prŏhibere* 'prohibit', *prŏhinc* 'hence', *prŏin* and *prŏinde* 'likewise'. Of these, *prŏinde* is regularly contracted in poetry to a disyllable,[281] *prŏin* and *prŏhinc* are not used in poetry, the other words are not contracted. Lexicalised contraction is found in *prōmere* 'bring forth' < *prō+emere*.

Surprisingly, the short form is also found with the majority of [f]-initial stems: *prŏfugus* 'fugitive', *prŏfanus* 'profane', *prŏfundere/prŏfusus* 'pour out', *prŏfiteri/prŏfessus* 'say publicly', *prŏficisci/prŏfectus* 'travel', *prŏfecto* 'really', *prŏfestus* 'common (scil. day)', *prŏfari/prŏfatus* 'speak out' (as opposed to *prōficere* 'go forward, affect',[282] *prōfluere* 'gush forth', *prōflare* 'blow forth', *prōferre* 'bring forth'). This is phonologically very strange, all the more so since the rare instances of internal [f] in simplex forms are preceded, with one exception, by long vowels (see 2.2.1).

---

[278] Including, as elsewhere in Latin phonology, [h]V-initial stems.

[279] The word *deorsum* 'downwards' was fairly popular with prose writers, but of the poets only Lucretius ever used it, thus the relevant aspects of its realisation are hard to guess. In Lucretius it is almost always disyllabic, which means that the sequence written ⟨deor⟩ constituted one syllable; but sometimes it is trisyllabic with a light first syllable, i.e. *dĕorsum*, which is more in line with the general tendency. Etymologically, a [w] was lost between the two vowels.

[280] Note that this verb has no third stem, where the stem vowel would be long on account of the rule explained in 5.4.2 and thus contraction precluded: **deāct-.

[281] But this may be skewed in that out of the 23 occurrences in poetry 20 are by Lucretius.

[282] Note the minimal pair *prōfectus* PASSPART of *prōficere* 'go forward, affect' vs. *prŏfectus* PASSPART of *prŏficisci* 'travel', or *prŏfecto* 'really'.

A vacillating prefix is found in the word *prŏpago* (sometimes *prōpago* 'issue'). This word may have been analogically influenced by the etymological family built around *prŏpe* 'near' or *prŏprius* 'own'. The word *propitius* 'favourable' is also believed to have *prŏ-* rather than *prō-*; the negative evidence for this is the complete absence of this word from poetry, which may be due to three consecutive light syllables (*prŏpĭtĭ-*), unfitting for any of the classical metres bar an exceedingly rare one (called galliamb).[283]

7.2.1.3. *sē-*

This prefix is significantly rarer than the preceding two and is never found before vowels or before [t b s f n r]. One reason for its rarity may have been a partial coincidence with *sē-*, the variant of *sex* 'six' in compounds before voiced consonants (e.g. *sēdecim* '16' from *sex+decem*).[284] There is only one form, *seorsus* 'separate', in which a vowel-initial (originally [w]-initial, see *deorsum* above) stem follows *sē-*. This form is not used by poets except Lucretius, and just like *deorsum*, it is overwhelmingly contracted. In the two instances when it is not contracted, the prefix scans as a light syllable, i.e. *sĕ.or.sum*.

7.2.1.4. *ne-*

The negative prefix *ne-* is one of the rarest prefixes. It only occurs in *nequire* 'be unable', *nescire* 'not know', *nefas* 'disallowed', *nefandus* 'unspeakable', *nefarius* 'outrageous', *negligere* 'neglect', *negotium* 'business' and preclassical *nefrens* 'toothless'. Apparently before sonorants (viz. in *neg-ligere* and *neg-otium*) the prefix is augmented to *neg-*.

7.2.1.5. *re-*

This is one of the most frequently used prefixes. It occurs before all kinds of stems except [r]-initial ones. As was mentioned in 4.11, this restriction (**#[r]V[r]) is generally true of Latin words, including simplexes as well as reduplicated perfectum forms; and this constraint appears to be rather stable, since the current reflexes of this prefix (*re-*, *ré-*, *ra-*, *ri-*) still do not combine with [r]-initial stems in Spanish, French or Italian. Before vowels a variant *red-* appears (similarly to *prod-*), as in the following words:

---

[283] The short-vowel variant of the prefix is also found in several obscured formations such as *procul* 'far', *probus* 'excellent'.

[284] Thus, for instance, there are two words *sēiugis*: one means 'separate' and is from *sē+iug-*, the other means 'six-horse' (scil. cart, etc.) and is from *sex+iug-*. The second half of both forms is the stem meaning 'bind'.

(79) Words prefixed with *red-*
    redigere 'drive back'
    redire 'go back'
    redundare 'overflow'
    redimere 'take back'
    redhibere 'take back'
    redhostire (preclass.) 'recompense'
    redhalat (hapax legomenon in Lucretius) 'exhale' PRES3SING

The variant *red-* is also found in *reddere* 'give back', which is a synchronically inexplicable oddity. The etymology of this word is generally believed to involve original infectum reduplication (**re-di-dare*, see Walde & Hoffmann 1956 s.v.; de Vaan 2008: 174–5 is silent about it), an explanation not without problems in view of the perfect *reddidi* (with perfectum reduplication *plus* the geminate [d]) and the third stem *reddit-*, though, of course, analogy may have interfered.

Around 200 AD, the preconsonantal variant *re-* appears before vowels in Tertullian's works, who has *reaedificare* 'rebuild', *reanimare* 'restore to life' and *reindutus* 'reclothed' next to regular *redaccendere* 'relight' and *redornare* 'reornate'. Even later, around and after 400 AD, further such forms make their appearance as *reordinatio* 'reordination', *reinterpretatus* 'reinterpreted', *reignire* 'relight' and *reaccendere* 'relight' in the Christian literature.

Throughout the classical period, the frequently occurring verb *reicere* (< *re+iacere*) 'throw back' scans with a heavy–light syllable sequence for the portion written ⟨rei⟩, which clearly shows the gemination of [j] ([rej.ji.ke.re]).[285] In all likelihood this is due to the analogy of simplex forms, where intervocalic [j] is redundantly geminated (see 2.2.1, also see Allen 1978: 39; Weiss 2009: 154).

7.2.1.6. ambi-

This very rare prefix occurs, strictly speaking, only with a handful of vowel-initial stems in the classical period, and in this environment it loses the final vowel:

(80) Words prefixed with *amb(i)-*
    ambire 'go round'
    ambigere 'go round'
    ambesse (< *amb+ed-*) 'gnaw around'
    amburere 'burn'
    ambago or *ambages* 'evasion'

---

[285] Contrary to Touratier (2005: 75), who claims that the phonetic representation of this word was [reːjikere].

Consonant-initial stems prefixed with *ambi-* are first found in a technical text by Apuleius (*ambifarius* 'ambiguous'), and then a few more well after the classical period (*ambiformiter* 'in two forms' in Arnobius, *ambidexter* 'ambidextrous' from the fifth c. AD on).

Since the etymologically related, synonymous prefix *an-* (see 7.2.3.3) occurs almost exclusively before consonants, the two prefixes can be regarded as variants of the same entity even in Classical Latin.

7.2.1.7. *ante-*

This prefix appears as *ante-* or *anti-* without any discernible regularity:

(81) Words prefixed with *ante-/anti-*
    antecellere 'surpass'
    antecedere 'precede'
    antesignani 'troops in front'
    anteferre 'carry in front'

    anticipare 'anticipate'
    antistes 'high priest'

There seems to be some evidence that when a vowel-initial stem was prefixed with *ante-*, the final [e] of *ante-* was lost, though such forms are few and far between. The only example with any frequency is *anteire* 'go before' in its attested forms *anteis, anteit, ante(e)at, anteeunt*. Both *anteis* and *anteit* scan in poetry as two heavy syllables; the same is true of the infinitive *anteire* (with the scansion of the third syllable depending on context). Whether this suggests [antejs], [antejt], [antejr(e)] or [anti:s], [anti:t], [anti:r(e)] is, in itself, difficult to determine, though the attested spelling ⟨antire⟩ suggests the latter, and generally speaking vowel elision is more frequent in Latin (morpho-)phonology than desyllabification.[286] The only occurrence (Ovid *Ars am.* 2.726.) of *ante(e)at* scans as heavy–light–light, thus clearly [an.te.at] and one of the two [e] vowels is lost. The participle *anteactus* 'past' occurs twice in the entire poetic corpus,[287] and scans as three syllables (heavy–heavy–X), which points to elision or desyllabification of the [e]. The occurrences of *anteambulo(-)*[288] 'who walks before' scan as four syllables (heavy–heavy–light–X) if one disregards the inflectional endings, which points to the same.

It would be interesting to see how the final vowel of *anti-/ante-* behaves in the environment of lowering before [r] (see 5.2.2.2), but this prefix does not combine with stems beginning with [r] at all.

---

[286] See the prevocalic deletion of back vowels in 5.3.2 or word-final deletion in hiatus in poetry, mentioned in 2.3.2.
[287] Ovid *Am.* 2.8.25, Tib. *El.* 3.7.189; it is also exceedingly rare in prose.
[288] Mart. *Epigr.* 2.18. 5 *anteambulo*, 3.7.2 *anteambulonis*, 10.74.3 *anteambulones*.

7.2.1.8. vē-

This marginal negative prefix is confined to a handful of forms:

(82) Words prefixed with *ve-*
      vecors 'frenzied'
      vepallidus 'very pale'
      vesanus 'mad'
      vegrandis 'undersized'
      Veiovis a deity

A number of etymologies involving this prefix were proposed earlier for further words, e.g. *vestigium* 'trace', *vemens/vehemens* 'vehement', *vesica* 'bladder', but these are not now generally accepted (see de Vaan 2008 s.vv.).

7.2.1.9. prae-

The only glide-final prefix is frequent and occurs with all consonants as well as vowels, though vowel-initial stems with *prae-* are not particularly numerous. In poetry, *prae-* tends to scan as a light syllable before vowels, though contraction with the stem-initial syllable also occurs, and neither pattern is attested in more than a handful of instances. For contraction the only clear example is Catullus *Carm.* 64.120, where *praeoptarit* 'prefer' scans as heavy–heavy–light, which means that the entire sequence spelled ⟨praeop⟩ counts as a single syllable. Uncontracted short scansion is found in Verg. *Aen.* 7.524 (*praeustis* 'burnt at the point' light–heavy–heavy), Ov. *Metam.* 7.131 (*praeacutae* 'sharpened to a point' light–light–heavy–heavy), and three occurring forms of *praeire* 'go before' (i.e. *praeeunt, praeeunte, praeeuntibus*) all scan with two initial light syllables ([pra.je.unt] and [pra.je.un.t-]), while *prae-iret* with two initial heavy syllables in Stat. *Theb.* 6.519 ([praj.ji:.ret] with gemination of [j] in line with its redundant gemination in simplex forms). Lexicalised contraction is found in *praebere* 'put forward' (< *prae+habere*, in Plautus the uncontracted form with weakened stem-vowel *praehibere* is found).

    The isolated verb *prehendere* 'grab' shows a variant *pre-* (as well as a stem unattested elsewhere in the language).

7.2.2. Prefixes ending in [r]

7.2.2.1. per-

This prefix is lexically frequent and combines, mostly without phonological interference, with any stem-initial segment. In three words the [r] sporadically and variably assimilates to [l]:

(83) [l]-initial stems prefixed with *per-*
      perlegere ~ *pellegere* (only in Plautus) 'scan'

perlucere (mostly) ~ *pellucere* 'transmit light'
perlicere ~ *pellicere* 'attract'

There is further the isolated verb *peierare* [pejjer-] next to its reassembled etymon *perjurare* (see 7.1).

7.2.2.2. *super-*

This prefix is rarer than the previous one, and is even more impervious to phonological alteration. There is only one item in which the final [r] assimilates to [l], *supellex/supellectilis* 'belongings'. In this word the assimilation of [r] to [l] is invariable; the form *superlectilis* without assimilation is attested altogether six times, all from the fourth–fifth centuries AD, clearly a symptom of the etymologising tendency in writing. In a few words the prefix appears as *supra-* (e.g. *suprascandere* 'surmount', also *superscandere*). Given that both *super* and *supra* are existing words ('over' preposition and adverb, respectively), this suggests that *super*-prefixed forms are closer to compounds than to other prefixed forms.

7.2.2.3. *subter-*

This prefix occurs in about ten words at most (e.g. *subterpositus* 'placed beneath', *subterfugere* 'run for shelter', *subterlabens* 'flowing beneath'); its final consonant remains intact in all of them.

7.2.2.4. *inter-*

This prefix is relatively frequent. Its final [r] only assimilates in the lexical item *intellegere* or *intelligere* 'understand'.[289]

7.2.2.5. *por-*

This moribund prefix occurs in *portendere* 'portend' and *porrigere* 'extend', *porricere* 'offer as sacrifice', and in *polliceri* 'promise' with assimilation of [r] to [l].

7.2.3. *Nasal-final prefixes*

7.2.3.1. *in-*

In- is two prefixes, not one. The negative prefix is found in e.g. *inscius* 'unaware', the directional in e.g. *incurrere* 'run up against/to'. Since there does

---

[289] Statius *Theb.* 7.571 uses the word *interligat*, which is not from *inter+legere* but from *inter+ligare* 'join'.

not seem to be any significant difference between the two in terms of their phonology (though Prinz 1953: 45–6 indicates a small discrepancy in their readiness to assimilate), I discuss them together here.

The behaviour of *in-* shows the following particularities. The coronal nasal at the end of the prefix undergoes place assimilation before stops (place assimilation 1) and before [m] (place assimilation 2, for both types see 4.8). Although in writing only assimilation to labials is directly indicated with the spellings ⟨imp-⟩, ⟨imb-⟩, ⟨imm-⟩, there is no reason to doubt that before velars assimilation to [ŋ] took place (place assimilation 1), and this is, in fact, quite clearly indicated by grammarians.[290] Before the fricatives [s], [f] place loss resulting in a placeless nasal is most likely (but vacillation must have been great, see 4.6), followed by coalescence resulting in a long nasal vowel (see 5.4.4).

The nasal may undergo total assimilation to [r] and [l], though lack of assimilation appears to be significantly more frequent, especially in the classical and the preclassical periods, as far as the writing indicates this (see also Prinz 1953: 45 sqq.). Before glides and vowels the written form of the prefix is unchanged (which implies a phonological [n]).

(84)   Words prefixed with *in-*

example	transcription	gloss	process
imponere	[imp-]	'put on'	place assimilation 1
inquirere	[iŋk-]	'inquire'	place assimilation 1
inscius	[ĩːs-] ([ins-]?)	'unaware'	place loss and coalescence
inferre	[ĩːf-] ([imɸ-]?)	'take in'	place loss and coalescence
immittere	[imm-]	'send in'	place assimilation 2
inrigare	[inr-] ~ [irr-]	'make wet'	total assimilation[291]
inlicere	[inl-] ~ [ill-]	'entice'	total assimilation

7.2.3.2. *con-*

The prefix *con-* was discussed in detail in 5.4.4, where the behaviour of the placeless nasal was explained. Here I recapitulate the main points of that section and add a number of others to make the picture full.

The behaviour of *con-* before consonants is somewhat similar to that of *in-*. The placeless nasal at the end of the prefix undergoes place assimilation before stops (place assimilation 1) and before [m] (place assimilation 2). As with *in-*, in writing only assimilation to labials is directly indicated with the spellings ⟨comp-⟩, ⟨comb-⟩, ⟨comm-⟩, but it is certain that before velars assimilation

---

[290] See the references in Allen (1978: 27 sqq). Note also that the usual etymologising tendency in the latter half of antiquity often replaces the ⟨imp-/imb-⟩ spellings with ⟨inp-/inb-⟩.

[291] As was remarked upon in 5.2.2.2, the [r] resulting from the assimilation does not induce the lowering of [i] (**errigare*) even though it is clearly derived environment, which may be yet another indication that the lowering came to be confined to non-initial syllables.

resulting in [ŋ] took place (place assimilation 1).[292] Before the fricatives [s], [f] coalescence resulting in a long nasal vowel is most likely. Total assimilation to [r] is usual except for the relatively rarely used words *conridere* 'laugh together', *conradere* 'rake together', *conrodere* 'gnaw'. Assimilation to [l] is almost exceptionless with the lexemes *colligere* 'collect' and *collega/collegium* 'partner in office', 'college'; with other [l]-initial stems the proportion of assimilated forms varies between 20–50 per cent in the corpus, see 7.3.3 for a more detailed presentation.

With [n]-initial stems no geminate [nn] results (as with *in-*) but a [koːn-] sequence instead with dropping of the prefix-final nasal and compensatory lengthening of the [o] (*conivere* 'close the eyes', *conectere* 'connect', *conubium* 'marriage', etc. vs. *innectere* 'tie', *inniti* 'lean upon'). It is also possible that the vowel was nasal rather than plain. The explanation I gave in 5.4.4 for the dropping of the nasal is that a sequence of a placeless nasal and [n] cannot undergo either place assimilation 1 or place assimilation 2, because such a sequence does not satisfy the structural description of either. Since a placeless segment is incomplete, it cannot surface and is thus deleted. I speculated in 5.4.4 that the placeless nasal may just possibly have coalesced with the preceding vowel instead of being deleted in this environment.

Before glides the nasal is present in the spelling, suggesting coalescence into a long nasal vowel. There is one exception: *con*[j]*icere* 'throw' is attested more than sporadically as ⟨coicere⟩, which probably suggests a totally assimilated nasal, i.e. [kojjikere]. Other words with glide-initial stems are occasionally found with no orthographic ⟨n⟩ in inscriptions (e.g. ⟨coiux⟩ 'spouse').

Before [w] there is some evidence of a labial pronunciation coming from the grammarian Marius Victorinus (fourth century AD). He explicitly claims that the relevant forms are ⟨comvalescit⟩ 'convalesce', ⟨comvocat⟩ 'summon' with ⟨m⟩ rather than ⟨n⟩ (*Ars Grammatica* 1.4.65). The problem is not only that such forms are extremely rare generally, but also that Marius Victorinus's other claims seem to be so far-fetched (e.g. ⟨ovvertit⟩ 'turn back' and ⟨ovvius⟩ ' facing' instead of ⟨obvertit⟩, ⟨obvius⟩) that one feels one has to take even this apparently plausible piece of information regarding ⟨comvocat⟩, etc. with a pinch of salt. Note, however, that he does not claim the same for *in-*, which seems to be in line

---

[292] Again similarly to *in-*, the usual etymologising tendency in the latter half of antiquity often replaces the ⟨comp-/comb-⟩ spellings with ⟨conp-/conb-⟩. Contrary to Prinz (1953: 36) I do not believe that Cicero's remarks in *Orator* 159 point to phonetically unassimilated [konp-]. The relevant portion of the text is this: 'Indoctus dicimus brevi prima littera, insatius producta, inhumanus brevi, infelix longa... quibus in verbis eae primae litterae sunt quae in sapiente atque felice, producte dicitur, in ceteris omnibus breviter; itemque composuit, consuevit, concrepuit, confecit' 'The first sound of *indoctus* is pronounced short, that of *insatius* long, that of *inhumanus* short, that of *infelix* long... in those words that begin with the same sound as *sapiens* and *felix* it is pronounced long, in all the others short; similarly *composuit, consuevit, concrepuit, confecit*' (translation mine). The point Cicero makes is simply that the vowel of the prefix is long in *consuevit* 'got used' and *confecit* 'accomplished' but short in *composuit* 'composed' and *concrepuit* 'creaked'. It does not follow, as Prinz believes, that 'the parallel is valid only if one assumes *n* in *conposuit*'.

with my assumption that *in-* ended in a coronal nasal (see 7.2.3.1), whereas *con-* ended in a placeless nasal.

Besides the empirical issue regarding putative [komw-] there is a theoretical issue as well: how could a place feature spread from a glide to a consonant if glides have the same structure as vowels (i.e. they have no C-Place node, only a V-Place node, as explained in 2.4) and so their place nodes and features are not on the same tier as those of consonants? The most plausible assumption is that there was no assimilation at all, and so the preconsonantal placeless nasal coalesced with the preceding vowel. Thus the spelling ⟨con⟩ stood for [kõ:] before glides as well as before fricatives. There was no spreading and no true labial nasal in the ⟨comvocat⟩/⟨convocat⟩-type words. This would also explain why Marius Victorinus gives examples of the ⟨in⟩ > ⟨im⟩ assimilation before the labial consonants [p b f m], but not before [w]: the glide does not induce assimilation in the nasal of either prefix, and the grammarian's variation in the spelling of the *con-* nasal is congruent with its lack of place, as opposed to that of *in-*.

As was pointed out in 4.8 and 5.4.4, before vowels the variant is *co-* with no nasal (*coarguere* 'prove', *coire* 'meet', etc.), thus hiatus is created by dropping an intervocalic consonant.[293] Metrical evidence does not show contraction in such cases. Lexicalised contraction is found in a few words (*cōgere* < *co+agere* 'coerce', *cōmere* < *co+emere* 'comb'),[294] but only with short vowels, thus the PassPart of *cōgere* is *coāctus* and its Perf is *coēgi*. Note, however, that the variant *com-* is also attested before vowels in certain words in the preclassical as well as the classical era (notably *comesse* 'eat', *comestus* 'eaten', *comes* 'companion'), and Romance languages also point to such formations (French *commencer* and Italian *cominciare* 'begin' go back to **com+initiare*). This shows very early lexicalisation, with the etymological *[m] intact in intervocalic position as opposed to its later development into a placeless nasal in word-final position (de Vaan 2008 s.v. *com*) and does not impinge on the synchronic phonology of the placeless nasal in any way.

(85) Words prefixed with *con-*

example	transcription	gloss	process
componere	[komp-]	'compose'	place assimilation 1
conquirere	[koŋk-]	'collect'	place assimilation 1
conscius	[kõ:s-]	'privy'	coalescence
conferre	[kõ:f-]	'carry'	coalescence
conubium	[ko:n-] ([kõ:n-]?)	'marriage'	loss with compensatory lengthening (or coalescence)

---

[293] The verb *urere* 'burn' gives *comburere* 'burn to ashes'. This may be due either to the analogical influence of *amburere*, or perhaps to the actual prefixation of *co-* to *amburere* rather than to *urere* (see Walde & Hoffmann 1956 s.v.). Actually, no [u]-initial stem was prefixed with *co(n)-* until the fourth century AD, when Marius Victorinus introduced the theological term *counitus/counitio* 'united/union'.

[294] But note the form *coemere* for the latter in Caesar *Bell. Gall.* 1.3.

committere	[komm-]	'bring together'	place assimilation 2
conrigere	[korr-] ([kõːr]?)	'correct'	total assimilation
conlocare	[koll-] ([kõːl]?)	'put in place'	total assimilation
convocare	[kõːw-]	'summon'	coalescence

7.2.3.3. an-

This prefix combines only with a handful of stems, all but one beginning with a consonant. It is historically a variant of *ambi-* (see 7.2.1.6); the phonological regularity governing their distribution (vowel- vs. consonant-initial stem) only broke down after the classical period. There is, I think, no reason to believe that its final nasal behaved differently from that of *in-*.[295]

(86) Words prefixed with *an-*

example	transcription	gloss	process
amputare	[amp-]	'cut off'	place assimilation 1
amplecti	[amp-]	'embrace'	place assimilation 1
anquirere	[aŋk-]	'inquire'	place assimilation 1
anceps	[aŋk-]	'equivocal'	place assimilation 1
anfractus	[ãːf-] ([aɱf-]?)[296]	'broken'	place loss and coalescence
amicire	[ami-]	'cover'	?

7.2.3.4. circum-

This prefix does not seem to be subject to any alternations before consonants. The spelling ⟨circum⟩ is invariable and is replaced by ⟨circu⟩ only before the stem *ire* 'go' (*circuire* 'go round') and its derivatives (mainly in *circuitus* 'circular motion', less frequently in other forms, e.g. *circuit* 'goes round', *circueunda* 'around which one turns'). *Circu(m)-* is exceedingly rare before other

---

[295] Two lexical items present interesting issues here. *Antestari* 'call as witness' appears to be *an+testari*, but Leumann (1977: 234) suggests an etymology (accepted by de Vaan 2008) *ante-testari* with haplology. While semantically as well as phonologically plausible, it is synchronically irrelevant in that the outcome of the putative haplology is, in fact, identical to the prefix *an-*. The other word is *amicire* 'cover', in which the verbal stem is [-ikiːre], an unusual deviation from original [jakere] 'throw' (see de Vaan 2008 s.v. *iacio*), and the prefix is *am-*, which is explicable diachronically from *amb-* (though not in a straightforward manner), but in a synchronic phonological description it is not easily reconciled with the other prefix variants. Kent (1912) and in his wake Zirin (1970: 38 sqq.) suggests that [ji] > [i] may have been a real sound change (on the basis of the light scansion of the first syllable of *adicere* 'throw', *conicere* in preclassical scenic poetry), and the [j] was restituted on the analogy of *jacere* (Kent 1912: 38–9) or of forms like *conficere* 'accomplish' (Zirin 1970: 39). If accepted, this would explain the stem-initial [i], but the stem-final [iː] would still be unaccounted for and unique among the many compunds of *iacere*, which regularly have [-jikere] (*reicere* 'throw back', *deicere* 'throw down', *conicere* 'throw', etc.).

[296] The labial rather than the coronal nasal is also indicated by Lucretius' spelling ⟨amfractus⟩, whereas ⟨imf-⟩ for *in+f-* is not found there.

vowels (e.g. *circumagere* 'drive/sail round'). With *ire* the forms in *circum-* are significantly more frequent than those in *circu-*, especially when the stem form begins with [e] (e.g. *circumeunt* 'they go round'), but the noun *circuitus*, alone of all derivatives, appears in the corpus overwhelmingly in this form.

As far as the last segment of the prefix is concerned, it is difficult to give a phonological interpretation of these data which is completely coherent with everything that has been said so far. The spelling without ⟨m⟩ before *ire* suggests a placeless nasal which is lost before a vowel much like that of *con-* (see 7.2.3.2 above). But a placeless nasal could not explain the spellings ⟨circumagere⟩ or ⟨circumeunt⟩ — add to this that the surface phonological form corresponding to these spellings is also uncertain. Did it include an actual [m] or a nasalised [u] before another vowel? Both would be somewhat problematic.

A non-phonological difference between *circum-* and *con-* may be relevant, however. Words prefixed with *circum-* are much more like compounds than words prefixed with *con-*: their meanings are usually more compositional, stem vowel weakening is hardly ever found in them (*circumcidere* 'cut around' and *circumcludere* 'enclose' were probably lexicalised early), and *circum-* can precede other prefixes (e.g. *circumobruere* 'wrap around' with *ob-*). In this respect *circum* resembles the other disyllables *retro* 'backwards', *intro* 'in', *extra* 'out', which formed compounds (if at all), but did not function as prefixes in the strict sense of the word. On the other hand, *circuire*, *circuitus* suggest prefixation rather than a compound boundary, and hence deletion of the placeless nasal just as is *coire*; thus the issue probably cannot be resolved definitively.

7.2.4. *Coronal obstruent-final prefixes*

7.2.4.1. *post-*

This prefix is rare in Classical Latin and shows no phonological interference with the stem. The only possible exception to this is *possidere* 'possess', which is believed to go back to *post+sedere* 'sit' (de Vaan 2008: 552). If this etymology is correct, the stem vowel has undergone weakening, which is untypical with *post-*.

7.2.4.2. *ex-*

One of the frequent prefixes, *ex-* appears in the form *ē-* before all voiced consonants (though occasional spellings with ⟨ex⟩ are found):

(87) Words prefixed with *ex-*
        extendere 'extend'
        expellere 'expel'
        excellere 'excel'
        exire 'go out'
        ēdere 'give out'
        ēmanere 'stay away'

ēicere [eːjikere] 'throw out'
ēvincere 'defeat'

The replacement of *ex-* by *ē-* follows from a sound change in the prehistory of Latin which deleted [s] before all voiced consonants with compensatory lengthening. As was explained in 4.2.1, the consequences of this sound change are visible in the allomorphic patterns of some prefixes as well as elsewhere in the morphology and the lexicon, but it is no longer an active phonological rule in Classical Latin (and, in itself, would not account for the loss of the [k] anyway). Note, however, that a sequence in which [s] is preceded by [k] and followed by anything other than a voiceless stop or a vowel would be unsyllabifiable under the terms explicated in Chapter 3. Thus some change in the shape of the prefix is forced by the phonotactics; but what exactly that change should be is not dictated by it.

With [s]-initial stems simplification of [kss] to [ks] took place (general degemination, see 4.5.1), and in the spelling the ⟨s⟩ of the stem is very often dropped in such cases:

(88) [s]-initial stem prefixed with *ex-*
⟨exilire⟩ 'jump out' < *ex+salire*, i.e. [ks] < [kss]

The only consonant which triggers assimilation in *ex-* is [f]. The spelling is either ⟨eff-⟩ or ⟨ecf-⟩ (*efferre/ecferre* 'take out', etc., though *effatus* 'who has spoken' and not **ecfatus* in classical and postclassical Latin). If the spelling ⟨ecf-⟩ is taken to represent [ekf-] (the most plausible choice), a third variant [ek-] is identified. This can be analysed as resulting from a reanalysis of the *ex-s-* forms triggered by the degemination of [s]:

(89) Reanalysis of *ex-s-*
[eks]+[saliːre] > [eksiliːre] (degemination) > [ek]+[siliːre]

The completely assimilated form ⟨eff-⟩ can, in theory, be analysed as including the variant [ek-], in which case the assimilation process only affects the consonant [k], not the sequence [ks].

On the other hand, since the [s] of *dis-* (see 7.2.4.3) assimilates systematically to [f] (and only to [f]), the emergence of the [ek-] variant can also be explained as resulting from assimilation (place assimilation 2) followed by degemination:

(90) Assimilation and degemination in *ex-f-*
[eks]+[ferre] > [ekfferre] (assimilation) > [ek]+[ferre] (degemination)

Under the latter analysis, [ek-] is not a morpheme variant at all, it is simply the automatic result of the independently motivated and attested phonological rule of degemination.

7.2.4.3. dis-

This prefix shows variation very similar to that of *ex-*, diachronically deriving from the change presented in 4.2.1. Before voiced consonants of all kinds except [j] *dī-* is found.

(91) Words prefixed with *dis-*
      distendere 'stretch'
      discurrere 'run away'
      disponere 'distribute'
      dissentire 'disagree'
      dis[j]*icere* 'scatter'

      dīgerere 'disperse'
      dīversus 'diverse'
      dīluere 'wash away'
      dīmittere 'send away'

Regarding [j], the exceptional voiced consonant, the following seems clear. The variant *dis-* is found in all forms of the verb *dis*[j]*icere* 'scatter' (perfect *disieci*, third form *disiectum* with different vowels following the [j]), in inscriptional *disiurgium* 'quarrel', and mostly in *disiungere* 'separate'. The only word that consistently shows the *s*-less form is *dīiudicare* 'judge'. In *dīrumpere* 'burst', assimilated (*dirrumpere*) as well as unchanged forms (*disrumpere*) are sporadically found in all ages from Plautus to St Augustine. In the archaic period a handful of assimilated forms of *dimminuere* ~ *dīminuere* 'shatter' are also found.

Only two vowel-initial stems appear to have combined with *dis-*, and in these the [s] historically underwent rhotacism:[297]

(92) Vowel-initial stems prefixed with *dis-*
      diribere < *dis+habere* 'sort (votes)'
      dirimere < *dis+emere* 'take away'

The only consonant to which the [s] assimilates regularly is [f] (place assimilation 2):

(93) [f]-initial stems prefixed with *dis-*
      differre 'scatter'
      diffundere 'pour out'
      diffidere 'have no confidence'

---

[297] Note, however, that stem-initial [s] does not undergo rhotacism: *prosilire* 'jump forth', *desinere* 'desist', and so on. In 4.4 I argued that *dirimere* and *diribere* were lexicalised remnants from an earlier period, and rhotacism does not affect intervocalic [s] at prefix–stem boundaries, hence the productive *prosilire*-type. Combinations of *dis-* with vowel-initial stems were apparently avoided, as opposed to combinations of [s]-final prefixes with vowel-initial stems.

7.2.4.4. trans-

This prefix also shows the loss of [s] before voiced consonants, but the consistent application of this regularity is only triggered by coronals and [j]. Assimilation of [s] is not attested at all. When a geminate [s] would result, it is shortened by the specific degemination discussed in 4.5.2.

(94) Words prefixed with *trans-*
  transportare 'carry over'
  transtuli 'took across'
  transcurrere 'run across'
  transcendere ([trãːskendere] < [trãːs]+[skandere]) 'step over, cross'
  transilire ([trãːsiliːre] < [trãːs]+[saliːre]) 'jump across'
  trā[j]icere (~ *transiicere* hapax leg.) 'throw across'

  trāducere (overwhelmingly) ~ *transducere* 'lead across'
  trādere (overwhelmingly) ~ *transdere* 'hand over'
  trālucere, -lucidus (overwhelmingly) ~ *translucere, -lucidus* 'transmit(ting) light'
  trānare ~ *transnare* (roughly equal) 'swim across'

  translatus (! overwhelmingly) ~ *trālatus* 'taken across'
  transvolare (overwhelmingly) ~ *trāvolare* 'fly across'
  transversus (overwhelmingly) ~ *trāversus* 'crosswise'
  transmittere (overwhelmingly) ~ *trāmittere* 'send over'
  transmeare (overwhelmingly) ~ *trāmeare* 'travel across'
  transgredi 'step over, cross'

The base variant *trans-* was used productively and independently of the phonological environment to form adjectives based on geographical names, e.g. *transrhenani*[298] 'those living beyond the Rhine' in Caesar, Tacitus and later historians or *transdanuviana* 'beyond the Danube' in Lactantius (fourth c. AD).

The word *trānquillus* 'calm' is unexplained phonologically, as is the sporadically attested *trāferre* 'take across' (besides the much more frequent *transferre*).[299]

---

[298] *Transrhenani* is the only word in the corpus in which any variant of *trans-* is found before [r]. This, however, is unrelated to the absence of **re-r-* words (see above), since [r]V:[r] is well formed in any position except final syllables, cf. *rārus* 'rare', *prōrumpere* 'jump forth'.

[299] Unless perhaps one assumes assimilation of [s] to [f] like with *dis-* in *differre*, etc. and then shortening of the long fricative after the long vowel like in *transilire*. The phenomena are too isolated to allow anything more than speculation and, at any rate, all other [f]-initial stems show *trans-* (*transfugere* 'run across', *transfigere* 'transfix', *transformare* 'transform', etc.). On *tranquillus* see Vine (2008).

7.2.4.5. ad-

With the exception of [j], [w] the [d] in the prefix *ad-* assimilates to all consonants, though with varying consistency. The cline along which stem-initial consonants can be arranged according to how forcefully they act on the [d] of *ad-* is the following, with examples below:[300]

(95) The consonants causing assimilation in *ad-*
    p t k >> l r >> g s f >> m n (>> w j)

(96) Words prefixed with *ad-*
    appetere ~ adpetere 'try to reach'
    attinere 'hold'
    accipere 'receive'
    alloqui ~ adloqui (roughly equal) 'speak to'
    alligare (more frequently) *~ adligare* 'tie'
    arripere (more frequently) *~ adripere* 'grasp'
    arrogare ~ adrogare (roughly equal) 'claim'
    (*abbibere ~ adbibere* 'drink')
    adgredi (more frequently) *~ aggredi* 'go up to'
    adferre (more frequently) *~ afferre* 'bring'
    adsiduus ~ assiduus (roughly equal) 'persistent'
    adsistere (more frequently) *~ assistere* 'stand near'
    admovere (overwhelmingly) *~ ammovere* 'move near'
    adnumerare (overwhelmingly) *~ annumerare* 'count'

The cline apparently has to do with sonority, though the relation is not straightforward, with liquids higher in the hierarchy than nasals and even fricatives and, as often, one has to count on analytic spelling. It also emerges from the manuscript tradition that assimilation to [k] was rare if it was followed by a second onset consonant (as in *adclamare* 'shout', *adclinis* 'inclined', *adclivis* 'sloping upwards', *adcredere* 'trust', *adcrescere* 'grow', *adquirere* 'acquire'). With some consonants, e.g. [p], the 'readiness' to assimilate was lexically gradient, thus in *apparere* 'appear' and *apparare* 'prepare' virtually exceptionless, in *appetere* 'try to reach' very frequent, rarer in *adponere* 'place near', much rarer in *adprobare* 'endorse' and in *adprehendere* 'grasp' (Prinz 1949–50: 91 sqq.; see also García González 1996).

The frequent verb *adesse* 'be present' seems to be lexically exempt from assimilation: the forms with the [s]-initial stem variant are almost always *adsum*

---

[300] Stems beginning with [b] almost never figure with this prefix. A few occurrences of *adbibere ~ abbibere* 'drink' and archaic *adbitere* 'approach' are recorded, and in postclassical Latin *adbreviare ~ abbreviare* 'shorten, abbreviate' makes its appearance. Because of the scarcity of data, the place of [b] in the cline is not so clear as that of the other consonants, hence the omission. Stem-initial [s] is likely to have effected the devoicing of [d] to [t].

Pres1Sing, *adsunt* Pres3Plur, *adsim* Subj1Sing, etc. The perfectum-based forms (which all begin with [f]) also mostly avoid assimilation (*adfui* Perf1Sing, etc.), but not as strictly as infectum-based forms (the incidence of *affui*, etc. is about 15% of all occurrences vs. about 3% for *assum*, etc.;[301] the general assimilation rate for *ad+s-* in other words is around 26% in the editions on which the Brepols-corpus is based, a proportion similar to that emerging from an investigation of manuscripts according to Prinz 1949–50: 98–99).

When a stem begins with [s]+stop, the prefix variably appears in writing as ⟨ad⟩ or ⟨a⟩. The latter of the two represents assimilation of [d] to [s] followed by degemination before the following stop:

(97) [s]+stop-initial word prefixed with *ad-*
      [ad]+[skandere] > [asskendere] > [askendere] (*ascendere* 'ascend')

The assimilation rate in these clusters is generally higher than for *ad+s*V-: for *ascendere* 'ascend', *aspicere* 'catch sight of', *aspergere* 'sprinkle' and *aspectare* 'watch' it is over 80 per cent, for *astare* 'stand near', *aspirare* 'breathe' and *ascire/asciscere* 'associate with oneself' over 30 per cent, and for *aspernari* 'despise' 100 per cent.[302] Only two words, *ascribere* 'add in writing' and *astringere* 'tie', at about 20 per cent, are below the non-pre-cluster average.

It is noteworthy that the tendency to assimilate is so sharply divergent in the case of stop+sonorant complex onsets (where *ad*+CC << *ad*+CV) vs. initial clusters of an extrasyllabic [s] and a stop (where *ad*+CC >> *ad*+CV).[303] Phonologically there are two important differences between the two structures. One is in the syllabic affiliation of the segments involved; the other is in the status of the resulting sequences. The geminate stop found in words like *approbare* 'endorse' apears to remain intact if assimilation has taken place. By contrast, the geminate [s] resulting from assimilation in words like *ascendere* is categorically degeminated by the rule described in 4.5.1. In that section I explained the difference with reference to the fact that a [ppr] sequence is syllabifiable whereas a [ssk] sequence is not. Interestingly, the behaviour of *ad-* before CC shows that assimilation is more frequent in cases when it produces an illicit configuration which, however, is categorically remedied (*ascendere*-type) than in cases when it produces a cluster which is legitimate in the sense that it is syllabifiable, but is untypical in the sense that it only ever emerges at prefix–stem boundaries.

---

[301] Though note that a pun is found in Plautus's *Poenulus* 279 which crucially assumes the assimilated pronunciation of *adsum* in spite of the manuscript tradition.

[302] *Aspernari* is relevant only if it historically includes *ad-* (as e.g. de Vaan 2008: s.v. assumes), and not *ab-*.

[303] As I pointed out in 2.2.2.9, the assimilation ratio of the only [sw]-initial stem prefixed with *ad-* (*adsuescere* 'get used to') is 24 per cent, nearly identical to the assimilation ratio of [s]V-initial stems (26%). Given that there is only this one lexical item respresenting this particular phonological configuration, no general conclusions can be drawn apart from the trivial one that it does not follow the pattern of extrasyllabic [s]+stop clusters.

7.2.5. Prefixes ending in [b]

7.2.5.1. ob-

The [b] in *ob-* usually undergoes assimilation to [k g f], occasionally to [m] with great differences in the degree of lexicalisation involved:[304]

(98) Words prefixed with *ob-*
    occupare 'seize'
    occulere, occultus 'hide/hidden'
    occidere 'fall'
    occīdere 'kill'
    occumbere (~ *obcumbere* sporadically from late fourth c. AD on) 'fall'
    occludere (mostly) ~ *obcludere* 'close'
    obcaecare (mostly) ~ *occaecare* 'blind'
    oggerere 'heap'
    offendere 'strike'
    offerre (~ sporadic *obferre*) 'put in one's path'
    offundere (~ sporadic *obfundere*) 'pour'
    offuscare (~ *obfuscare* from fourth c. AD on) 'darken'
    obfui, -fuit, etc. (overwhelmingly) ~ *offui, offuit*, etc. 'hinder'
    obmutescere (mostly) ~ *ommutescere* 'become dumb'
    obmurmurare 'murmur in protest'[305]

The [b] underwent voice assimilation before [p t s]; before all other consonants and all vowels the prefix appears as *ob-*. Voice assimilation to [p t s] is not always indicated in writing, and the relation of written form to phonetic form is particularly difficult to disentangle at this point. Normally ⟨op⟩ is written before ⟨p⟩ but ⟨ob⟩ is written before ⟨t⟩ and ⟨s⟩:[306]

(99) Voice assimilation with *ob-*
    ⟨oppetere⟩ (overwhelmingly) ~ ⟨obpetere⟩ 'encounter'
    ⟨obtinere⟩ (overwhelmingly) ~ ⟨optinere⟩ 'maintain'
    ⟨obsidere⟩ (overwhelmingly) ~ ⟨opsidere⟩ 'occupy'

[304] In *omittere* < **ommittere* < *ob+mittere* 'release' degemination followed the assimilation. This historic degemination, triggered by the following heavy syllable, is referred to as the Mamilla-Law, see Tucker (1922).

[305] Note that the verbs that show overwhelmingly unassimilated *ob-* (*obcaecare, obfui, obmutescere, obmurmurare*) also show unweakened stem vowels.

[306] The standard etymology of the verb *ostendere* 'show' involves the prefix *ob-* in the form **obs-* plus the verb *tendere* 'stretch' with loss of the [b] in the cluster [bst] (or more likely [pst]). Note, however, that the cluster [pst] occurs without simplification both at prefix-stem boundaries (*abstinere* 'keep away') and in simplex forms (*depstum* 'pastry', *consumpsti* 'you consumed'). Admittedly, though, the other two [b]-final prefixes show [s]-final variants before [t] (see the following two sections on *ab-* and *sub-*). A form analogous in etymology to *ostendere* is *oscen* 'divining bird' < **obs+can-* 'sing'.

Is this a phonological difference indicating that voice assimilation was compulsory when voice was the only difference between the two adjacent stops, but optional when there was also a difference in place? Or is it merely a spelling convention? In the latter case, does it mean that voice assimilation was general but was not indicated in the spelling unless it resulted in a geminate? The problem is that parallels cannot be found within the language. In simplex forms voice assimilation is very often indicated, as in *actus* 'driven' and *scriptus* 'written', *scripsi* 'I wrote' (cf. 4.2). The prefix *ad-* (7.2.4.5) shows extensive assimilations, but that probably has to do with the fact that it ends in a coronal stop, which is strongly dispreferred in syllable coda. There are two other [b]-final prefixes (see the following two sections), but they generally behave differently from *ob-*.

7.2.5.2. ab-

This prefix occurs before all consonants except [b g]. Before the voiceless stops [k t] it appears as *abs-*:[307]

(100) Words prefixed with *ab-*
      abesse 'be absent'
      abire 'go away'
      abstinere 'keep away'
      abstrahere 'drag away'
      abscondere 'conceal'

Before [p] it appears as *as-*, a form apparently dissimilated from *abs-* (these two verbs are the only examples):

(101) [p]-initial stems prefixed with *ab-*
      asportare 'take away'
      aspellere 'drive away'

Before [m] and [w] the variant form is *ā-*:

(102) [m]- and [w]-initial stems prefixed with *ab-*
      āmovere 'remove'
      āmittere 'send away'
      āvertere 'turn away'
      āvocare 'call away'

Before [f] this prefix only occurs in three verbs. Of these, *fui* is accompanied by *ā-*, as are the other labial consonants, but the other two, *fugere* and *ferre* combine

---

[307] Note that as a preposition, *ab* also shows the variant *abs*, almost exclusively before *te* 'you', plus a handful of instances of *abs* before [t]- and [k]-initial words.

with a prefix *au-*, which only occurs in these two words. Whether *au-* is etymologically related to *ab-* is a matter of debate (for the literature and a thorough discussion of the question see de Vaan 2009).

(103) [f]-initial stems prefixed with *ab-*
      āfui (PERF of *abesse*) 'be absent'
      aufugere 'run away'
      auferre[308] 'carry away'

With the prefix *ab-* no assimilation takes place except for voice assimilation.

It seems clear that the stop-final form of *ab-* was avoided before labial consonants: the prefix does not occur with labial stop-initial stems except *asportare* and *aspellere*, and with the other labial consonants it occurs in the form *ā-* (and *au-*). This looks like a case of phonologically conditioned allomorphy; the odd thing about it is that it does not affect the other two [b]-final prefixes (*obvertere* 'turn against/facing', *subvertere* 'overturn', *obmutescere* 'become dumb' vs. *āvertere* 'turn away', *āmovere* 'remove'). The tendency that seems to be very powerfully at work in the case of *ab-* is not so much the avoidance of a sequence of two labial consonants as the avoidance of homophony with the most strongly assimilating prefix *ad-*. The fact that *ab-* does not occur (or does not occur in its [b]-final form) before labials is probably due to the fact that such forms would have been very hard to distinguish from *ad* + labial consonant sequences.[309] Note that the two prefixes produce semantic opposites in several cases:

(104) *Ad-* and *ab-*prefixed semantic opposites
      afferre (< *ad+ferre*) 'take there, to sb.' vs. *auferre* 'take from, away'
      affuit (< *ad+fuit*) 'was present' vs. *āfuit* 'was absent'
      admovere 'take, move there' vs. *āmovere* 'take away'

What would a putative **ab+ponere* have sounded like? And what would have distinguished it from *apponere* (< *ad+ponere*)?

The same drive to avoid homophony cannot be invoked to explain the [s] of the *abs-* that appears before [t k] for at least two reasons. One is that with a putative **abtinere* vs. *attinere* there is more room for differentiation; the other is that [s]-final variants before [t] (and occasionally before [p k]) appear with *sub-* as well (see next section), and marginally with *ob-* (see note 306), where there is no danger whatever of homophony.

---

[308] *Auferre* being a three-way suppletive verb, it shows all the three variants of the prefix: *auferre* (INF), *abstuli* (PERF), *ablatum* (SUP).

[309] This was pointed out already by ancient grammarians, see for instance Priscian's *Institutiones* 2.5,6 (Keil 1857: 46), cf. Álvarez Huerta (2005).

7.2.5.3. sub-

This prefix has a variant *sus-* before voiceless stops, and also shows assimilation of [b] to peripheral consonants and [r]. The assimilation of [b] to [f] and [g] is practically compulsory, assimilation to [m] seems to be simply variable, and assimilation to [k] and [r] is lexically determined.

The choice of the *sus-* variant before voiceless stops is also lexically determined. Before [s] the variant *sub-* is found, but before [sp]-initial stems only *su-* is written, which represents the *sus-*variant with degemination. (Alternatively, such forms may be analysed as including *sub-* but with simplification of the [psp] cluster to [sp], similarly to the *asporto-*type variation seen above.) Historically *sumere* 'take' also includes the *sus-*variant (< *su(b)s-emere*).

(105) Words prefixed with *sub-*
 subire 'go down'

 sufferre (~ *subferre* sporadically from the fourth c. AD) 'endure'
 suffundere (overwhelmingly) ~ *subfundere* 'pour'
 suggredi 'approach'
 suggerere (~ *subgerere* sporadically) 'pile up'

 submergere (mostly) ~ *summergere* 'submerge'
 submovere ~ *summovere* (roughly equal) 'remove'
 submittere ~ *summittere* (roughly equal) 'put forth'
 surripere 'steal'
 surgere ~ *surrexi* PERF 'rise' (< *sub+regere*)
 subrogare 'substitute'
 subrepere (overwhelmingly) ~ *surrepere* 'creep'

 succumbere 'sink/collapse'
 succlamare 'shout'
 succurrere 'run to'
 succedere 'move below, approach'
 suscipere 'support'
 suscitare 'cause to rise'
 succensere (more frequently) ~ *suscensere* 'be angry'

 suspendere 'hang'
 supponere 'place under'
 supplicare 'implore'
 supprimere 'press down'

 sustinere 'support'
 sustuli 'endure' PERF
 subtemen 'weft'
 subtilis 'fine'

 subterere 'wear away'
 subsidium 'reserves'

substruere 'build up'
subscribere (mostly) ~ *suscribere* 'inscribe'
suspicere (< *sus+spicere*) 'look up'
suspirare (< *sus+spirare*) 'sigh'

7.3. Generalisations

7.3.1. *Assimilations*

7.3.1.1. *Voice assimilation*

As was explained in 4.2, voice assimilation is always regressive and only the feature specification [–voice] appears to spread, mainly because environments in which a voiced obstruent would follow a voiceless obstruent do not emerge. This is largely true of prefixed forms as well:

(106) Voice assimilation in prefixed forms
    ad+tenere → *attinere* 'hold'
    ad+serere → [atserere] (or *asserere*) 'claim (for)'

The only prefix-final voiceless obstruent is [s], which is hardly ever found before any voiced consonant (see the discussion of *ex-*, *dis-* and *trans-* above) because of the historical *s*-deletion discussed in 4.2.1. How the regularly undeleted *transgredi* was actually realised is impossible to determine with certainty. There is further the word *postgenitus* 'born later', the only word in which *post-* is followed by a voiced obstruent. The realisation of this word is again uncertain, though a phonetic cluster [zdg] is, I think, very unlikely.[310]

7.3.1.2. *Place assimilation*

Both types of place assimilations are found with prefixed forms. In particular, they involve the assimilation of [n], [d] and the placeless nasal of *con-* to peripheral stops, of [b] to velar stops, and of [s] to [f]. In the case of [b] and [d] place and voice assimilation co-occur:

(107) Place assimilation in prefixed forms
    con+ponere → *componere* 'compose' (place assimilation 1)
    in+quaerere → [iŋkwiːrere] 'inquire' (place assimilation 1)
    ad+ponere → *apponere* 'place near' (place assimilation 2, voice
        assimilation)
    ad+capere → *accipere* 'receive' (place assimilation 2, voice
        assimilation)
    sub+gerere → *suggerere* 'pile up' (place assimilation 2)
    dis+ferre → *differre* 'scatter' (place assimilation 2)

---

[310] Note Cicero's interesting remark in *Orator* 157 in which he claims to prefer *posmeridianus* to *postmeridianus* 'afternoon'; this word is attested as *pomeridianus* in postclassical Latin.

In line with what was said about place assimilation processes in 4.8, it is generally true that coronal consonants undergo but do not trigger place assimilation, and non-coronals systematically trigger it but undergo it less frequently than coronals. No prefix in the relevant environment ends in a velar consonant (the [ek-] variant of *ex-* only occurs before fricatives).

7.3.1.3. Total assimilation

In Figure 37 I summarise the total assimilations that take place between prefix-final consonants and stem-initial consonants. Place assimilations and voicing assimilations are not indicated (see the previous two sections). A distinction is made between systematically attested assimilations (1, darker shade), sporadic assimilations (2, medium shade), isolates (3, lighter shade) and non-assimilating types (empty box);[311] in the last type the cluster surfaces unchanged or is only affected by place and/or voicing assimilation. The marking *n/a* means that the clusters in question do not emerge for some reason (nasal place loss and coalescence before fricatives and historical [s]-deletion before voiced segments).

Figure 38 highlights the place assimilations that take place in the stop/stop and the fricative/fricative relations. It summarises information given in 7.3.1.2 as well as 4.8.

It is clear from the data in Figure 37 that the assimilations are governed largely by the Syllable Contact Law (cf. 3.4). Total assimilation is likely to take place if

C_1 \ C_2			stop	fricative		nasal		liquid		glide	
				s	f	n	m	l	r	j	w
stop	d					1					
	b	(*ob-*)									
		(*sub-*)							1		
fricative	s	(*dis-*)				n/a		n/a			n/a
		(*trans-*)				n/a			n/a		
nasal				n/a				1	2		
liquid								2	3		
glide	j	(*prae-*)									

Legend: 1 – systematically attested assimilations
2 – sporadically attested assimilations
3 – isolated instances of assimilation
empty box – no assimilation
n/a – cluster does not emerge for independent reasons

Figure 37. Total assimilations at prefix–stem boundary

[311] Admittedly, this four-way categorisation is an oversimplification, since what I call sporadic here in some cases conflates type-level and token-level variability, and also lexically determined allomorph selection. The data are explained in the relevant sections on each prefix separately.

C₁	C₂	d t	b p	g k	s	f
d			▨	▨		
b				▨		
s						▨

Figure 38. Systematically attested place assimilations between stops and between fricatives at prefix–stem boundary

the sonority of C_1 is lower than the sonority of C_2.[312] This is borne out by the fact that nothing assimilates (totally) to stops, only stops assimilate to fricatives and nasals, both stops and nasals assimilate to liquids, and the glide [j] does not assimilate to anything. That is, Figure 37 is by and large the inverse of Figure 12 given in 3.4. On the other hand, nothing ever assimilates to [w], and assimilation to [j] is sporadic, which means that C+glide clusters are tolerated much better at prefix–stem boundaries than in simplex forms.

Thus the Syllable Contact Law, a sonority-based principle, appears to operate as a static filter in the case of simplex forms and as a filter inducing assimilation processes at these morpheme boundaries. The clusters that are of special interest at this point are those which are rising-sonority or equal-sonority clusters (i.e. at variance with the Syllable Contact Law) *and* which are practically never remedied by assimilation.[313] Some of these clusters are identical in both segmental composition and syllabification to clusters found in simplex forms (viz. [pt], [ps] and [rw], as in *obtinere* 'maintain', *obsidere* 'occupy' and *pervadere* 'go through', respectively). But some are not; in particular, these latter are [bd bn sm] (e.g. *subdere* 'put underneath', *obnunciare* 'bring bad news', *transmittere* 'send over', respectively), and the glide-final clusters [dj dw bj bw sw[314] nw rj]. The cluster [bl] is found internally too, but at prefix–stem boundary it is always heterosyllabic (*oblectare* 'delight'), thus in spite of the identical segmental composition its syllabification is not the same as that of its word-internal counterpart (see 3.3).

If one wishes to make a phonologically based generalisation about these stable, categorically non-assimilating equal- and rising-sonority clusters, they clearly present two separate issues. One is that given the lack of active assimilatory capacity on the part of glides, and the compulsory regressive direction of assimilations in Latin,[315] most C+glide clusters that emerge at

---

[312] More formally we could say that the condition on total assimilation is that the [son] and [cont] features of C_2 must have more [+] specifications that those of C_1.

[313] Thus I do not include here clusters such as [bm], [dn] or [rl] because these are variably repaired to [mm], [nn], [ll], respectively, e.g. *submovere* ~ *summovere* 'remove', *adnumerare* ~ *annumerare* 'count' and *perlucere* ~ *pellucere* 'transmit light'. By contrast, I include [rj] in the list of non-remedied clusters in spite of the single item *peierare* 'forswear' discussed above.

[314] The cluster [sw] is found in simplex forms too, but only word-initially as a complex onset, never as a heterosyllabic cluster.

[315] Which is, of course, not to deny that some progressive assimilations are generally believed to have happened in the prehistory of the language, e.g. *wel-si* > *velle* 'want'.

prefix–stem boundaries surface intact. If we discount these, we are left with [ps pt bd bn sm bl].[316] Of these, the coronal-final clusters (i.e. all except [sm][317]) are covered by what can be termed Generalised Place Condition (cf. 11 in 3.4), which is no longer restricted to [obs][obs] and [nas][nas] clusters:

(108)   The Generalised Place Condition (valid at prefix–stem boundary; cf. Cser
        2012a: 61)
        Heterosyllabic clusters are well-formed irrespective of sonority relations
        if C_1 is non-coronal and C_2 is coronal (i.e. [ps pt bd bn bl] do not undergo
        assimilation). If C_2 is a non-coronal other than [w], only sonority
        relations are decisive (i.e. [bf df bm dm] undergo obligatory or optional/
        variable assimilation, but the falling sonority clusters do not; by
        undergoing place assimilation, the clusters [bg dg sf nm] and the
        placeless nasal + [m] comply with the same clause).

7.3.2. Non-assimilatory allomorphy

7.3.2.1. [s]-allomorphy

The allomorphy displayed by *dis-/dī-*, *trans-/trā-* and *ex-/ē-* is diachronically explicable as resulting from the loss of [s] in [s] + C[voiced] sequences, which, however, is no longer an active rule in the synchronic phonology of Classical Latin (see 4.2.1). With *trans-/trā-*, the regularity is already relaxed so that only coronal consonants trigger the dropping of [s] (*trā-ducere* vs. *trans-gredi*, on the assumption that the spelling of the latter represents phonological reality). By contrast, the loss of [s] in *dis-* fails to be triggered by [j] in the majority of eligible forms.

7.3.2.2. Vowel-triggered allomorphy

Whenever a vowel-initial stem combines with a vowel-final prefix, one of three things happens: (i) the two adjacent vowels are contracted to a single long vowel, as in *dē(e)st* 'is absent', *prōmere* 'take out'; (ii) the resulting hiatus is filled with the stop [d], as in *red-ire* 'go back', *prod-ire* 'go forth', or (iii) the resulting hiatus is made to templatically (but not melodically) conform to the hiatus pattern whereby V_1 must be short, as in *prŏ-avus* 'great-grandfather', *dĕ-hinc* 'hence'.

As was seen, the prefix *con-* loses its final (placeless) consonant before vowels and thereby hiatus is created, as in *co-actus* 'coerced'. (Also note the strange *circu-it* ~ *circum-eunt* 'go round' 3Sing ~ 3Plur quasi-alternation.)

---

[316] Although [br] should fall under the generalisation to be made, it is not included here because it variably undergoes assimilation with *sub-*, though not with *ob-*.

[317] This [sm] is that found with *trans-* only. This prefix ends in a non-assimilating [s], and thus it creates the only exception to the Generalised Place Condition in (108).

7.3.2.3. [b]-allomorphy

The [b]-final prefixes *ab-* and *sub-* show the [s]-final variants *abs-/as-* and *sus-*, respectively, before voiceless stops, and *sub-* also before [sp] (*abstinere* 'keep away', *suscipere* 'support', *suspicere* 'look up'); for *ob-* a variant *os-* can only be identified etymologically *(ostendere* 'show', *oscen* 'divining bird'). It is difficult to bring this allomorphy into the orbit of phonological generalisations (as opposed to the hiatus-triggered allomorphy above). While a [pk] cluster is certainly ill-formed phonotactically, the cluster [psk] (as in *abscondere* 'conceal') is also unattested in simplex forms, though with respect to the latter one could argue that the insertion of an extrasyllabic [s] somehow improves the cluster by separating the two stops from each other. On the other hand, the *sustinere* 'support' vs. *subterere* 'wear away' allomorphy results in clusters that are equally well-formed in simplex forms ([st] and [pt]).

The appearance of *ā-* (and *au-*) instead of *ab-* before labial consonants, which was discussed above, can be attributed to the homophonic clash with the prefix *ad-*.

7.3.3. On the nature of prefix-variation

As we have seen, variation is a pervasive feature of prefixes and prefixed forms. This variation itself is of several kinds and several factors contribute to its patterns. In this section I will summarily describe four such factors.

In some cases variation is determined lexically. The choice of *sus-* vs. (assimilating) *sub-* depends entirely on the lexical identity of the stem: e.g. *suscitare* 'cause to rise' vs. *succumbere* 'sink/collapse' and *sustinere* 'support' vs. *subterere* 'wear away' in spite of the identical stem-initial consonants. However, when the variant *sub-* is picked by a [k]-initial stem, as in *succumbere*, the [b] → [k] assimilation is no longer variable, it is obligatory. In the case of the exceptional stem *censere* 'assess' the choice is not determined: both *succensere* and *suscensere* 'be angry' exist.[318]

Most instances of prefix-variation are not, or largely not, lexically determined. The assimilation of the nasal to stem-initial liquids, as in *con-* and *in-*, is a case in point. What I will take a closer look at here, for exemplification, is the *conl-* ~ *coll-* assimilation, which appears to present a mixture of lexical vs. non-lexical (probably frequency-based) conditioning.

The facts are the following.[319] The words *collega/collegium* 'partner in office', 'college', which are together attested 1,231 times in the corpus, show assimilated forms in 95 per cent of their occurrences, which is much higher than the ratio of

---

[318] But note that this verb may well represent historical contamination from two unrelated stems, cf. de Vaan (2008 s.vv. *-cendo* and *-censeo*).

[319] The data presented here were culled from the corpus. The pattern they display generally coincides with that reported in Prinz (1949–50; 1953).

assimilated forms for the other *conl*-words except one, *colligere* 'collect', which shows 90 per cent. This probably means that in *collega/collegium* the assimilated form was by this time lexicalised.[320] The data for the rest of the most frequent *conl*-words are given in Figure 39.[321] These words assimilate between 20–90 per cent of all occurrences, and the more frequent a word is, the higher this ratio. This makes it at least plausible that the variation is a reflection of the phonological properties of the forms, since sound changes are known to be often

lexical item	number of occurrences in the corpus	proportion of assimilated forms (%)
conligere 'collect'[322]	4500	90
conlocare 'put in place'	1903	48
conlatus 'carried'	1387	37
conloqui 'speak to'	970	32
conlaudare 'praise'	312	31
conlabi 'collapse'	290	20

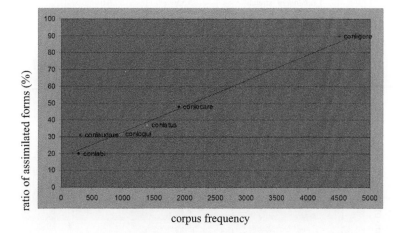

Figure 39. Ratio of *con-l*-assimilation

[320] An independent argument for the lexicalised status of these words is that their stem is not used productively either in itself or with other prefixes (as opposed to *dilaudare* 'distinguish by praise', *adlabi* 'glide towards', *delabi* 'sink', *elocare* 'let out', *eligere* 'choose' and many others, with relatively compositional meanings). Apart from a distant etymological relationship with *lex* 'law' and *privilegium* 'law concerning an individual', nothing can be said about the stem; as a consequence, the meanings of the two words cannot be regarded as compositional.

[321] The lexical items in the chart subsume derivatives like *collaudatio*, *collocatus*, etc.

conditioned or influenced by word frequency. If we compare these data to the assimilation patterns of *ad-* before [t]-initial stems (Figure 40), a very different picture emerges where there is clearly no correlation and what one sees is, in all likelihood, genuine spelling variation.

The third point to be considered is that some prefixes were used in and after the classical era to create new lexical items, and in some such cases complex forms were produced in palpable disharmony with the observable phonological regularities. A case in point is Caesar's designation for the tribes that inhabited the region beyond the river Rhine: *trans-rhenani*.[323] For non-linguistic reasons it seems highly probable that this word was made up by him (or someone in his

lexical item	number of occurrences in the corpus	proportion of assimilated forms (%)
adtribuere 'assign'	610	54
adtingere 'touch'	873	63
adtinere 'belong'	672	65
adtrahere 'draw'	515	43
adtendere 'stretch'	3534	46
adterere 'rub'	423	58

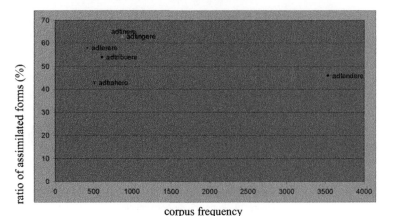

Figure 40. Ratio of *ad-t*-assimilation

[322] With *colligere* there is an uncertainty in that the database does not distinguish between homographous (and homophonous) forms of *colligere* 'collect' and *colligare* 'bind'. The number 4500 was conjectured on the basis of the number of non-homographous forms.

[323] First occurrence: *Bell. Gall.* 4.16.

environment). Its formation is completely transparent by the standards of Latin morphology as it existed in the first century BC. But phonologically, the choice of the prefix variant *trans-* is infelicitous: not only is *trans-* incompatible with a following voiced coronal (see *trā-ducere, trā-lucere, trā-nare*), neither form of the prefix ever combines with an [r]-initial word. Similarly, when Suetonius described the colour of Augustus' and Nero's hair as being of a particular shade of colour, he used *sub-flavus* (from *flavus* 'yellowish, fair'). This word, which is attested only at these two loci in the entire corpus (*De vita Caesarum. Augustus* 79.2 and *Nero* 51.1.), is again completely transparent and at the same time phonologically irregular in that *sub-f-* overwhelmingly gives *suff-*.[324]

The last point is, in all likelihood, a diachronic extension of the third. It is clear from the historical lexicology of Latin that in the late period, especially in the language of Christianity, where a plethora of new words were coined to render religious and theological notions, the allomorphic rules relevant to prefixes often ceased to apply. Mention has been made of the *re*+vowel formations beginning with Tertullian around 200 AD and then multiplying in the fourth–fifth centuries (cf. 7.2.1.5), and also of the *ambi*+consonant formations that begin with a hapax by Apuleius and then gain some currency in the last two centuries of Antiquity (cf. 7.2.1.6). These forms, the distant ancestors of modern English words like *reinforce* or *co-defendant*, clearly show that these points of grammar inherited from Classical Latin were given up with the passage of time.[325]

7.4. CONCLUSION

This chapter has surveyed the phonological and morphological features that prefixed forms show. These are important partly because they are specific to such forms, partly because they represent generalisations of, or variations on, regularities that obtain in simplex forms. They also represent a plethora of historical and etymological issues that are beyond the purview of the present work. The variability that is attested in such forms furthermore provides a fertile ground for the testing of current models of variation and its relation to other aspects of the organisation of language.

---

[324] But note that the prefix *sub-* tends to combine unassimilated with adjectives to produce diminutives, cf. Prinz (1949–50: 102).

[325] Another interesting example is provided by Cl. Mamertus (fifth c. AD) in his *De statu animae* 1.21: *anima ... vitam corporis nec anticipat nec posticipat* 'the soul neither precedes nor survives life in the body' (translation mine). The neologism *posticipat* cca. 'survive, exist after', a word occurring only here in the entire corpus, is parallel in form to its time-honoured semantic opposite *anticipat* 'get ahead of, anticipate', but since it involves a bound morpheme after *posti-* (itself an otherwise unattested variant of *post-*), which is unusual, it actually increases the cohesion between stem and prefix, contrary to the general trend.

CONCLUSION AND CONSPECTUS OF THE PHONOLOGICAL RULES

The goal of this book has been to give a comprehensive description and analysis of the segmental phonology of Classical Latin. Data have been gathered, patterns have been identified, analyses have been proposed. Generally speaking, I have adopted a certain theoretical stance regarding both the representation of phonological entities and the properties of rules. I trust that the tenor of the book and the particular arguments found in it have shown that these theoretical underpinnings are helpful in capturing and articulating meaningful generalisations about the structure of the language. But I also hope that the findings encapsulated in the preceding chapters will provide useful insights for those working in other models.

In Table 20, the phonological rules discussed in the book are summarised. Ordering relations, where relevant, have been taken into account. P means the rule applies to prefixed forms; (P) means the rule applies optionally to prefixed forms.

Table 20. A conspectus of the phonological rules

Rule name	Rule form	Reference	Example	Remarks
Epenthesis after [m]	$\emptyset \rightarrow$ [p] / [m] _ {[s,t]}	4.7	*compsi, comptus*	
E-insertion	$\emptyset \rightarrow$ [e] / [−son, −cont] _ [r] {C, #}	5.3.1	*pater, ager*	
Final stop deletion	[−son, −cont] $\rightarrow \emptyset$ / _# if unsyllabifiable	4.10	*cor, lac*	
Rhotacism	[s] $\rightarrow$ [r] / V_V	4.4	*muris*	
Lowering before [r]	[i, e] $\rightarrow$ [u, o] / _ [r]	5.2.2.2	*cineris, temporis*	fed by rhotacism
Coalescence with empty vowel	V_i + empty V $\rightarrow V:_i$	5.4.3	*puellā*	
Prevocalic deletion of back vowels	V[+back, −high] $\rightarrow \emptyset$ / _V	5.3.2	*aris, amo*	precedes prefixation
Contact voice assimilation	[−son] $\rightarrow$ [−voice] / _ [−voice]	4.2	*scriptus*	P
Lengthening before voiced stops	V $\rightarrow$ V: / _[−son, −cont, +voice] [−voice]	5.4.2	*āctus*	simultaneous with contact voice assimilation

(continued)

Table 20. (continued)

Rule name	Rule form	Reference	Example	Remarks
Word-final lowering	[i] → [e] / _ #	5.2.2.3	*mare*	
Assimilation of [t] to [s]	[t] → [s] / _ [s]	4.3	*miles*	(P); fed by contact voice assimilation
Total assimilation of consonants	C_iC_j → C_jC_j if son(C_i) < son(C_j)	7.3.1.3	*alligare*	(P)
General degemination	C_iC_i → C_i if unsyllabifiable	4.5.1	*falsus*	P; fed by assimilation of [t] to [s]
Degemination of [s]	[ss] → [s] / {V:, C}_	4.5.2	*casus*	fed by assimilation of [t] to [s]
Nasal place loss before fricatives	[n] → placeless nasal / _ [−voice, +cont]	4.6	*inscius, frons*	P; fed by assimilation of [t] to [s]
Vowel shortening	V: → V / _{t#, nt, nd, V, l#, r#}	5.4.1	*proavus*	P
Place assimilation 1, 2	C($Place_i$) → C($Place_j$) / _ C($Place_j$)	4.8	*imbibere, immittere*	P; postlexical (works even with clitics)
Coalescence with placeless nasal	V_i+placeless nasal → Ṽ:	5.4.4	*frons*	P; postlexical; fed by nasal place loss before fricatives, bled by place assimilation

THE TEXTUAL FREQUENCY OF CONSONANTS IN CLASSICAL LATIN

The textual frequency of consonants was calculated from a selective corpus of texts representing a variety of authors and genres from the first century BC and the first century AD. The texts in particular are the following:

Res gestae divi Augusti (also known as the Monumentum Ancyranum)

Julius Caesar's Commentarii de bello civili

Cicero's Brutus, De legibus, Pro Archia poeta and Pro Quinctio

Ovid's Amores

Persius's Saturae

Sallust's Bellum Catilinae

Statius's Silvae

Vergil's Georgica

These texts altogether comprise 191,025 words and 1,101,173 characters. The frequencies of consonants are given in the following charts. The notes provide details that may be useful for those who assume a segmental analysis different from mine (in particular, monosegmental [kʷ] ⟨qu⟩, [gʷ] ⟨(n)gu⟩, [aj] ⟨ae⟩, [oj] ⟨oe⟩, [aw] ⟨au⟩ instead of the biphonemic sequences that I argued for in Chapter 2, and VN sequences instead of the long nasal vowels).

---

[326] The data for [t] include 235 initial and 373 medial ⟨th⟩.

[327] The data for [p] include 244 initial and 303 medial ⟨ph⟩.

[328] The data for [k] include the 20,225 occurrences of ⟨qu⟩; of these, 9723 are initial, 10,502 are medial. The data for [k] also include 111 initial and 497 medial occurrences of ⟨ch⟩.

[329] The data for medial [j] include the 592 occurrences of tautosyllabic [oj]. The data for [j] also include the 9045 occurrences of ⟨ae⟩, of which 3,944 are final, 5101 are medial (with respect to the [j], not the ⟨ae⟩).

[330] The data for [n] do not include the 3,527 occurrences of ⟨ns⟩ and the 565 occurrences of ⟨nf⟩.

[331] The data for [w] include the 20,225 occurrences of ⟨qu⟩, all medial (scil. with respect to [w], not to ⟨qu⟩). They also include the 282 occurrences of [ŋgw], all medial. Furthermore, they include the 3676 tautosyllabic [aw] sequences, all medial (with respect to [w], not to ⟨au⟩). The 144 final occurrences of [w] are all made up by the four [ew]-final words (e)heu, neu, seu, ceu. The word hau does not occur in the corpus at all.

[332] The data for [m] do not include the 27,475 final occurrences of graphic ⟨m⟩.

	#_	_#	X_X	Σ
s	15691	38716	35781	90188
t[326]	8958	26203	54468	89629
r	5330	6981	57476	69787
k[328]	25515	4046	40119	69680
n[330]	10146	6655	45504	62305
w[331]	7444	144	31277	38865
l	5620	711	29374	35705
m[332]	10260	0	20859	31119

	#_	_#	X_X	Σ
d	9083	5194	16789	31066
p[327]	15993	0	14388	30381
b	1678	689	14273	16640
j[329]	2131	4085	9297	15513
g	2281	0	9819	12100
f	6907	0	3277	10184
h	5324	0	1490	6814

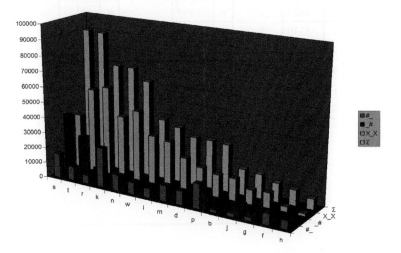

Figure 41. The frequency of consonants, in order of decreasing overall frequency

	#_
k	25515
p	15993
s	15691
m	10260
n	10146
d	9083
t	8958
w	7444
f	6907
l	5620
r	5330
h	5324
g	2281
j	2131
b	1678

	_#
s	38716
t	26203
r	6981
n	6655
d	5194
j	4085
k	4046
l	711
b	689
w	144
m	
p	
g	0
f	
h	

	X_X
r	57476
t	54468
n	45504
k	40119
s	35781
w	31277
l	29374
m	20859
d	16789
p	14388
b	14273
g	9819
j	9297
f	3277
h	1490

Figure 42. Initial, final and medial frequency separately

Here I give the list of all the authors mentioned in the text. Only those of their works are mentioned by title to which specific reference was made. The list is given alphabetically as well as chronologically.

Table 21. Alphabetical list of authors

Name in commonly used form	Full name	Works referred to	Date
Accius	Lucius Accius		second c. BC
Apuleius	Lucius Apuleius (Platonicus)	*Florida*	second c. AD
Arnobius	Arnobius		cca 300 AD
St Augustine	Aurelius Augustinus (Hipponensis)		354–430 AD
Boethius	Anicius Manlius Severinus Boethius		480–524/525 AD
Cato	Marcus Porcius Cato		234–149 BC
Catullus	Gaius Valerius Catullus	*Carmina*	cca 85–55 BC
Cicero	Marcus Tullius Cicero	*Brutus, De legibus, Pro Archia poeta, Pro Quinctio*	106–43 BC
Claudianus Mamertus	Claudianus Mamertus	*De statu animae*	fifth c. AD
Claudius Claudianus	Claudius Claudianus		cca 400 AD
Commodianus	Commodianus		third c. AD
Ennius	Quintus Ennius	*(Annalium fragmenta)*	cca 239–169 BC
Festus	Sextus Pompeius Festus	*Epitoma operis de verborum significatu Verrii Flacci*	second c. AD?
Horace	Quintus Horatius Flaccus	*Saturae (=Sermones), Epodi*	65–8 BC
St Jerome	Eusebius Sophronius Hieronymus		cca 340–420 AD
Julius Caesar	Gaius Julius Caesar	*Commentarii de bello gallico, Commentarii de bello civili*	100–44 BC
Juvenal	Decimus Junius Juvenalis	*Saturae*	late first c. – early second c. AD
Lactantius	Lucius Caecilius Firmianus Lactantius		cca 300 AD
Livy	Titus Livius		59 BC – 17 AD
Lucanus	Marcus Annaeus Lucanus	*Bellum civile (=Pharsalia)*	39–65 AD

(continued)

Table 21. (continued)

Name in commonly used form	Full name	Works referred to	Date
Lucilius	Gaius Lucilius	*(Saturarum fragmenta)*	second c. BC
Lucretius	Titus Lucretius Carus	*De rerum natura*	cca 97–55 BC
Marius Victorinus	Marius Victorinus	*Ars grammatica*	fourth c. AD
Martialis	Marcus Valerius Martialis	*Epigrammata*	cca 40–103 AD
Martianus Cappella	Martianus Minneius Felix Cappella	*De nuptiis Philologiae et Mercurii*	fifth c. AD
Ovid	Publius Ovidius Naso	*Amores, Ars amatoria, Heroides, Metamorphoses, Tristia*	43 BC–17/18 AD
Pacuvius	Marcus Pacuvius		early second c. BC
Paulinus Nolanus, St Paul of Nola	Pontius Meropius Anicius Paulinus	*Carmina*	353–431 AD
Persius	Aulus Persius Flaccus	*Saturae*	34–62 AD
Petronius	Gaius Petronius Arbiter	*Satyrica*	cca 27–66 AD
Plautus	Titus Maccius Plautus	*Casina, Miles gloriosus, Poenulus*	cca 254–184 BC
Pliny (the elder)	Gaius Plinius Secundus (Plinius Maior)	*Naturalis historia*	23–79 AD
Pomponius Bononiensis	Lucius Pomponius Bononiensis	*(Atellanarum fragmenta)*	early first c. BC
Propertius	Sextus Propertius	*Elegiae*	first c. BC
Prudentius	Aurelius Prudentius Clemens	*Liber Peristephanon*	348 – cca 405 AD
Quintilian	Marcus Fabius Quintilianus		first c. AD
Sallust	Gaius Sallustius Crispus	*Bellum Catilinae*	86–34 BC
Seneca	Lucius Annaeus Seneca		cca 4–65 AD
Silius Italicus	Tiberius Catius Asconius Silius Italicus	*Punica*	cca 25–100/101 AD
Statius	Publius Papinius Statius	*Silvae, Thebais*	first c. AD
Suetonius	Caius Suetonius Tranquillus	*De vita Caesarum*	cca 75–150 AD
Terence	Publius Terentius Afer		first half of second c. BC
Tertullian	Quintus Septimius Florens Tertullianus		cca 150/170–230 AD
Tibullus	Albius Tibullus	*Elegiae*	first c. BC
Valerius Flaccus	Gaius Valerius Flaccus Setinus Balbus	*Argonautica*	first c. AD
Varro	Marcus Terentius Varro		116–27 BC

(continued)

Table 21. (continued)

Name in commonly used form	Full name	Works referred to	Date
Velius Longus	Velius Longus	*De orthographia*	first half of second c. AD
Vergil	Publius Vergilius Maro	*Aeneis, Georgica*	70–19 BC
Vitruvius	Marcus Vitruvius Pollio	*De architectura*	beg. of first c. BC – beg. of first c. AD
(unknown author — Quintus Cornificius?)		*Rhetorica ad Herennium (De ratione dicendi ad C. Herennium)*	early first c. BC
(unknown author(s))		*Historia Augusta*	fourth–fifth c. AD?

Table 22. Chronological list of authors

Name in commonly used form	Full name	Works referred to	Date
Plautus	Titus Maccius Plautus	*Casina, Miles gloriosus, Poenulus*	cca 254–184 BC
Ennius	Quintus Ennius	*(Annalium fragmenta)*	cca 239–169 BC
Cato	Marcus Porcius Cato		234–149 BC
Terence	Publius Terentius Afer		first half of second c. BC
Pacuvius	Marcus Pacuvius		early second c. BC
Accius	Lucius Accius		second c. BC
Lucilius	Gaius Lucilius	*(Saturarum fragmenta)*	second c. BC
Varro	Marcus Terentius Varro		116–27 BC
Pomponius Bononiensis	Lucius Pomponius Bononiensis	*(Atellanarum fragmenta)*	early first c. BC
(unknown author — Quintus Cornificius?)		*Rhetorica ad Herennium (De ratione dicendi ad C. Herennium)*	early first c. BC
Cicero	Marcus Tullius Cicero	*Brutus, De legibus, Pro Archia poeta, Pro Quinctio*	106–43 BC
Julius Caesar	Gaius Julius Caesar	*Commentarii de bello gallico, Commentarii de bello civili*	100–44 BC
Lucretius	Titus Lucretius Carus	*De rerum natura*	cca 97–55 BC
Sallust	Gaius Sallustius Crispus	*Bellum Catilinae*	86–34 BC
Catullus	Gaius Valerius Catullus	*Carmina*	cca 85–55 BC
Vitruvius	Marcus Vitruvius Pollio	*De architectura*	early first c. BC – early AD first c.

(continued)

Table 22. (continued)

Name in commonly used form	Full name	Works referred to	Date
Vergil	Publius Vergilius Maro	*Aeneis, Georgica*	70–19 BC
Horace	Quintus Horatius Flaccus	*Saturae (=Sermones), Epodi*	65–8 BC
Livy	Titus Livius		59 BC–17 AD
Propertius	Sextus Propertius	*Elegiae*	first c. BC
Tibullus	Albius Tibullus	*Elegiae*	first c. BC
Ovid	Publius Ovidius Naso	*Amores, Ars amatoria, Heroides, Metamorphoses, Tristia*	43 BC–17/18 AD
Seneca	Lucius Annaeus Seneca		cca 4–65 AD
Pliny	Gaius Plinius Secundus (Plinius Maior)	*Naturalis historia*	23–79 AD
Silius Italicus	Tiberius Catius Asconius Silius Italicus	*Punica*	cca 25–100/101 AD
Petronius	Gaius Petronius Arbiter	*Satyrica*	cca 27–66 AD
Persius	Aulus Persius Flaccus	*Saturae*	34–62 AD
Lucanus	Marcus Annaeus Lucanus	*Bellum civile (=Pharsalia)*	39–65 AD
Martialis	Marcus Valerius Martialis	*Epigrammata*	cca 40–103 AD
Quintilian	Marcus Fabius Quintilianus		first c. AD
Statius	Publius Papinius Statius	*Silvae, Thebais*	first c. AD
Valerius Flaccus	Gaius Valerius Flaccus Setinus Balbus	*Argonautica*	first c. AD
Suetonius	Caius Suetonius Tranquillus	*De vita Caesarum*	cca 75–150 AD
Juvenal	Decimus Junius Juvenalis	*Saturae*	late first c. – early second c. AD
Festus	Sextus Pompeius Festus	*Epitoma operis de verborum significatu Verrii Flacci*	second c. AD?
Velius Longus	Velius Longus	*De orthographia*	first half of second c. AD
Tertullian	Quintus Septimius Florens Tertullianus		cca 150/170–230 AD
Apuleius	Lucius Apuleius (Platonicus)	*Florida*	second c. AD
Commodianus	Commodianus		third c. AD
Arnobius	Arnobius		cca 300 AD
Lactantius	Lucius Caecilius Firmianus Lactantius		cca 300 AD
Marius Victorinus	Marius Victorinus	*Ars grammatica*	fourth c. AD

(continued)

Table 22. (continued)

Name in commonly used form	Full name	Works referred to	Date
St Jerome	Eusebius Sophronius Hieronymus		cca 340–420 AD
Prudentius	Aurelius Prudentius Clemens	*Liber Peristephanon*	348 – cca 405 AD
Paulinus Nolanus, St Paul of Nola	Pontius Meropius Anicius Paulinus	*Carmina*	353–431 AD
St Augustine	Aurelius Augustinus (Hipponensis)		354–430 AD
(unknown author(s))		*Historia Augusta*	fourth–fifth c. AD?
Claudius Claudianus	Claudius Claudianus		cca 400 AD
Claudianus Mamertus	Claudianus Mamertus	*De statu animae*	fifth c. AD
Martianus Cappella	Martianus Minneius Felix Cappella	*De nuptiis Philologiae et Mercurii*	fifth c. AD
Boethius	Anicius Manlius Severinus Boethius		480–524/525 AD

REFERENCES

ADAMS, JAMES N., 2003. *Bilingualism and the Latin language.* Cambridge: Cambridge University Press.

ADAMS, JAMES N., 2007. *The regional diversification of Latin 200 bc – ad 600.* Cambridge: Cambridge University Press.

ADAMS, JAMES N., 2013. *Social variation and the Latin language.* Cambridge: Cambridge University Press.

ALBRIGHT, ADAM, 2005. The morphological basis of paradigm leveling, in Laura J. Downing, Tracy A. Hall & Renate Raffelsiefen (eds.), *Paradigms in phonological theory.* Oxford: Oxford University Press. 17–43.

ALDERETE, JOHN D. & STEFAN A. FRISCH, 2006. Dissimilation in grammar and the lexicon, in Paul de Lacy (ed.), *The Cambridge handbook of phonology.* Cambridge: Cambridge University Press. 379–398.

ALLEN, WILLIAM S., 1973. *Accent and rhythm.* Cambridge: Cambridge University Press.

ALLEN, WILLIAM S., 1978²[1965]. *Vox Latina.* Cambridge: Cambridge University Press.

ÁLVAREZ HUERTA, OLGA, 2005. Neutralisation consonantique en latin, in Christian Touratier (ed.), *Essais de phonologie latine.* Aix-en-Provence: Université de Provence. 135–155.

ANDERSON, ANDREW R., 1909. Some questions of Plautine pronunciation. *Transactions of the American Philological Association* 40. 99–107.

ANTTILA, ARTO, 1997. Deriving variation from grammar, in Frans Hiskens, Roeland van Hout & W. Leo Wetzels, (eds.), *Variation, Change and Phonological Theory.* Amsterdam: John Benjamins. 35–68.

ARONOFF, MARK, 1994. *Morphology by itself.* Cambridge, MA: MIT Press.

BAILEY, CHARLES-JAMES N., 1970. Towards specifying constraints on phonological metathesis. *Linguistic Inquiry* 1(3). 347–349.

BAKKUM, GABRIËL C. L. M., 1989. Complex s-onsets in Latin and Italic, in Marius Lavency & Dominique Longrée (eds.), *Actes du ve colloque de linguistique Latine.* Louvain-la-Neuve: Peeters. 17–27.

BAKOVIĆ, ERIC, 2011. Opacity and ordering, in Goldsmith John, Jason Riggle & Alan C. L. Yu (eds.), *The handbook of phonological Theory* (2nd edn). Oxford: Wiley-Blackwell. 40–67.

BALDI, PHILIP, 1994. Some thoughts on Latin rhotacism. *General Linguistics* 34. 209–215.

BALDI, PHILIP, 2002. *The foundations of Latin.* Berlin-New York: Gruyter.

BALLESTER, XAVÉRIO, 1996. *Fonemática del Latín Clásico. Consonantismo. Monografías de filología latina.* [Zaragoza] Departamento de Ciencias de la Antigüedad, Universidad de Zaragoza.

BENNETT, WILLIAM G., 2015. *The phonology of consonants: Harmony, dissimilation and correspondence.* Cambridge: Cambridge University Press.

BENUA, LAURA, 1995. Identity effects in morphological truncation, in Jill Beckman, Suzanne Urbanczyk & Laura Walsh (eds.), *Papers in optimality theory*. Amherst, MA: University of Massachusetts Graduate Linguistic Student Association. 77–136.

BERMÚDEZ-OTERO, RICARDO, 2006. Diachronic phonology, in Paul de Lacy (ed.), *The Cambridge handbook of phonology*. Cambridge: Cambridge University Press. 497–518.

BERMÚDEZ-OTERO, RICARDO, 2012. The architecture of grammar and the division of labor in exponence, in Jochen Trommer (ed.), *The morphology and phonology of exponence*. Oxford: Oxford University Press. 8–83.

BERMÚDEZ-OTERO, RICARDO & GRAEME TROUSDALE, 2012. Cycles and continua: On unidirectionality and gradualness in language change, in Terttu Nevalainen & Elizabeth C. Traugott (eds.), *The Oxford handbook of the history of English*. New York: Oxford University Press. 691–720.

BIVILLE, FRÉDÉRIQUE, 1994. Existait-il une diphthongue *ui* en latin?, in Herman József (ed.), *Linguistic studies on Latin*. Amsterdam: Benjamins. 3–18.

BLEVINS, JULIETTE, 1995. The syllable, in John A. Goldsmith (ed.), *The Handbook of Phonological Theory*. Oxford: Blackwell. 206–244.

BOERSMA, PAUL, 1998. *Functional phonology*. The Hague: Holland Academic Graphics.

BOLDRINI, SANDRO, 2004. *Fondamenti di prosodia e metrica latina*. Roma: Carocci.

BOOIJ, GEERT, 1995. *The phonology of Dutch*. Oxford: Oxford University Press.

BRANDENSTEIN, WILHELM, 1951. *Kurze phonologie des Lateinischen. Appendix to Franz Althelm's Geschichte der lateinischen Sprache*. Frankfurt am Main: Klostermann.

BUCK, CARL DARLING, 1899. Notes on Latin orthography. *The Classical Review* 13(2, 3). 116–119, 156–167.

BURTON, SIR RICHARD FRANCIS, 1894. Translation of C. Valerius Catullus' *Carmina*. London: Private edition.

BUTLER, HAROLD E., 1912. Translation of Propertius' *Elegies*. Loeb Classical Library. London: Heinemann.

BUTLER, HAROLD E., 1920. *Quintilian. With an English translation*. Cambridge, MA/ London: Harvard University Press/ Heinemann.

CASTILLO HERRERA, MARINA DEL, 2009. Las formas de perfecto de indicativo en -*iit* en la versificación latina: ¿una cuestión métrica o una cuestión morfológica? *Cuadernos de Filología Clásica. Estudios Latinos* 29(2). 5–20.

CIL = *Corpus inscriptionum latinarum, 1862–* various editors. Leipzig and Berlin.

CLACKSON, JAMES, 2007. *Indo-European Linguistics. An introduction*. Cambridge: Cambridge University Press.

CLACKSON, JAMES, 2011. The forms of Latin: Inflectional morphology, in James Clackson (ed.), *A Companion to the Latin Language*. Oxford: Wiley-Blackwell. 105–117.

CLACKSON, JAMES & GEOFFREY HORROCKS, 2007. *The Blackwell history of the Latin language*. Oxford: Blackwell.

CLCLT-5 – Library of Latin Texts by Brepols Publishers, Release, 2002.

CLEMENTS, GEORGE N., 1990. The role of the sonority cycle in core syllabification, in John Kingston & Mary E. Beckman (eds.), *Papers in laboratory phonology I*. Cambridge: Cambridge University Press. 283–333.

CLEMENTS, GEORGE N., 2009. Does sonority have a phonetic basis?, in Eric Raimy & Charles A. Cairns (eds.), *Contemporary views on architecture and representation in phonology*. Cambridge, MA: MIT Press. 165–175.

CLEMENTS, GEORGE N. & ELIZABETH HUME, 1995. The internal organization of speech sounds, in John A. Goldsmith (ed.), *The handbook of phonological theory*. Oxford: Blackwell. 245–306.

CLEMENTS, GEORGE N. & S. JAY KEYSER, 1983. *CV phonology: A generative Theory of syllable structure*. Cambridge, MA: MIT Press.

COLE, JENNIFER, 1995. The cycle in phonology, in John A. Goldsmith (ed.), *The handbook of phonological theory*. Oxford: Blackwell. 70–113.

COLLINGE, NEVILLE E., 1985. *The laws of Indo-European*. Amsterdam: John Benjamins.

CORTE, FRANCESCO DELLA (ed.), 1984–1991. *Enciclopedia Virgiliana* 5 vols. Roma: Istituto della Enciclopedia Italiana.

CÔTÉ, MARIE-HÉLÈNE, 2000. *Consonant cluster phonotactics: A perceptual approach*. PhD Thesis, Massachusetts Institute of Technology.

CSER, ANDRÁS, 1999. Diphthongs in the syllable structure of Latin. *Glotta* 75(3/4). 172–193.

CSER, ANDRÁS, 2003. *The typology and modelling of obstruent lenition and fortition processes*. Budapest: Akadémiai.

CSER, ANDRÁS, 2010. The Latin -*alis/aris* allomorphy revisited, in Franz Rainer, Wolfgang U. Dressler, Dieter Kastovsky & Hans Christian Luschützky (eds.), *Variation and change in morphology: Selected papers from the 13th International Morphology Meeting*. Amsterdam: John Benjamins. 33–52.

CSER, ANDRÁS, 2011. The floating C-place node in Latin. *Journal of Linguistics* 47(1). 65–85.

CSER, ANDRÁS, 2012a. The role of sonority in the phonology of Latin, in Steve Parker (ed.), *The Sonority Controversy*. Berlin: De Gruyter. 39–63.

CSER, ANDRÁS, 2012b. Resyllabification and metre: The issue of *s impurum* revisited, *Acta Antiqua Academiae Scientiarum Hungaricae* 52(4). 363–373.

CSER, ANDRÁS, 2013. Segmental identity and the issue of complex segments, *Acta Linguistica* 60(3). 247–264.

CSER, ANDRÁS, 2015. The nature of phonological conditioning in Latin inflectional allomorphy, *Acta Linguistica Hungarica* 62(1). 1–35.

CSER, ANDRÁS, 2020. Prefix allomorphy and the phonologisation of *s*-deletion in Latin. *Transactions of the Philological Society* 118(1). 159–171. https://doi.org/10.1111/1467-968X.12178

DAVIDSON, JOSEPH, 1813. Translation of the *Epistles* of Ovid. London: Nunn.

DE SAUSSURE, FERDINAND, 1916. *Cours de linguistique générale.* Lausanne: Payot.

DE LACY, PAUL, 2006. *Markedness: Reduction and preservation in phonology.* Cambridge: Cambridge University Press.

DE VAAN, MICHIEL, 2008. *Etymological dictionary of Latin and the other Italic languages.* Leiden: Brill.

DE VAAN, MICHIEL, 2009. Latin *au-* 'away', an allomorph of *ab-*. *Anuari de Filologia* 25–26 [2003–2004], 141–147.

DENNISON, WALTER, 1906. Syllabification in Latin inscriptions. *Classical Philology* 1(1). 47–68.

DEROY, LOUIS, 1980. La prononciation du graphème ⟨AE⟩ en latin. *Revue de philologie, de littérature et d'histoire anciennes.* III. 54(106). 209–225.

DEVINE, ANDREW M. & LAURENCE D. STEPHENS, 1977. *Two studies in Latin phonology.* Saratoga, CA: Anma Libri.

DEVINE, ANDREW M. & LAURENCE D. STEPHENS, 1994. *The prosody of Greek speech.* Oxford: Oxford University Press.

DRESSLER, WOLFGANG, 1971. An alleged case of non-chronological rule insertion, *Linguistic Inquiry* 2(4). 597–599.

DUFF, JAMES, 1927. *Translation of Punica by Silius Italicus.* Cambridge, MA: Harvard University Press.

EICHNER, HEINER, 1992. Indogermanische phonemsystem und lateinische lautgeschichte, in Oswald Panagl & Thomas Krisch (eds.), *Latein und Indogermanisch. Akten des Kollokviums der Indogermanischen Gesellschaft, Salzburg 23–26. September, 1986.* Innsbruck: Institut für Sprachwissenschaft. 55–79.

EMBICK, DAVID, 2010. *Localism versus globalism in morphology and phonology.* Cambridge, MA: MIT Press.

EMONDS, JOSEPH EMBLEY, 2014. The phonological basis of Latin case patterns. *Topics in Linguistics* 14. https://doi.org/10.2478/topling-2014-0011.

EMONDS, JOSEPH EMBLEY & PHILLIP SPAELTI, 2005. Fully distributing morphology: The phonology and syntax of Latin case inflections. *Theoretical and Applied Linguistics at Kobe Shoin* 8. 1–20.

FABB, NIGEL & MORRIS HALLE, 2008. *Meter in poetry.* Cambridge: Cambridge University Press.

FLOBERT, PIERRE, 1990. Le témoignage épigraphique des apices et des I longae sur les quantités vocalique en latin impérial, in Gualtiero Calboli (ed.), *Latin vulgaire, Latin tardif II.* Niemeyer: Tübingen. 101–110. .

GARCÍA GONZÁLEZ, JUAN JOSÉ, 1996. Asimilación de prefijos en inscripciones latinas, in Alfred Bammesberger & Friedrich Heberlein (eds.), *Akten des VIII. Internationalen Kolloquiums zur Lateinischen Linguistik.* Heidelberg: Winter. 94–107.

GESS, RANDALL, 2004. Phonetics, phonology and phonological change in OT: Another look at the reduction of three-consonant sequences in Late Latin. *Probus* 16(1). 21–41.

GIANNINI, STEFANIA & GIOVANNA MAROTTA, 1989. *Fra gammatica e pragmatica: La geminazione consonantica in latino*. Pisa: Giardini.

GODEL, ROBERT, 1953. Les semi-voyelles en latin. *Studia Linguistica* 7(1/2). 90–114.

GOLDSMITH, JOHN A., 1990. *Autosegmental and metrical phonology*. Oxford: Blackwell.

GORDON, MATTHEW, 2002. A phonetically driven account of syllable weight. *Language* 78(1). 51–80.

GORDON, MATTHEW, 2004. Syllable Weight, in Bruce Hayes, Robert Kirchner & Donca Steriade (eds.), *Phonetically based phonology*. Cambridge: Cambridge University Press. 277–312.

GORDON, MATTHEW, 2006. *Syllable weight. Phonetics, phonology, typology*. New York: Routledge.

GORDON, MATTHEW, EDITA GHUSHCHYAN, BRADLEY MCDONNELL, DAISY ROSENBLUM & PATRICIA A. SHAW, 2012. Sonority and central vowels: A cross-linguistic phonetic study, in Steve Parker (ed.), *The sonority controversy*. Berlin: De Gruyter. 219–256.

GORMAN, KYLE, 2012. Exceptions to rhotacism. *Proceedings from the Annual Meeting of the Chicago Linguistic Society* 48. 279–293.

GREENOUGH, JAMES B., 1900. *Bucolics, Aeneid*, and *Georgics* of Vergil. Edition and translation. Boston, MA: Ginn.

GRUBER, JAMES F., 2006. The prosodic domain of roots: Output oriented faithfulness in Classical Latin. *Georgetown University Working Papers in Theoretical Linguistics* 6. 127–165.

GUSSENHOVEN, CARLOS, 2007. A vowel height split explained: Compensatory listening and speaker control, in Jennifer Cole & José I. Hualde (eds.), *Laboratory phonology 9*. Berlin: Mouton de Gruyter. 145–172.

GUSSMANN, EDMUND, 2002. *Phonology: Analysis and theory*. Cambridge: Cambridge University Press.

HALL, TRACY ALLAN, 2006. Segmental features, in Paul de Lacy (ed.), *The Cambridge handbook of phonology*. Cambridge: Cambridge University Press. 311–334.

HALPORN, JAMES W., MARTIN OSTWALD & THOMAS G. ROSENMEYER, 1963. *The meters of Greek and Latin poetry*. London: Methuen.

HARRIS, JAMES W., 1983. *Syllable structure and stress in Spanish: A nonlinear analysis*. Cambridge, MA: MIT Press.

HARRIS, JOHN, 1994. *English sound structure*. Oxford: Blackwell.

HAYES, BRUCE, ROBERT KIRCHNER & DONCA STERIADE (eds.), 2004. *Phonetically based phonology*. Cambridge: Cambridge University Press.

HERMAN, JÓZSEF, 1996. The end of the history of Latin. *Romance Philology* 49 (4). 364–382.

HERMAN, JÓZSEF, 2000. *Vulgar Latin*. Translated by R. Wright. University Park, PA: Pennsylvania University Press.

HOENIGSWALD, HENRY M., 1949a. Antevocalic u-diphthongs in Latin. *Language* 25(4). 392–394.

HOENIGSWALD, HENRY M., 1949b. A note on Latin prosody: Initial s impure after short vowel. *Transactions and Proceedings of the American Philological Association* 80. 271–280.

HOENIGSWALD, HENRY M., 1992. Silbengrenze und vokalschwächung im Lateinischen, in Oswald Panagl & Thomas Krisch (eds.), *Latein und Indogermanisch. Akten des Kollokviums der Indogermanischen Gesellschaft, Salzburg 23–26. September, 1986.* Innsbruck: Institut für Sprachwissenschaft. 81–85.

HOOPER, JOAN B., 1976. *An Introduction to natural generative phonology*. New York: Academic Press.

HURCH, BERNARD, 1991. On adjacency and related concepts, in Pier Marco Bertinetto, Michael Kenstowicz & Michele Loporcaro (eds.), *Certamen phonologicum II*. Torino: Rosenberg & Sellier. 43–63.

HUSBAND, RICHARD WELLINGTON, 1910. The diphthong -ui in Latin. *Transactions and Proceedings of the American Philological Association* 41. 19–23.

INKELAS, SHARON, 2011. The interaction between morphology and phonology, in John Goldsmith, Jason Riggle & Alan C. L. Yu (eds.), *The handbook of phonological theory* (2nd edn). Oxford: Wiley-Blackwell. 103–140.

ITÔ, JUNKO & ARMIN MESTER, 1993. Licensed segments and safe paths. *Canadian Journal of Linguistics* 38(2). 197–213.

JACOBS, HAIKE, 1992. The interaction between the evolution of syllable structure and foot structure in the evolution from Classical Latin to Old French, in Christiane Laeufer & Terrell Morgan (eds.), *Theoretical analyses in Romance linguistics*. Amsterdam: Benjamins. 55–79.

JANY, CARMEN, MATTHEW GORDON, CARLOS M. NASH & NOBUTAKA TAKARA, 2007. How universal is the sonority hierarchy? A cross-linguistic acoustic study, in Jürgen Trouvain (ed.) *Proceedings of the 16th International Congress of Phonetic Sciences*, Saarbrücken, Germany, 6–10 August, 2007. Saarbrücken: University of Saarbrücken. 1401–04.

JARDINE, ADAM, 2016. Learning tiers for long-distance phonotactics, in Laurel Perkins, Rachel Dudley, Juliana Gerard & Kasia Hitczenko (eds.) Proceedings of the 6th Conference on Generative Approaches to Language Acquisition North America (GALANA 15). Somerville: Cascadilla Proceedings Project, 2016. 60–72.

JASANOFF, JAY H., 2004. *Plus ça change...*: Lachmann's law in Latin, in John H. W. Penney (ed.), *Indo-European perspectives – studies in honour of Anna Morpurgo Davies*. Oxford: Oxford University Press. 405–416.

JURET, (ABEL-)CLAUDE, 1913. *Dominance et résistance dans la phonétique latine*. Heidelberg: Winter.

JURET, (ABEL-)CLAUDE, 1921. *Manuel de phonétique latine*. Paris: Hachette.

KEIL, HENRICUS (ed.), 1855–78. *Grammatici Latini*. Leipzig: Teubner.

KENSTOWICZ, MICHAEL, 1994. *Phonology in generative grammar.* Oxford: Basil Blackwell.

KENSTOWICZ, MICHAEL, 1997. Quality-sensitive stress. *Rivista di Linguistica* 9(1). 157–187.

KENT, ROLAND G., 1912. Dissimilative writings for ii and iii in Latin. *Transactions and Proceedings of the American Philological Association* 43. 35–56.

KENT, ROLAND G., 1932. *The sounds of Latin. A descriptive and historical phonology.* Linguistic Society of America (=*Language* 8(3). 11–216, *Language Monograph* 12).

KENT, ROLAND G., 1936. Assimilation and dissimilation. *Language* 12(4). 245–258.

KIPARSKY, PAUL, 1982a. From cyclic phonology to lexical phonology, in Harry van der Hulst & Norval Smith (eds.), *The structure of phonological representations* vol 1. Dordrecht: Foris. 131–175.

KIPARSKY, PAUL, 1982b. Lexical phonology and morphology, in In-Seok Yang (ed.), *Linguistics in the morning calm.* Hanshin: Seoul. 3–91.

KIPARSKY, PAUL, 2017. *Paradigms and opacity.* Stanford, CA: CSLI.

KISS, ZOLTÁN, 2007. *The phonetics–phonology interface.* PhD Dissertation, Eötvös Loránd University.

LABRUNE, LAURENCE, 2012. *The phonology of Japanese.* Oxford: Oxford University Press.

LEHMANN, WINFRED P., 1994. Gothic and the reconstruction of Proto-Germanic, in Ekkehard König & Johan van der Auwera (eds.), *The Germanic languages.* New York: Routledge. 19–37.

LEHMANN, CHRISTIAN, 2005. La structure de la syllabe latine, in Christian Touratier (ed.), *Essais de phonologie latine.* Aix-en-Provence: Université de Provence. 157–206.

LEONARD, WILLIAM E., 1921. *Lucretius: On the nature of things.* New York: E. P. Dutton.

LEUMANN, MANU, 1917. *Die lateinischen adjektiva auf -lis.* Strassburg: Trübner.

LEUMANN, MANU, 1977. *Lateinische laut- und formenlehre.* München: Beck.

LEVIN, JULIETTE, 1985. *A metrical theory of syllabicity.* PhD dissertation, MIT.

LINDSAY, WILLIAM M., 1894. *The Latin language: An historical account of Latin sounds, stems and flexions.* Oxford: Clarendon.

LODGE, KEN, 2009. *Fundamental concepts in phonology.* Edinburgh: Edinburgh University Press.

LOPORCARO, MICHELE, 2015. *Vowel length from Latin to Romance.* Oxford: Oxford University Press.

LOWENSTAMM, JEAN, 1981. On the maximal cluster approach to syllable structure. *Linguistic Inquiry* 12(4). 575–604.

MANIET, ALBERT, 1955. *L'évolution phonétique et les sons du latin ancien dans le cadre des langues indo-européennes.* Louvain: Nauwelaerts.

MAROTTA, GIOVANNA, 1999. The Latin syllable, in Harry van der Hulst & Nancy A. Ritter (eds.), *The syllable: Views and facts*. Berlin: Mouton de Gruyter. 285–310.

MASCARÓ, JOAN, 1976. *Catalan phonology and the phonological cycle*. PhD dissertation, MIT.

MATTHEWS, PETER H., 1974. *Morphology: An introduction to the theory of word structure*. Cambridge: Cambridge University Press.

MCCARTHY, JOHN J., 2003. Comparative markedness. *Theoretical Linguistics* 29 (1). 1–51.

MEILLET, ANTOINE, 1928. *Esquisse d'une histoire de la langue latine*. Paris: Hachette.

MEISER, GERHARD, 1998. *Historische laut- und formenlehre der lateinischen sprache*. Darmstadt: Wissenschaftliche Buchgesellschaft.

MEISER, GERHARD, 2003. *Veni vidi vici. Die vorgeschichte des lateinischen perfektsystems*. München: Beck.

MESTER, R. ARMIN, 1994. The quantitative trochee in Latin. *Natural Language and Linguistic Theory* 12(1). 1–61.

MILLER, BRETT, 2012. Sonority and the larynx, in Steve Parker (ed.), *The sonority controversy*. Berlin: De Gruyter. 257–288.

MOHANAN, KARUVANNUR PUTHANVEETTIL, 1986. *The theory of lexical phonology*. Dordrecht: Reidel.

MORALEJO, JOSÉ-LUIS, 1991. Vocalis ante vocalem: Corripitur an distrahitur?, in Robert Coleman (ed.), *New studies in Latin linguistics*. Amsterdam: John Benjamins. 35–45.

MORE, BROOKES, 1922. Translation of Ovid's *Metamorphoses*. Boston, MA: Cornhill.

MORÉN, BRUCE, 2003. The parallel structures model of feature geometry, in Johanna Brugmann & Anastasia Riehl (eds.), *Working papers of the Cornell Phonetics Laboratory*, vol. 15. Ithaca, NY. Cornell University. 194–270.

MOZLEY, JOHN H., 1928. *Statius. With an English translation*. London: Heinemann; New York: Putnam's.

MÜLLER, DANIELA, 2013. Liquid dissimilation with a special regard to Latin, in Fernando Sánchez Miret & Daniel Recasens (eds.) *Studies in phonetics, phonology and sound change in Romance*. München: Lincom. 95–109.

MURRAY, ROBERT & THEO VENNEMANN, 1983. Sound change and syllable structure in Germanic Phonology. *Language* 59(3). 514–528.

MYNORS, ROGER A. B., 1972. *P. Vergili Maronis opera*. Oxford: Clarendon.

NEVINS, ANDREW, 2011. Phonologically conditioned allomorph selection, in Marc van Oostendorp, Colin J. Ewen, Elizabeth Hume & Keren Rice (eds.), *The Blackwell companion to phonology*. Wiley-Blackwell: Malden, MA. 2357–2382.

NIEDERMANN, MAX, 1953[3][1906]. *Précis de phonétique historique du latin*. Paris: Klincksieck.

ODDEN, DAVID, 2005. *Introducing phonology*. Cambridge: Cambridge University Press.

ONIGA, RENATO, 2014. *Latin: A linguistic introduction*. Oxford: Oxford University Press.

PADGETT, JAYE, 2008. Glides, vowels, and features. *Lingua* 118(12). 1841–2030.

PALMER, LEONARD R., 1954. *The Latin language*. London: Faber and Faber.

PARKER, STEPHEN GEORGE, 2002. *Quantifying the sonority hierarchy*. PhD dissertation, University of Massachusetts Amherst.

PARKER, STEVE, 2003. The psychological reality of sonority in English. *Word* 54 (3). 359–399.

PARKER, STEVE, 2008. Sound level protrusions as physical correlates of sonority. *Journal of Phonetics* 36: 55–90.

PARKER, STEVE, 2011. Sonority, in Marc van Oostendorp, Colin J. Ewen, Elizabeth Hume & Keren Rice (eds.), *The Blackwell companion to phonology*. Wiley-Blackwell: Malden, MA. 1160–1184.

PARSONS, JED, 1999. A new approach to saturnian verse and its relation to Latin prosody. *Transactions of the American Philological Association* 129. 117–137.

PAUCKER, CARL, 1885. Materialien zur lateinischen wörterbildungsgescgichte V. Die Nomina derivata auf alis (aris und arius). *Zeitschrift für Vergleichende Sprachforschung* 27(2). 113–156.

PAYNE, AMANDA, 2017. All dissimilation is computationally subsequential. *Language* 93(4). e353–e371.

PIGGOTT, GLYNE L., 1999. At the right edge of words. *Linguistic Review* 16(2). 143–85.

PILLINGER, O. STEPHEN, 1983. Latin degemination: an autosegmental approach, in Harm Pinkster (ed.), *Latin linguistics and linguistic theory*. Amsterdam: John Benjamins. 243–260.

PLATNAUER, MAURICE, 1951. *Latin elegiac verse. A study of the metrical usages of Propertius, Tibullus and Ovid*. Cambridge: Cambridge University Press.

PRINZ, OTTO, 1949–50. Zur präfixassimilation im antiken und im frühmittelalterlichen latein. *Archivum Latinitatis Mediae Aevi* 21. 87–115.

PRINZ, OTTO, 1953. Zur präfixassimilation im antiken und im frühmittelalterlichen latein. *Archivum Latinitatis Mediae Aevi* 23. 35–60.

PULGRAM, ERNST, 1970. *Syllable, word, nexus, cursus*. The Hague: Mouton.

PULGRAM, ERNST, 1975. *Latin-Romance phonology: Prosodics and metrics*. Munich: Wilhelm Fink.

RAMSAY, GEORGE GILBERT, 1918. *Translation of Juvenal and Persius*. Loeb Classical Library, London: Heinemann.

RAVEN, DAVID S., 1965. *Latin metre: An introduction*. London: Faber and Faber.

REBRUS, PÉTER & MIKLÓS TÖRKENCZY, 2015a. Monotonicity and the typology of front/back harmony. *Theoretical Linguistics* 41(1–2). 1–61.

REBRUS, PÉTER & MIKLÓS TÖRKENCZY, 2015b. The monotonic behaviour of language patterns. *Theoretical Linguistics* 41(3–4). 241–268.

REYNOLDS, LEIGHTON DURHAM & NIGEL GUY WILSON, 1991³[1974]. *Scribes and scholars: A guide to the transmission of Greek and Latin literature.* Oxford: Clarendon.

RIBBECK, OTTO (ed.), 1894. *Vergilii opera.* Leipzig: Teubner.

RIDLEY, SIR EDWARD, 1905. *Translation of Pharsalia by M. Annaeus Lucanus.* London: Longmans, Green, and Co..

RINGE, DON, 2006. *A Linguistic History of English. Volume I: From Proto-Indo-European to Proto-Germanic.* Oxford: Oxford University Press.

RIX, HELMUT, MARTIN KÜMMEL, THOMAS ZEHNDER, REINER LIPP & BRIGITTE SCHIRMER, 2001² [1998]. *Lexikon der indogermanischen verben: Die wurzeln und ihre primärstammbildungen.* Wiesbaden: Reichert.

ROBERTS, PHILIP J., 2009. *An optimality-theoretic analysis of Lachmann's law.* MPhil Thesis, University of Oxford.

ROBERTS, PHILIP J., 2012. Latin rhotacism: A case study in the life cycle of phonological processes, *Transactions of the Philological Society* 110(1). 80–93.

ROCA, IGGY, 1994. *Generative phonology.* London: Routledge.

ROSÉN, HANNA, 1999. *Latine loqui. Trends and directions in the crystallisation of Classical Latin.* München: Wilhelm Fink.

SAFAREWICZ, JAN, 1974. *Linguistic studies.* The Hague: Mouton.

SEEBOLD, ELMAR, 1967. Die Vertretung idg. *gᵘh* im Germanischen. *Zeitschrift für Vergleichende Sprachwissenschaft* 81(1/2). 104–133.

SELKIRK, ELISABETH, 1984. On the major class features and syllable theory, in Mark Aronoff & Richard T. Oehrle (eds.), *Language sound structure.* Cambridge, MA: MIT Press. 107–136.

SEN, RANJAN, 2006. Vowel weakening before *muta cum liquidā* sequences in Latin: A problem of syllabification? *Oxford University Working Papers in Linguistics, Philology and Phonetics* 11. 143–161.

SEN, RANJAN, 2012. Reconstructing phonological change: Duration and syllable structure in Latin vowel reduction. *Phonology* 29(3). 465–504.

SEN, RANJAN, 2014. Inverse compensatory lengthening in Latin: Weight preservation or phonologisation? Talk given at Symposium on Historical Phonology, Edinburgh, 13–14 January, 2014.

SEN, RANJAN, 2015. *Syllable and segment in Latin.* Oxford: Oxford University Press.

SEO, MISUN, 2011. Syllable contact, in Marc van Oostendorp, Colin J. Ewen, Elizabeth Hume & Keren Rice (eds.), *The Blackwell companion to phonology.* Malden, MA: Wiley-Blackwell. 1245–1262.

Shackleton Bailey David Roy (ed.), 1997. *M. Annaei Lucani De bello civili libri X.* Stuttgart: Teubner.

SIHLER, ANDREW L., 1995. *New comparative grammar of Greek and Latin.* Oxford: Oxford University Press.

SIPTÁR, PÉTER & TÖRKENCZY MIKLÓS, 2000. *The phonology of Hungarian.* Oxford: Oxford University Press.

SMART, CHRISTOPHER & THEODORE ALOIS BUCKLEY, 1863. *Translation of the works of Horace*. New York: Harper & Brothers.

SOMMER, FERDINAND, 1902. *Handbuch der lateinischen laut- und Fformenlehre: Eine einführung in das sprachwissenschaftliche studium des Lateins*. Heidelberg: Winter.

SPAELTI, PHILLIP, 2004. Some phonological and morphological patterns in the Latin noun declension system. *Theoretical and Applied Linguistics at Kobe Shoin* 7. 131–137.

STANTON, JULIET, 2017. Segmental blocking in dissimilation: An argument for co-occurrence constraints, in *Proceedings of the 2016 annual meeting on phonology*. Washington DC: Linguistic Society of America, (no page numbering)

STAUSLAND JOHNSEN, SVERRE, 2009. The development of voiced labiovelars in Germanic, in Stephanie W. Jamison, H. Craig Melchert & Brent Vine (eds.), *Proceedings of the 20th Annual UCLA Indo-European Conference*. Bremen: Hempen. 197–211.

STERIADE, DONCA, 1982. *Greek prosodies and the nature of syllabification*. PhD dissertation, MIT.

STERIADE, DONCA, 1984. Glides and vowels in Romanian. *Papers from the Berkeley Linguistics Society* 10. 47–64.

STERIADE, DONCA, 1987. Redundant values, in Anna Bosch, Barbara Need & Eric Schiller (eds.), *Papers from the 23rd Annual Regional Meeting of the Chicago Linguistic Society. Part two: Parasession of Autosegmental and Metrical Phonology*. Chicago, IL: Chicago Linguistic Society. 339–362.

STERIADE, DONCA, 1988. Gemination and the Proto-Romance syllable shift, in David Birdsong & Jean-Pierre Montreuil (eds.), *Advances in Romance linguistics*. Dordrecht: Foris. 371–409.

STERIADE, DONCA, 1995. Underspecification and markedness, in John A. Goldsmith (ed.), *The handbook of phonological theory*. Oxford: Blackwell. 114–174.

STERIADE, DONCA, 1999. Alternatives to syllable-based accounts of consonantal phonotactics, in Osamu Fujimura, Brian D. Joseph & Bohumil Palek (eds.), *Proceedings of the 1998 Linguistics and Phonetics Conference*. Prague: Karolinum. 205–242.

STERIADE, DONCA, 2012. The cycle without containment: Latin perfect stems. unpublished manuscript, http://lingphil.mit.edu/papers/steriade/Steriade2012 LatinPerfect.pdf

STUART-SMITH, JANE, 2004. *Phonetics and philology. Sound change in Italic*. Oxford: Oxford University Press.

STURTEVANT, EDGAR H., 1912. The Pronunciation of cui and huic. *Transactions and Proceedings of the American Philological Association* 43. 57–66.

STURTEVANT, EDGAR H., 1916. The monophthongization of Latin ae. *Transactions and Proceedings of the American Philological Association* 47. 107–116.

STURTEVANT, EDGAR H., 1920. *The pronunciation of Greek and Latin*. Chicago, IL: Chicago University Press.

STURTEVANT, EDGAR H., 1939. The pronunciation of Latin qu and gu. *Language* 15(4). 221–223.

STURTEVANT, EDGAR H. & ROLAND G. KENT, 1915. Elision and hiatus in Latin prose and verse. *Transactions and Proceedings of the American Philological Association* 46. 129–155.

SZEMERÉNYI, OSWALD, 1980. Latin verbs in *-uō -uere*, in Herbert J. Izzo (ed.), *Italic and Romance: Linguistic studies in honour of Ernst Pulgram*. John Benjamins: Amstedam. 9–32.

SZIGETVÁRI, PÉTER, 2008. What and where?, in Joaquim Brandão de Carvalho, Tobias Scheer & Philippe Ségéral (eds.), *Lenition and fortition*. Berlin: Mouton de Gruyter. 93–129.

TOURATIER, CHRISTIAN, 2005. Système des consonnes, in Christian Touratier (ed.), *Essais de phonologie latine*. Aix-en-Provence: Université de Provence. 61–134.

TRUBETZKOY, NIKOLAI S., 1969 *Principles of phonology*. Translated by C. A. M. Baltaxe. Berkeley, CA: University of California Press.

TUCKER, THOMAS GEORGE, 1922. On a Latin phonetic rule. *The Classical Quarterly* 16(2). 102–103.

UFFMANN, CHRISTIAN, 2007. *Vowel epenthesis in loanword adaptation*. Tübingen: Max Niemeyer.

VÄÄNÄNEN, VEIKKO, 1981[3]. *Introduction au Latin Vulgaire*. Paris: Klincksieck.

VAINIO, RAIJA, 1999. *Latinitas and Barbarismus according to the Roman grammarians*. Turku: Department of Classics, University of Turku.

VENNEMANN, THEO, 1988. *Preference laws for syllable structure and the explanation of Ssound change: With special reference to German, Germanic, Italian and Latin*. Berlin: Mouton de Gruyter.

VINE, BRENT, 2008. On the etymology of Latin *tranquillus* "calm". *International Journal of Diachronic Linguistics and Linguistic Reconstruction* 5. 1–24.

WALDE, ALOIS & JOHANN B. HOFMANN, 1956. *Lateinisches etymologisches wörterbuch*. Heidelberg: Winter.

WARD, RALPH L., 1951. Stop plus liquid and the position of the Latin accent. *Language* 27(4). 477–484.

WATBLED, JEAN-PHILIPPE, 2005. Théories phonologiques et questions de phonologie latine, in Christian Touratier (ed.), *Essais de phonologie latine*. Aix-en-Provence: Université de Provence. 25–57.

WATKINS, CALVERT, 1970. A case of non-chronological rule insertion. *Linguistic Inquiry* 1(4). 525–7.

WEISS, MICHAEL, 2009. *Outline of the historical and comparative grammar of Latin*. Ann Arbor, MI: Beech Stave Press.

WEST, MARTIN LITCHFIELD, 1982. *Greek metre*. Oxford: Oxford University Press.

WIESE, BERND, 2013. On Latin nominal inflection: The form–function relationship. *Morphology* 23(2). 179–200.

WILLIAMS, THEODORE C., 1910. *Translation of Vergil's Aeneid.* Boston, MA: Houghton Mifflin.

WRIGHT, ROGER H. P., 2002. *A sociophilological study of Late Latin.* Turnhout: Brepols.

YIP, MOIRA, 1991. Coronals, consonant clusters and the coda condition, in Carole Paradis & Jean-François Prunet (eds.), *The special status of coronals: Internal and external evidence.* San Diego, CA: Academic Press. 61–78.

ZEC, DRAGA, 2007. The syllable, in Paul de Lacy (ed.), *The Cambridge handbook of phonology.* Cambridge: Cambridge University Press. 161–194.

ZIRIN, ANDREW R., 1970. *The phonological basis of Latin prosody.* The Hague: Mouton.

INDEX OF LATIN WORDS

(not including inflected forms and verb stems; prefixed forms that show variable assimilation are given in their more usual form, e.g. *accedere* and *adclamare*, not *adcedere* or *acclamare*)

-cumque 85
-dam 83, 84, 96
-dem 33, 83, 84, 96
-libet 85
-met 85
-nam 84
-piam 85, 119
-quam 85
-que 22, 75, 85
-vis 85
ab 18, 19
abicere 17
abies 24, 25, 43, 122
abire 70, 71, 133–139, 173
abscondere173, 180
absorbere 56, 57
abstinere 172, 173, 180
abstrahere 173
absumere 93
ac 18, 20
accedere 135
accipere 30, 95, 107, 170, 176
acer 54, 66, 111, 146
acies 43,122
acuere 14, 29
adbibere 170
adbitere 170
adbreviare 170
adclamare 30, 170
adclinis 170
adclivis 170
adcredere 170
adcrescere 170
adducere 105
adesse 95, 118, 170, 171

adferre 170, 174
adgredi 170
adicere 165
adimere 93
adiungere 57
adlabi 181
adloqui 170
admittere 135
admovere 170, 174
adnumerare 170, 178
adolescere 106
adponere 174, 176
adprehendere 30 170
adprobare 90, 170, 171
adquiescere 23
adquirere 23, 30, 90, 170
adripere 60, 170
adrogare 170
adsiduus 170
adsistere 83, 170
adsuescere 30, 90, 171
adsumere 93
adtendere 182
adtrahere 89, 90, 182
aeger 18, 55, 56
aemulus 55
aeneus 44
aequus 21, 36, 56
aereus 54
aes 14, 53, 87, 91
aestus 56, 91
aeternus 54
aevum 54, 68
afer 17, 54, 66
agellus 97
ager 54, 111, 145, 184

agere 9, 27–29, 41, 54, 68, 116, 118, 128–130, 140, 153, 156, 164, 173, 184
agger 14, 16
aggredi 107, 170
agmen 55
agnus 16, 54, 80
ait 17, 44
alacer
albus 27, 55, 68, 97
alere 106
alimentum 114
alligare 170, 185
almus 54, 114
alnus 54
alter 97
altrix 67
alvus 54
amare 8, 9, 28, 35, 113, 115, 128–130, 134, 137, 139, 140, 184
ambages / ambago 158
ambesse 158
ambidexter 159
ambifarius 159
ambiformiter 159
ambigere 158
ambire 158
amburere 158, 164
amicire 165
amiculus 97
amicus 8
amittere 173
amnis 54, 68, 143
amor 8, 41
amovere 173, 174

amplecti 165
amplus 56, 93
amputare 57, 165
anceps 165
anfractus 165
angor 16
anguis 21
animal 17, 100, 115
annus 14–16, 143–148
anquirere 165
anser 36, 119
ante 55, 67
anteactus 159
anteambulo 159
antecedere 159
antecellere 159
anteferre 159
anteire 159
antesignanus 159
antestari 165
anticipare 159, 183
antiquus 31
antistes 159
antrum 27, 56, 67
apparare 170
apparere 170
appetere 30, 95, 170
aptus 54, 68
aqua 14, 30, 31, 66
ara 113, 143–148, 184
ardere 55
arguere 21, 29
aries 122
arma 54
armentum 114
arripere 60, 170
arx 53
ascendere 171
asci(sce)re 171
ascribere 171
aspectare 171
aspellere 173, 174
aspergere 171
aspernari 171

aspicere 171
aspirare 171
asportare 173, 174
aspritudo 56
ast 53
astare 171
astringere 171
attat 18
atterere 182
attinere 154, 170, 174,
  176, 182
attingere 182
attribuere 182
audax 53, 145
audire 55, 137, 139, 140
auferre 174
aufugere 174
augere 42, 55–57
augmen(tum) 56, 66,
  114
augur 55
Augustalis 100
aula 54
aura 54
aureus 110
aurum 54
auscultare 57, 91
auspicium 57
Auster 57, 91
aut 53
autem 54
autumnalis 100
auxilium 57
avertere 173, 174
avocare 173
balbus 55
barbaria 142
basis 87
bellulus 102
belua 14
bestia 92
bibere 14
blandus 52
blaterare 52

blatta 52
bos 29, 37
bracchium 4, 5
brevis 52
bruma 52
brutus 52
bufo 17
caedere 41, 42, 55, 106
caelebs 54
caelum 54
caementum 54
caesaries 122
caespes 57, 66, 91
caestus 56, 91
caetra 56
calcar 101
calix 107
calx 53
cancer 56
capere 9, 108, 110,
  128–130, 140
capital 100
capra 54
caput 14, 17, 18, 105,
  115, 143–148
carpere 55–57, 66, 130
castrum 56
causa 55, 87
cavere 29, 40
cedere 41, 86
cedrus 60
celeber 111
celebritas 111
celer 18, 110, 145
cernere 54, 68, 133
ceu 19, 38–40, 200
cicer 14, 112
cicur 109
cingere 56
cinis 41, 108, 184
circuire 165, 166, 179
circuitus 165, 166
circum 165, 166
circumagere 166

circumcidere 166
circumcludere 166
circumobruere 166
cito 100
clades 142
clamare 41
claudere 41, 52, 55, 106
Claudilla 102
claustrum 57
clemens 52
cliens 52
clitellae 102
coarguere 33, 34, 164
coemere 93, 164
coepisse 55, 56
cogere 44, 114, 164, 179
cognatus 79
cohors 17
coire 14, 33, 34, 95, 96,
    121, 164
coitus 14, 42
collega 163, 180
collegium 163, 180
colligare 182
colligere 163, 181, 182
columella 102
comburere 164
comere 93, 120, 164,
    184
comes 107, 164
comesse 164
comis 35
committere 95, 165
commixtrix 57
complere 134, 139
componere 95, 163,
    164, 176
concrepere 163
condimentum 114
condonare 95
conectere 33, 063
conferre 35, 164
conficere 20, 105, 163,
    165

conicere 163, 165
coniunctrix 57
coniunx 53, 163
conivere 163
conlabi 181
conlaudare 181
conlocare 165, 181
conloqui 181
conquirere 95, 164
conradere 163
conridere 163
conrodere 163
conscius 36, 164
consecrare 15
consuescere 163
consul 18, 35, 36
consularis 101
consumere 57, 93, 172
contemptrix 57
contrarietas 111
contrarius 111
conubium 95, 96, 121,
    163, 164
convalescere 163
convocare 163, 165
coquere 27–29
cornu 143–148
corpus 108
counitio 164
counitus 164
crescere 52, 54, 67, 92
crines 52
crispus 54
crista 54
cruor 14, 52
cubiculum 102
cubital 100
cucumis 109
culpa 27, 55
cultellus 102
cumbere 55, 116
cupiditas 105
cupidus 105
cur 115

currere 103
cylindrus 27
dare 14, 35, 37, 115
dea 148
debere 156
deesse 156, 179
degere 153, 156
dehinc 44, 156
dehiscere 156
deicere 165
dein(de) 38, 42, 43, 53
deinceps 38, 42, 43
delabi 181
delere 126
demere 93
dens 35–37, 88
deorsum 156, 157
depingere 57
depstum 57, 172
derigere 135
deses 107
desinere 44, 88, 133,
    137–139, 168
detrimentum 114
deunx 53, 156
deus 148
dexter 57
dicere 18, 20, 28, 41
dies 43, 143–148
differre 168, 176
difficilis 111
difficultas 111
diffidere 168
diffundere 168
digerere 84, 168
dignus 15, 54, 68, 80
diiudicare 168
dilaudare 181
diluere 84, 168
diminuere 168
dimittere 84, 168
diribere 88, 109, 168
dirimere 88, 109, 168
dirumpere 168

discurrere 84, 168
disicere 168
disiungere 168
disiurgium 168
disponere 84, 168
dissentire 168
distendere 84, 168
diversus 168
dividere 116, 135, 139
divus 27, 28, 36
dodrans 54
dominus 113
domus 142, 144
Drusus 52
ducere 18, 20, 57,105
duellum 43
dux 14
ebrietas 111
ebrius 111
edere 166
effari 167
efferre 167
eheu 17–19, 38–40, 44
eho 17
eicere 167
eiusmodi 84
elephantus 142
eligere 105, 181
elocare 181
emanere 84, 166
emblema 27
emere 9,10, 42, 56, 66, 93
emungere 57
ensis 36, 87,119, 120
equus 6, 27
ergo 55
error 100, 103
esse 14, 18, 36, 53, 66,126, 140
ēsse 53
et 18, 86
evincere 167
excellere 84,166

exemplar 101
exemplum 56, 93
exfafillatus 5
exiguus 14, 113
exilire 62, 90, 167
eximere 93
eximius 110
exire 138, 166
expellere 166
expunctrix 57
extendere 84, 166
extingere 57
extra 57, 166
facere 18, 20, 28,40, 41, 100, 105, 132
facies 43, 122
faex 42, 53, 55
fafae 18, 19
fallere 89, 185
falx 42, 53
fames 142–148
familia 97
famulus 97
Faunus 54
faustus 57, 66, 91
fautrix 56
faux 37, 53
favere 29, 40
febris 54
felix 163
feminal 101
ferctum 56
ferire 128–131
fermentum 114
ferre 17, 18, 28, 53, 126, 173
fieri 43, 115
figlina 55
filia 148
filiolus 97,102
filius 148
fingere 27–29
finire 136, 137
firmus 109

fiscus 54
flagellum 102
flamma 52, 66
Flavialis 101
flavus 183
floralis 101
fluere 28, 52, 54
fluvialis 101
fodere 9
fore 108, 130, 150
forma 35, 39, 42, 54
forsan 33, 35
fortis 35, 39
fovere 133
fragmentum 114
frangere 14, 17
frater 52, 66
fraus 53, 91
frigidus 52
frons 36, 119–121, 185
fructus 52
fuga 8
fugare 8
fugere 8, 173
fulcrum 56
fulgur 109
fulmen 119
fulminalis 102
funebris 70
funerepus 109
fur 17, 35, 115
furor 35, 103, 109
galbeus 55
gemitus 35
genetivus 23
genus 145
gerere 86
glacialis 101
gladiolus 102
gladius 52
glaeba 55
glandula 102
glebalis 102
gliscere 52

globus 52
Gnaeus 78
gnarus 78
gradus 52
gravis 14, 52
grex 52, 53, 116
Hadria 60
hau/haud 14, 19, 39, 40, 53
haurire 87
haustus 57, 87, 91
hebes 108
herctum 56
hiascere 92
hic 16, 18, 38, 53, 90
hiemalis 100
hiems 35, 43, 53, 57, 64, 91, 93, 122
hilarulus 102
hinc 14, 18, 53
hircus 108, 109
homo 14, 17, 18
honestus 54
honos 18
hospes 54, 67
hostis 54, 58, 59, 61, 67, 91, 143
huiusmodi 84, 85
hydrus 60
iacere 20, 165
iam 18
ieiunus 14
ignis 15
ignoscere 16, 70, 79
illac 18
ille 39, 43, 71, 100
illepidus 16
illic 53
illinc 18
imber 14
imberbis 16
imbibere 95, 185
immittere 95, 162
immortalis 16

impetrare 51, 54
impolitus 16
imponere 162
incelebratus 16
incipere 154
incohare 17
incola 29
incrementum 114
incurrere 161
indecens 46
indoctus 163
inermis 16
iners 53
inesse 33, 95
infamis 35
infelix 163
inferus 35
infra 54
inguen 21, 31, 56
inhumanus 163
inicere 15
iniquus 15
inlicere 117, 162
innectere 33, 163
inniti 163
inquilinus 29
inquirere 95, 162, 176
inrevocabilis 16
inrigare 109, 162
insatius 162
inscius 36, 92, 161, 162, 185
insulsus 106
intellectualis 101
intellegere 116, 161
interficere 105
interligare 161
internatus 79
intingere 57
intro 166
inultus 92
ipse 54, 68
ire 105, 133, 137, 138

is 17, 33, 40, 83, 85, 96, 119
iuglans 55
iungere 14, 56
iustus 92
Kalendae 14
labellum 102
labi 54, 116
lac 17, 18, 20, 99, 112, 184
lacunar 101
laevus 24, 25, 54
languor 21
lanx 53
lapis 107, 122
laquear 101
largus 55
larva 54
later 112
lateralis 101
Latiaris 102
latrare 35
latro 35
laurus 54
laus 42, 53, 91
lavare 40
lectus 15
legalis 101
legere 105
legerupa 109
lepor 35
lepus 35
letalis 102
levir 109
lex 181
liber 111
līber 112
lien 18, 35
lingua 14, 21, 27, 56
linquere 14, 26, 27
litoralis 101
litterulae 102
localis 102
loqui 28, 29

lucerna 54
ludicrum 102
lunaris 101
lupanar 101
Lupercal 101
luteolus 102
maeror 54, 87
maestus 56, 87, 91
maior 40
mancus 55
mane 35
manere 35, 36, 87, 88, 92
manus 36, 144
mare 110, 142–148, 185
mater 111
materia 142
mel 89
meminisse 125
mens 125
mensis 14, 87
mergere 55
merx 53
metuere 108
miles 15, 36, 86, 90, 107, 121, 144, 185
militaris 101
mille 39
milvus 39
miser 87
misericors 53, 92
mittere 10, 91
moenia 54
monere 26, 125, 126, 134, 139
monstrare 26
monstrum 36, 56
mori 103
movere 29, 133
mufrius 54
mulctra 57, 89
mulgeo 56, 66
mulier 18
multitudo 18

mus 86, 91, 184
musca 54
naevus 54
nare 8, 115
natus 78
navalis 100
navus 78
nefandus 157
nefarius 157
nefas 157
nefrens 157
negligere 15, 157
negotium 157
nequire 133, 157
nescire 74, 157
neu/neve 19, 38–40
neuter 38
nihil 17
ninguit 21, 26, 27, 31
nisi 87, 110
nobilis 78
nomen 14, 107
non 35
nondum 36
noscere 78, 92, 133, 134, 137–139, 150
novitas 111, 131, 137
novus 111
nubes 142
nubilar 101
numquam 23
nunc 18
ob 18
obcaecare 172
obesse 172
obire 137, 138
oblectare 178
obmurmurare 172
obmutescere 172, 174
obnunciare 178
obruere 70, 71
obses 90, 107, 116
obsidere 105, 172, 178
obstare 70

obstupescere 105
obtinere 83, 118, 172, 178
obvertere 163, 174
obvius 163
occidere 172
occīdere 172
occludere 95, 172
occulere 172
occumbere 172
occupare 172
ocellus 97
octo 54
offa 17
offendere 172
offerre 172
officium 147
offundere 172
offuscare 172
oggerere 172
ollula 102
omittere 172
oppetere 83, 172
ops 53
optare 54
opulentus 142
opus 17
orator 115
origo 145
oriri 143
os 17, 90
oscen 172, 180
ostendere 172, 180
paelex 54
paene 54
palam 34, 35, 119
pallidulus 102
palliolum 102
palmaris 102
pandere 42
par 115
parcere 55
parere 105
paries 122

pars 14, 42, 53, 55
parvus 24, 25, 54, 68
pater 54, 58, 59, 111, 112, 143–148, 184
paternus 111
paucus 55
paullulum 102
paulum 54
pauper 55, 111
paupertas 111
pauxillum 57
pecten 17, 33, 35, 41, 107, 119
pedere 82
peierare 154, 155, 161, 178
pellere 55, 68, 97
penes 18
per 18
peragere 118
perargutus 103
pererro 103
perficere 107, 152
peric(u)lum 60
periclitari 55, 60
perimere 93
perire 133, 137, 138
periurare 154, 155, 161
periurium 154, 155
periurus 154, 155
perlegere 160
perlicere 161
perlucere 161, 178
pernicies 43
perpes 108
perpeti 106, 107
perpolitus 153
perurbanus 103
pervadere 178
petere 133, 137, 138
piger 146
pigmentum 114
pignus 108
pilum 143–148

pinguis 21
pinnirapus 109
pisum 87
planta 52
plaustrum 57
plebs 53, 82, 93
plenus 52, 66
pluralis 101
plus 52
pluvialis 101
pneumaticus 4
poena 4, 42, 54
politus 153
polliceri 161
Pompeius 17
pons 36, 50
pontifex 107
poples 54
popularis 101
porricere 161
porrigere 90, 161
portendere 161
portus 113, 148
posse 35
possidere 166
post 53, 166
postgenitus 83, 176
posticipare 183
postmeridianus 176
postscribere 86
postsignanus 86
potare 35
prae 18, 19
praeacutus 41, 160
praebere 160
praecinere 107
praeire 160
praenoscere 79
praeoptare 160
praes 53, 91
praesumere 93
praeustus 160
prehendere 17, 160
premere 10, 52, 93

primitivus 23
primus 52
priscus 92
privilegium 181
proavus 44, 113, 156, 179, 185
probare 133
probus 157
procul 157
prodesse 156
prodigere 156
prodire 44, 156, 179
proelium 54
profanus 156
profari 156
profecto 156
proferre 156
profestus 156
proficere 156
proficisci 156
profiteri 156
proflare 156
profluere 156
profugus 156
profundere 156
prohibere 156
prohinc 156
proin(de) 42, 43, 53, 156
promere 93, 156, 179
promittere 44
propago 157
prope 157
propitius 157
proprius 157
prorumpere 169
prosilire 88, 168
prout 37
prurire 52
publicus 55
puella 35, 36, 39, 43, 100, 118, 119, 184
puellula 14, 19, 102
puer 6, 18, 35, 43

pugil 100
pugna 54
pulcer 56
pullulus 102
pulmo 42, 54
puls 53, 91
pulvinar 17, 101
pulvis 109
pungere 55
puppis 143–148
purpureus 38
purus 145
quadrantal 101
quadratus 54, 60
quadriiuga 60
quadrupes 60
quaerere 54, 56, 87, 91
quando 27, 55
quantus 27, 52
quasi 19
quatere 86, 117
querela 52, 100
queri 103
qui 14, 22, 30, 96
quid 22
quies 24, 52
quincunx 53
quinque 15, 21, 56
quippe 14
quis 22–24, 38–40, 42, 66, 85
quo 22
quoad 44
quod 14
quotiens 36
rabies 43
rapere 105
rarus 14
re(d)accendere 158
reaedificare 158
reanimare 158
recedere 41
receptrix 56

recidere 41,106
reclamare 41
recludere 41, 106
reddere 158
redhalat 158
redhibere 158
redhostire 158
redigere 118, 158
redimere 93, 158
redire 44, 137, 138, 158, 179
redornare 158
redundare 158
refrangere 70
regalis 100
regere 14, 116
reicere 17, 158, 165
reignire 158
reindutus 158
reinterpretatus 158
relinquere 28, 29
remittere 44
reordinatio 158
repetere 137–139
res 18, 43, 71, 146
resecare 88
respicere 20
restare 62, 70, 74
resumere 93
retinere 154
retrahere 62
retro 166
rex 27, 53, 82, 143–148
rostrum 92
Rufrae 60
rufus 17
rumpere 55
saeculum 55
saepe 55
saepes 53
saepire 56, 57
saevus 54
Safronius 60
Saliaris 101

salsus 106
sanguis 18, 21, 36, 66, 107
sapiens 163
satura 109
scabies 43
scaevus 54
scalpellum 52
scalpere 56, 57
scalprum 56
scelus 52
scindere 62, 116
scire 31, 52
scribere 52, 54, 82, 173, 184
scriblita 55
sculpere 56, 57, 66
secare 8, 27
sedecim 84, 85, 157
sedere 105, 116, 166
sedimentum 114
seges 108, 122
segmentum 8, 27
seiugis 157
semirasus 109
semirotundus 109
semper 15
Sempronius 56, 66
senatus 146
sentire 15
seorsus 157
sepelire 97, 98, 106
septunx 53
sepulcrum 97
sequi 28, 29, 55
sermo 54
serpere 57
servus 6, 54
sesqui- 56
seu/sive 18, 19, 38–40
sex 84, 157
si 86
siccus 94
sicut 19

silva 14, 24, 25, 31, 39, 54, 68
simplex 15, 27, 94
singuli 94
siremps 53
sitis 94
socer 112
societas 111, 122, 131, 136, 137
socius 111
sol 115
solvere 28, 29, 54
somnus 15, 54
spargere 52
specere 20
species 43
spernere 28, 29, 52, 133
spirare 52
spissus 14
splendor 52
spondere 52, 62, 91
squalor 21, 24, 52
squama 52
squilla 52
stare 48, 52, 61, 62
statim 34
stella 14
stellaris 101
sternere 28
stinguere 21
stipendium 52
stirps 53
stridor 52
studium 52
stupere 105
suadere 31, 52, 66
suavis 14, 24, 25, 52
sub 18
subdere 178
subflavus 183
subire 175
submergere 175
submittere 175
submovere 175, 178

subrepere 57, 175
subrogare 175
subscribere
subsidium 175
substruere 175
subtemen 175
subterere 175, 180
subterfugere 161
subterlabi 161
subterpositus 161
subtilis 175
subvertere 174
succedere 175
succensere 175, 180
succlamare 175
succumbere 175, 180
succurrere 175
suescere 52
sufferre 175
suffundere 175
suggerere 175, 176
suggredi 175
sulcus 55
sumere 10, 33, 35, 56, 90, 93
summus 14
supellex/supellectilis 161
super 112, 161
superare 112
superus 112
supplicare 175
supponere 175
supprimere 175
supra 112, 161
suprascandere / superscandere 161
surgere 90, 175
surripere 105, 175
suscipere 180
suscitare 180
suspendere 175
suspicere 176, 180
suspirare 62, 90, 176
sustinere 175, 180

suus 14
tablinum 55
taeter 55, 56
tamen 86
tametsi 86
tamquam 23
tangere 134, 139
tardus 55
taurus 54
tegere 14
teges 108
temnere 54
temperare 105
templum 56
tempus 105, 108, 184
tener 145
tibicen 18
tinguere 15, 21, 26
tiro 145
tofus 17
tondere 36
torcular 101
torquere 21, 26, 28, 56
trabs 53
tradere 84, 169
traducere 169, 179, 183
trahere 15, 17, 44, 52
traicere 169
tralucere 169, 183
tranare 84, 169, 183
tranquillus 169
transcendere 169
transcurrere 169
transdanuviana 169
transferre 84, 169
transfigere 169
transformare 169
transfugere 169
transgredi 83–85, 169, 176, 179
transilire 91, 169
transire 88
transmeare 169
transmittere 84, 169, 178

transportare 169
transrhenani 169, 182
transversus 169
transvolare 84, 169
tribuere 29, 128–130
tribunal 100
tribus 113, 143–148
tristis 52
triumvir 109
truncus 52
tundere 36
uber 112
ulmus 54, 68, 114
ulna 54
uls 53, 91
ultra 67
ultrix 67
ultro 56
umbilicalis 101
umbra 56
unguere 21, 27, 31
unguis 21
urbs 53, 142, 143
urere 103, 164
ursus 109
usquam 56

usque 21, 56
ut 19
vae 18, 19
vafer 17, 37, 54, 60
vafritia 60
valde 55
valens 23
varietas 111
varius 111
vastitas 111
vastus 111
vecors 160
vectigal 100
vegrandis 160
vehemens 17, 160
vehere 14, 15, 17, 54, 68
Veiovis 160
velle 14, 35, 53, 97, 98,
  126, 178
velut 19
venire 35, 140
vepallidus 160
verbum 55
verrere 89, 91
vertere 91
vesanus 160

vesica 160
vestigium 160
vetus 145
victrix 56
videre 9, 71, 115, 128–
  130, 140
villula 102
vincere 28
vinclum 56
vir 35, 108, 109
viridis 145
vis 35
vitulus 23
viveradix 109
vivere 130
volucer 143
volup 18
volvere 14, 29
vomere 10, 93
vovere 29
Vulcanalis 101
vulgaris 102
vulgus 25, 55
vulnus 54
vulpes 142
vultus 6, 25, 55

SUBJECT INDEX

allomorphy   8–10, 124–152, 156–183

analogy   28, 93, 104, 109, 122, 143, 157

assimilation (place, voice, total)   30, 33, 79–80, 82–89, 94–99, 115–121, 144, 154, 160–183

coalescence   87, 92, 96, 114, 118–121, 162–165

consonant clusters   4, 15, 20–32, 48–86, 89–96, 99, 114, 143, 171–180

consonants   13–34, 82–103, 149–152, 160–183

contiguity   124, 152

coronal(ity)   13–19, 25, 36, 44, 64–70, 84–86, 90, 94, 96, 120–121, 162–173, 177, 179

degemination   11, 62, 86–92, 116, 121, 135, 144, 167–172, 175

deletion   32–34, 79–80, 84–85, 99, 112–113, 117–118, 121, 129, 133–139, 145–147, 163, 166

Derived Environment Condition   7, 10, 86–88, 108–113, 131, 133

diphthongs   37–46

dissimilation   100–103, 173

epenthesis   35, 92–94, 111–112, 145–146

extrasyllabic *s*   48, 62–66, 70–77, 86, 89, 90, 171, 180

feature geometry   44–47, 79–80, 93–94

floating C-Place node   78–80

geminates   16–17, 22–25, 33, 62, 83, 86, 89–92, 167–175

heteroclisy   113, 128–129, 142–148

hiatus   17, 38, 43–44, 96, 121, 131, 136–137, 146–147, 156, 164, 179

inflectional morphology   8–11, 17–18, 27, 124–152

labiovelars   20–32

lengthening   33, 84–85, 118–123, 147, 148, 163–164, 167

morphological structure   7–11, 124–127, 153–155

nasal vowels   18, 32–37, 39, 87–88, 92, 96, 119–121, 144, 162, 163

Place Condition   68–70, 94, 179

place of articulation   13–20, 64, 67–70, 94–96, 176–177

placeless nasal   32–37, 47, 79–80, 92, 94–96, 119–121, 128, 143–144, 162–166, 176, 179

prefixation   16, 23, 30, 33, 41, 44, 62, 70, 79–80, 83–96,
                               103, 105–106, 109, 113, 118, 120–121, 153–
                               183
resyllabification   19, 41, 70–77, 90
s impurum   70–77
shortening   43–44, 115, 131, 136, 146–147, 156
sonority   24–26, 48–50, 61–70, 99, 112, 150–152,
                               170, 177–179
Syllable Contact Law   48, 67–70, 85, 177–178
vocalic scale   124, 149–152
voice   13–14, 26–27, 44, 49, 59, 64–69, 82–85, 88,
                               115–118, 176
vowels   34–46, 104–123, 149–152